Between Sea and Sky

Strange and Unique Stories of the Sea

From the Shipping Files of Robert C. Parsons

Other Books Available by
Robert Parsons

Toll of the Sea	ISBN 1-895387-51-5	$14.95
Vignettes of a Small Town	ISBN 1-895387-82-5	$19.95
Survive the Savage Sea	ISBN 1-895387-96-5	$19.95
Committed to the Deep	ISBN 1-894294-09-2	$16.95
Raging Winds...Roaring Sea	ISBN 1-894294-29-7	$16.95
Lost at Sea — A Compilation	ISBN 1-894294-34-3	$19.95

Ask your favourite bookstore or order directly from the publisher.

Creative Book Publishing
P.O. Box 8660
36 Austin Street
St. John's, NF
A1B 3T7

phone: (709) 722-8500
fax: (709) 722-2228
e-mail: books@rb.nf.ca

Between Sea and Sky

Strange and Unique Stories of the Sea

To: Wayne
In memory of Capt. George Belg.

From the Shipping Files of Robert C. Parsons

Robert Parsons
July 27, 06

CREATIVE PUBLISHERS

St. John's, Newfoundland
2002

Le Conseil des Arts | The Canada Council
du Canada | for the Arts

We acknowledge the support of The Canada Council for the Arts for our publishing
program.

We acknowledge the financial support of the Government of Canada through the Book
Publishing Industry Development Program (BPIDP) for our publishing
program.

Cover Art: "The *Marion*" by Lloyd Pretty
Cover Design: John Andrews

∞ Printed on acid-free paper

Published by
CREATIVE BOOK PUBLISHING
a division of 10366 Newfoundland Limited
a Robinson-Blackmore Printing & Publishing associated company
P.O. Box 8660, St. John's, Newfoundland A1B 3T7

Printed in Canada by:
ROBINSON-BLACKMORE PRINTING & PUBLISHING

First Edition

National Library of Canada Cataloguing in Publication Data

Parsons, Robert Charles, 1944-
        Between sea and sky : strange and unique stories of the sea : from the
shipping files of Robert C. Parsons.

ISBN 1-894294-43-2

        1. Navigation–Newfoundland–History. 2. Shipwrecks–Newfoundland.
3. Seafaring life–Newfoundland. 4. Ships–Newfoundland. I. Title.

FC2170.S5P36 2002   971.8   C2002-901541-3
F1122.P37 2002

Between Sea and Sky is dedicated to all those story bearers who sent or brought me tales of our fearless seamen and hardy pioneers—our ancestors.

CONTENTS

CHAPTER FOUR - DISAPPEARANCE

CHAPTER FIVE - DEBRIS

CHAPTER SIX - SURVIVAL

CHAPTER SEVEN - ABANDONMENT

CHAPTER EIGHT - WAR

CHAPTER NINE - PEOPLE

CHAPTER TEN - MURDER

Author's Notes and Introduction

"Preserving Newfoundland and Labrador's Maritime History, One Tale at a Time"

The era we live in now cannot be fully understood except in relation to a knowledge of the events which helped shape our past. Much of that awareness is oral history, the stories passed on from generation to generation. Newfoundland is rich with oral history: the oral has to be recorded and preserved before the singers, poets, sealers and bank fishers pass on. Their knowledge of ideas and things now past holds the key to much of our unwritten history. The written constantly has to be publicized and reassessed.

The great events of discovery, exploration, governance, politics and economics are relatively well-documented, but what of the "little", the more obscure, tales of the outports — the ships, the people, the losses, the will to survive whatever the odds against them. The lore of island marine history — from the loss of John Cabot's *Matthew* in 1498, to the years of high losses of sailing ships of the 1920s (especially 1921-22), and the marine disasters of the twentieth century — is rich; much remains to be documented.

These are the people's stories; tales which never made newspaper headlines and often not even the back pages, but were told years ago around kitchen tables. The heroic and tragic are part of a social fabric interwoven on the main loom of an island cloth.

The stories in this volume, many of which were compiled from a combination of oral and written sources, are true. Often the storyteller may have forgotten specific details or misconstrued certain facts (or the interviewer may not have asked the relevant questions), but the event did happen in some form many years ago. There are tales in *Between Sea and Sky* which border close to the unbelievable or at least seem doubtful — especially to the hard-core historian or researcher. Again, each depends on the whims of individual memory or on the notions of newspaper reporting. And reporters are prone to human mistakes. On the final pages of this volume I have written the "After Word" to show where the stories originated. As one can see many stories were sparked by a story (or a fragment) I would receive from correspondents and to these I shall say Thank You!

As well, should any reader find any error in the text/photos or should anyone like to add to or augment a story, contact the author at the address below; I will accept them with pleasure.

Robert C. Parsons
32 Pearson Place
Grand Bank, NF
A0E 1W0
E-mail: robert.parsons2@nf.sympatico.ca
Website: http://shipwrecks.nf.ca

Chapter One

Unusual

This collection of material ranges from the mysterious, unsolved disappearances at sea, unusual exploits of unique Newfoundland people, the amazing stories of feats and accomplishments to the almost unbelievable events of memorable, heroic, and tragic proportion. All are based on research, written documentation in old newspapers and oral history found in stories, songs, and poems or passed on through family history.

Adrift Six Months on an Ice Pan

While searching for seals off Labrador, the Newfoundland sealing steamer *Tigress* accidentally stumbled upon nineteen people — men, women, and children — living on an ice pan. They had been adrift with little food for six months — 196 days from October 15, 1872, to April 30 the next year. As the ice pan was breaking up in the warmer temperatures of April, the sealing ship appeared out of the fog and rescued them. The nineteen — nine European men and ten Eskimos, (today Innu) consisting of two men, two women, five children and one infant born on the ice pan — were part of the crew of the American steamer *Polaris*. *Polaris*, a ship of Charles Francis Hall's Arctic expedition, sailed north to find the North Pole several decades before Peary. Hall had engaged some Eskimo families to help him and the other explorers survive in the north.

Victims of *Tigress* explosion, April 2, 1874
John Rorke, wife, 1 child, Bay Roberts
Elijah Mercer, wife, 7 children, Bay Roberts
Henry Holmes, wife, 4 children, Bay Roberts
James Snow, wife, 5 children, Bay Roberts
Edward Snow, wife, Bay Roberts
Isaac Kierley, wife, Bay Roberts
James Bartlett, single, Bay Roberts
James Walsh, single, Bay Roberts
John Snow, single, Bay Roberts
John Jones, wife, 2 children, Upper Is. Cove
John Barrett, wife, 3 children, Upper Is. Cove
Garland Courage, wife, 6 children, Harbour Grace
G. Butler, wife, 1 child, Port-de-Grave
William Batten, wife, 1 child, Bareneed
James Buick, wife, 5 children, St. John's
Pat Pettigree, single, St. John's
John Hollahan, single, Holyrood
Michael McAbe, single, Southern Gut
William Hurley, Liverpool, England
William Reynolds, Dublin, Ireland
Samuel Booth, Philadelphia, US

In October 1872, thinking the vessel was sinking while stuck in ice off Northumberland Island, some expedition members got onto a large (approximately four mile square) sheet of ice and eventually drifted away.

The native people in the group built an igloo, blocks of

ice cemented with snow. Water was thrown over the shelter and when it froze, made the structure solid and warm. The group had some food and provisions from *Polaris* as well as two boats, two kayaks and fur bedding. When food ran out, they were faced with starvation, but subsisted off hides and the tops of their skin boots. One of the Eskimos killed a polar bear which lasted until they had drifted with the Labrador current off northern Labrador where seals were plentiful.

One of the boats was used for fuel. No deaths occurred during their ordeal; in fact one of the Eskimo women gave birth on the ice pan. Just as food was running short again, and as the ice pan was disintegrating slowly, the sealer *Tigress*, which was hunting for seals in that area, came by and brought the castaways to Newfoundland. They were landed in Bay Roberts on May 12, 1873.

Meanwhile *Polaris* escaped the crush of the ice fields, but ran out of coal and was beached near Etah, Greenland. The crew built two boats and sailed south until they were eventually picked up by a Scottish whaler.

Tigress, owned by Harvey and Company of St. John's, was only in service for two years. On her third trip to the ice, under the command of Captain Isaac Bartlett, *Tigress* was again the centre of a dramatic event. On April 2, 1874, in nearly the same place as she had located the castaways, her boilers blew up on the ice field. Twenty-one men, mostly from Bay Roberts, were killed.

According to Bay Roberts community history, seven of these men were buried, uncoffined, in a common grave. Several men were scalded and mutilated beyond recognition. One report states that eleven men were standing on the grating above the engine room when the boilers exploded. The victims had been literally blown to pieces. *The Harbour Grace Standard*, April 18, 1874, says, "... those standing over the engine room ... were instantly ushered into eternity, either scalded or mangled ..."

Another oddity connected with icebergs off Newfoundland happened on June 24, 1875, when the schooner *Caledonia* struck an iceberg ninety miles off Fogo. Captain P. Delaney left Cupids for Batteau, Labrador, with eighty-two people — men, women and children — aboard and all their supplies intended for the Labrador summer fishery.

At nine P.M.,two days out and off Fogo, *Caledonia* ran into an iceberg and sank in a half hour. It can only be supposed there weren't enough life boats to accommodate all. Taking nothing but a few blankets, guns, and a little food, the passengers and crew climbed onto the iceberg. At seven the next morning, the Carbonear schooner *Jane Ainsley*, commanded by Captain Kennedy of Carbonear, sailed past, also headed for the Labrador.

Kennedy and his crew may have passed the berg, which was off in the distance without giving it much attention, but they heard noises which, as they investigated, turned out to be the firing of guns and terrible screams from the people on the iceberg. *Jane Ainsley* took them off and carried them to Seldom Come By. Had there been any wind or heavy frost or had the berg rolled over, it is likely all would have been lost and nothing would ever have been heard of their fate.

Businessman Walter B. Grieve of Baine Johnson & Company heard of the plight of the unfortunate victims, helped purchase new supplies and, without charge, chartered two vessels to take them to Labrador.

Wrackers or Salvors at Little Placentia?

On the evening of August 7, 1888, the brigantine *Morna*, en route from Glace Bay, Nova Scotia, to St. John's with a load of coal, ran aground on Point

Latine, about two miles from Little Placentia. The ship was under the command of Captain Bartlett and was owned by John Woods and Sons, merchants and shipowners, of St. John's. At the time there was a dense fog and the brigantine veered off course.

Boats and men from nearby came, removed the coal and carried it away. Such was the excitement and quick removal of her precious fuel, that within two hours every man's face was black with coal dust. It was jokingly said that a father couldn't recognize his own son. There was a public outcry from St. John's that this was a case of "wracking" not legal salvage. According to evidence Captain Bartlett tried to stop men from coming aboard but his entreaties went unheeded.

On August 17 Judge Daniel Prowse was sent to investigate the allegations of wracking and plundering. On August 22 he and Magistrate Thomas O'Reilly conducted court proceedings in Placentia in relation to the wrackers.

On August 28, the *Evening Telegram* reported the plundering trial had concluded and that David Bruce was convicted and sentenced to four months. Richard Sparrow received six months, James Cunningham two months, and Denis King paid a fine of fifty dollars to avoid imprisonment.

In Memoriam:
Lines on the Loss of *Morna*

The staunch-built brigantine *Morna*
At the close of July hove in sight
An on the eve of the seventh of August
Came to grief on Latania Point.

She struck, and in less than ten minutes
Was boarded by hands from the shore,
Who soon shortened sail on the *Morna*
She was destined to leave us no more.

The news soon reached men in each harbour,
Who were soon to the scene of the wreck,
They looked anxious to render assistance,
But, alas, her sad fate was there met.

The *Morna* was, I believe, coal laden,
From Glace Bay to St. John's, Newfoundland
But her coal at this port was much needed,
As fuel is scarce at our command.

Unsparred and dismantled she lies here,
On a sea-beaten strand to remain
And we only regret that the *Morna*
Will not go to Glace Bay again!

Written: Placentia, Nov. 20th, 1888

This wasn't exactly the last word. In November *The Telegram* published an anonymous poem from a writer in Placentia expressing regret only for the fact that the *Morna* would never again be able to go to Glace Bay for coal.

Perhaps shipwreck and salvage — legal or otherwise — is not new in maritime history. But to publish a poem boasting of the event is unusual. The local wit and poet wrote "In Memoriam."

Photo courtesy of Conrad Clarke

Newfoundland Island (above) in Sydney Harbour. In the era of the coal trade between Newfoundland and Nova Scotia hundreds of vessels came to North Sydney laden with rock ballast in their holds. Before the coal was loaded, the rocks were dumped at one location in North Sydney harbour. Over the years the great accumulation of rock became known as "Newfoundland Island" and eventually grassed over.

A St. Shotts Mystery Solved

Two reports of a wrecked schooner circulated around the southern Avalon Peninsula in early October, 1900. The first knowledge of tragedy came on October 3 when news detailed that a fishing schooner, owned in Burin, had been lost at Cape Pine. Six of her eight crew were saved and had been taken to Sydney, Nova Scotia. At that time no one knew how or under what conditions the schooner had been wrecked.

Some of the answers unfolded at St. Shotts on October 6th when the forward half of a schooner, complete with anchor and chains aboard, drifted to shore near the town. The nameplate on the bow was broken and only "*Martin*" could be seen; there was no sign of the crew. Authorities in the town wired St. John's to say the vessel would have been about forty ton and had apparently been cut down. It had been foggy for several days.

The next day, the steamer *Netherholme*, travelling from England to Saint John, New Brunswick, arrived in Sydney to refuel. She had on board six crew of the Burin schooner *Henry M. Martin*. Although the details out of Sydney were not clear, apparently the schooner had been run down by *Netherholme* one mile west-northwest of Cape Pine.

The steamer struck just forward of the main chain and the schooner went down by the stern almost instantly. Two were drowned: Frank Martin, the captain's brother, who was one of the watch on deck, and William Riggs, who was below. Martin had a wife and two children; Riggs was single. The remainder of the crew forced their way to the deck and clung to the wreckage till picked up by a boat from the steamer.

Henry M. Martin, thirty-one ton, was not insured. The survivors, including Captain John Martin, George Martin and Thomas Martin returned to Newfoundland by the S.S. *Bruce*.

Over the years, the people of St. Shotts have seen many shipwrecks, tragedies and victims of the sea. In the era of sail and steam, St. Shotts, located on the headland between St. Mary's Bay and Trepassey Bay on the southern Avalon Peninsula, earned a widespread notoriety from a tragic succession of shipwrecks. The rugged coast, strong currents and tides, storms and dense fogs contributed to ship losses.

Another added element is its proximity to the shipping

lanes off Cape Race. For decades prior to the 1930s ocean liners passed relatively close to "shipwreck coast" in the great circle routes to and from North America. No respecter of title, the shipwreck coast claimed ships bearing HMS, His (or Her) Majesty's Ship, fell prey — *Drake*, *Harpooner* and *Comus*.

The sinking and re-appearance of the frigate HMS *Drake* (or *Little Drake* as she is called in a report of July 14, 1864) became one of the most unusual sea dramas pertaining to St. Shotts. By the 1790s the first English people settled in St. Shotts. The *Census* of 1869 shows the population that year as thirty. Over the years common surnames have been Best, Cahill, Corrigan, Davis, Finlay, Gibbons, Hayward, Hewitt, Knox, Lewis, Martin, McNeill, Molloy, Myrick and Nemec.

These early settlers knew about the armed frigate HMS *Drake* which grounded and sank on a ledge near the eastern head of St. Shotts on June 23, 1822. Many of the ship's company, as well as the women passengers, managed to clamber unto a small rock awash in the heavy seas. Thirteen, including one woman, were drowned getting to shore; forty-four survived.

Drake sank almost immediately in thirty feet of water. Local people knew of her location, but there was not much to salvage from the sunken vessel. However, on Monday, June 28, 1864, *Drake* re-appeared under unusual circumstances. About seven o'clock that evening, a slight earthquake shock echoed throughout Newfoundland. It was felt all over the island, but was especially strong near St. Shotts.

Accompanying the sea quake were other phenomena. The sea in St. Shotts harbour receded 250 yards, well beyond the point where the wreck of *Drake* lay. *Drake* was distinctly visible even to the point where the St. Shotts people saw her shot bolts and some of the cannon protruding from the ports. This ship had been five fathoms (or thirty feet) down, but for a few moments became an eerie kelp-strewn sight.

The sea gradually ebbed for ten to twelve minutes and then returned with awesome velocity bringing large stones and gravel with it. The gravel filled the St. Shotts Gut; the rush of water overturned several boats and sank one or two. Then, as quickly as the nightmarish experience came, it went leaving the terrified people to speculate that a severe submarine volcanic eruption or mud slide had happened not too far from St. Shotts.

Author's Collection

With the rugged coastal waters of St. Shotts (above showing Epworth a part of Burin) as backdrop, signs describe local wrecks near the town. The author stands by signage for the wreck of the Splinter Fleet vessel *Bonne Bay*, lost in 1947 at Finlay's Cove.

Brazilian Pirates and a Newfoundland Ship

It has been said that anything that could happen on the high seas has happened to a Newfoundland schooner, including piracy. In 1911 a report surfaced in St. John's that A.S. Rendell's *Helen F. Stewart* had been attacked by pirates and that was only one in a string of bad luck incidents the Newfoundland ship went through.

Under the command of Captain George Berg, *Helen F. Stewart* sailed from St. John's on December 5, 1910, headed for Pernambuco (today Recife), Brazil. She carried a cargo of fish from Smith Company Limited and arrived without any incident early in the new year, 1911. After discharging cargo she sailed for Barbados perhaps to load molasses for Newfoundland. The next report — an unusual one — or sighting of the *Helen F. Stewart* surfaces in April and the news was not good for the owners.

On April 27, 1911, the West Indies and Panama Telegram Company cable ship *Henry Holmes* steamed along about sixty miles off St. Lucia in the West Indies. The cable ship sailed slowly in calm seas laying or repairing telegraph cable. The man on the bridge saw a three-masted (tern) schooner making signals of distress and reported this to the captain. What could be the problem? Seas were clam, winds light, the wooden ship had her sails up, but was barely moving. Captain Morrell changed course and positioned *Henry Holmes* near the distressed tern.

Through the megaphone he learned this was *Helen F. Stewart* of St. John's bound for Barbados from Brazil. She would not make headway for she had lost part of her keel. The schooner was also short of provisions, for she had been to sea longer than expected and had run into an unusual problem. Finally Captain Berg asked the cable ship to tow the *Stewart* to Barbados. Barbados was too far out of *Henry Holmes'* route, but the cable ship did tow her to St. Lucia, one of the Windward islands of the Caribbean. Captain Morrell also supplied *Stewart* with enough provisions to last a few days.

The island newspaper *Voice of St. Lucia* carried a story in its April 1912 edition which outlined the misadventures of the hapless Newfoundland tern schooner. *Helen F.*

Stewart had arrived in time at Brazil, discharged and sailed for Barbados. Misfortune caught up with the schooner when she ran aground on the northern Brazilian coast.

To be aground in itself was not unusual. Many a Newfoundland captain has been in the same situation and, through experience and ingenuity, managed to free a schooner from sandbars or rocky ledges. Cargo can be lightened, repairs made, the captain can engage the services of a tug and unless there is severe weather or structural damage, perhaps a ship can live to sail again.

However, while aground, Brazilian men from the coast — termed "pirates" by the St. Lucian newspaper — boarded *Helen F. Stewart*. They proceeded to rob the ship of everything moveable. The ship's crew could only stand by, perhaps under the threat of death, while the pirates carried away sails, rope, lamps, dishes, food and provisions. No doubt things could have been much worse but the thieves, while in the act, were frightened off by someone who appeared on the shore.

For weeks, prior to the piracy and some time after, *Helen F. Stewart* lay aground until a passing steamer towed her off and gave the crew enough food to last a few days. Fortunately, the tern had an extra set of sails below which the pirates had overlooked. Captain Berg and crew fitted the sails on the *Stewart* and quickly sailed away from the coast. They didn't get far for the schooner's keel, damaged in the accident, had fallen off in the pounding of high seas.

It was in this unmanageable condition she was found by *Henry Holmes*. At St. Lucia, *Helen F. Stewart* was examined, found unseaworthy and condemned. After a few weeks, her crew of seven reached Barbados — without their ship — and five months after leaving St. John's, they arrived back in Newfoundland.

Captain George Berg went back to sea, but his life ended tragically as recounted in Chapter Four.

Photo courtesy of John Peacock

The power of New York advertising in Burin, Newfoundland. The Bugden business and Captain Thomas Bugden (standing at wheel to the left) of Burin owned at least two vessels: *Antelope*, and *Flying Cloud* (above) which has the words "The Mutual Life Insurance Co. of New York" painted on the side. Although it is not known what eventually happened to *Flying Cloud*, Bugden's banking schooner *Anelope* was cut down by the White Star liner *Majestic* in August 1894. William Woundy and Gabriel Mitchell of Burin died in the accident.

The picture postcard (above, showing Epworth, a part of Burin) has the vertical wording on the right saying "Geo. M. Goddard, Burin, Newfoundland." The Goddard salt fish enterprise in Burin was once prominent however the name doesn't exist today.

Reward for Rescue

Quite often in the annals of sea disasters and rescues off the coasts of Newfoundland the subject of reward surfaces — money, medals or recognition — for bravery or courage beyond the call of duty. There is an unwritten code of the sea that says if a ship needs help you give it. A reward is not foremost in the minds of sailors and fishermen who realize all too well the demands and claims of the relentless ocean. They believe a rescue favour will someday be returned in kind. Yet there are many instances where rewards were passed out for bravery in rescue operations off Newfoundland.

In 1846 George Lake and five other men of Fortune saved the lives of two French seamen on the ice off Fortune. The Governor of St. Pierre and Miquelon wrote the Newfoundland Governor, praising the rescuers and suggesting an award for them.

The fishermen of Ferryland, who had rescued the crew of the brigantine *Heather*, were awarded £50 by the Government of Newfoundland. *Heather* was owned by Baine Johnson and Company and was lost in 1856 on a voyage from Baltimore to St. John's.

The brigantine *Pursuit* commanded by Captain Ebsary of St. John's rescued the crew of the waterlogged barque *Helen* on January 29, 1856. To compensate the owners of *Pursuit*, which in the course of the rescue reached St. John's too late to engage in the seal fishery, the British Government awarded Ebsary and crew £592.

In 1911 a man named John Dower of Conche was awarded two silver medals by the French Emperor Napoleon III for having, on different occasions, saved the lives of French fishermen at Conche.

Several men of Harbour Grace received awards in 1909. Captain Valentine O'Neil of Harbour Grace was in charge of the Gloucester schooner *Vanessa*. He had other Harbour Grace men with him: his brother Richard, James Slocum, Thomas Furlong, Thomas Duggan, Thomas Clancy, James Jones, John Hayes and Patrick Smallcombe. These men saved the lives of the crew of the schooner *L.A.B.* on the Grand Banks the previous year.

A rescue which is more widely known came as a result of the wreck of the Norwegian ship *Snorre* on September 19, 1907. When *Snorre* grounded at Canallie Head near Bonavista, all her crew, except one man, were saved by Bonavista men James Ford, Eli Paul, Lewis Little, William Ford, Robert Brown and James Little, son of John Little. Recognition came in 1911. Lewis Little, who was lowered over a cliff in the rescue, was given the gold Carnegie

Lifesaving medal and fifteen-hundred dollars; the others, bronze medals and one-thousand dollars each. Chapter Four, Story Six, features the recognition given to Captain William Fitzgerald of Carbonear.

Recently, the details of another rescue and compensation became available. The incident happened on May 17, 1911, when the schooner *Maple Leaf* foundered on the Grand Banks. Captain Thomas Norman skippered the *Maple Leaf*, owned by brothers D.J. (Denis John) and T. (Thomas) Burke of St. Jacques. While *Maple Leaf* lay at anchor on Quero (Banquero) fishing grounds, she filled with water and went down. Her crew of fourteen signalled to the *Alerte*, a French vessel fishing nearby. *Alerte's* chief officer and four seamen carried out the rescue. Most likely, as is the case with most transfers, they rowed over to the Newfoundland schooner and took the men off.

In the first months of 1912, the Mercantile Marine Service Association, based in St. John's, met to discuss the matter of reward for the ship *Alerte*. Captain Edward English, the harbour master of St. John's and a member of the association (and who later became captain of the steamer *Ethie* and was himself given a reward in 1919), suggested £18: To Captain Francis Oribie was to be given £5, to the chief officer £3 and the four seamen £2 10s each. Accordingly, he sent a letter of explanation and a bank draft for £18 to the French consul at Liverpool, England.

In early February, the Consul for France sent a letter to the secretary of the Mercantile Association, Mr. Grylls, in St. John's which read:

> Dear Sir:
> I have the honour to acknowledge the receipt of your letter of February 25, enclosing, with a draft of £18 with reference to the presentation to the sum for distribution to the master and crew of the French fishing schooner *Alerte*

for rescuing the crew of the Newfoundland fishing schooner *Maple Leaf* on the 17th of May, 1911.

I shall feel greatly obliged if you will kindly express my sincere thanks to the Government of Newfoundland for their generous donation, the amount of which I shall immediately forward to the Minister of Marine at Paris to be distributed in accordance with the wishes of the Newfoundland Government.

(Signed) R. Boeufve,
Consul for France.

Not much has been written of the loss of *Maple Leaf*, her crew or any hardships they endured, but the story of the quest for adequate compensation for bravery is a glimpse into the world of rescue in the era of sail.

Photo courtesy of Capt. Hubert Hall

Wreckage of the coastal steamer *Ethie* lost on December 11, 1919, near Cow Head, while under the command of Captain Edward English. He successfully beached the steamer in a storm and helped saved the lives of all ninety-two people on board. For his skill and courage, English was awarded a Silver Cup by Governor Harris.

One of the few paddlewheel ships in Newfoundland; this one was used on Red Indian Lake to push logs into the Exploits River system.

Clothes for the Dead on Christmas Day

A cold and weary Newfoundland crew were given clothes normally used to dress the dead, but these men were very much alive. In fact it was Christmas Day when they touched solid earth again — grateful to be in the land of the living.

They had been plucked off their sinking schooner *Wilfred Marcus*, but their extra clothes went down with the vessel. Usually when a lifeboat, manned by four to seven men, is sent from a rescue ship to pick up a schooner crew there is no room for personal effects. As well, in the rush and trauma of rescue, crews leave a sinking ship as soon as possible. And this was the case when on December 25, 1918, the tern schooner *Wilfred Marcus*, laden with salt from Portugal, went down in a violent winter storm and the men were rescued in the nick of time by a passing steamer.

Wilfred Marcus, measuring 107 feet long and twenty-eight feet wide, was built in Shelburne, Nova Scotia, in 1914 and was named for the son of co-owner Aaron

Buffett of Grand Bank. At one point in her career the salt-laden *Wilfred Marcus* sank and turned on her side in Grand Bank harbour. After the salt melted and she was pumped out, the tern was refloated and lived to sail again.

G & A Buffett established a branch business in Mortier Bay in 1912 and the tern sailed out of that spacious port. Apart from her cook, Stephen Lovell of Grand Bank, the crew hailed from Marystown: Captain Robert Anderson, mate Ambrose King, seamen Leo J. Walsh, John Hooper, John Baker and Amos Hilby. The latter, an unusual name, may have been recorded incorrectly from Kirby.

Wilfred Marcus, deeply laden with 200 ton of fishery salt, left Oporto on November first. Stormy weather tossed the 123 ton vessel so severely, that on her twenty-fifth day out of port, all sails and rigging were carried away. Vainly the crew fought to keep their schooner afloat — constantly pumping, mending sail and attempting to buck headwinds.

Totally disabled and wallowing in heavy seas, the crew knew the schooner was doomed. On the fifteenth of December, they spotted a passing ship and hoisted distress signals to the masthead. The ship, the American steamer *Lynchburg*, headed east to France, turned to help the troubled schooner.

Lynchburg's captain sent out a lifeboat to help the men to safety. Although seas were high and the steamer's crew risked their lives, the steamer's lifeboat, with a crew of six or seven, rescued the schooner's men. There was no room for extra baggage; thus *Wilfred Marcus*' crew left their clothes bags and personal possessions behind.

On Christmas Day they were landed in France — a festive season the shipwrecked sailors were not likely to forget. No doubt, each would rather have spent the time with their families in Newfoundland. From France the men found transportation to England and then to Halifax, reaching home in February 1919.

Leo J. Walsh, one of six brothers and six sisters in the Walsh family, had married Catherine Ducey. Captain Patrick "Paddy" Walsh, who was lost with his crew in the schooner *Anna Anita* during the 1935 August Gale, was one of Leo J.'s brothers.

Sometime after his rescue from the *Wilfred Marcus*, Leo J. Walsh captained the tern schooner *Ria* and, on at least one occasion had taken her to Oporto. There, a Portuguese waterfront artist asked Captain Walsh if he could paint the schooner. Walsh laughed and said, "My schooner does not need to be painted." The next day the painter showed up with a canvas of the *Ria* which Captain Walsh purchased.

Photo courtesy of Harold Simms

Tern schooner *Wilfred Marcus* at Shelburne. For four years this tern sailed out of Mortier Bay delivering fish to Europe and bringing salt westward to Buffett's premises at Mortier Bay.

As far as his timely rescue from *Wilfred Marcus* was concerned, Leo J. Walsh remembered that when he landed in France he and his crewmates were given clean clothes — clothes normally reserved for those being buried, complete with cardboard shoes.

Unexpected Meeting

In February, 1922 two schooners — *Lowell F. Parks* and *Elizabeth Rodway* — ran into violent storms in the Atlantic. *Elizabeth Rodway* was captained by David Robertson and *Lowell F. Parks* was commanded by David's brother, William; both of Carbonear. The *Parks* was owned by A.S. Rendell and Company of St. John's.

Lowell F. Parks took on a partial load of fish from G.M. Barr's premises and left St. John's for Harbour Buffett to complete her cargo. She sailed for Oporto in mid-January but was gone so long that fears for her safety arose. She had been several weeks unreported and no other ship had spoken to her. Unknown to those waiting in St. John's and Carbonear, Captain William Robertson and his crew had fought a vicious Atlantic storm which tore the sails from the masts and pounded the schooner.

With his ship leaking and making little headway, Robertson decided to try to reach Barbados, but about 200 miles from land the decks of *Lowell F. Parks* were awash in the heavy seas. He soon realized his schooner was sinking and gave orders to abandon ship. The five men rowed and sailed south for Barbados and in five days, covering about 100 miles a day, they reached their destination.

When William Robertson reached Bridgetown, Barbados, he saw, to his surprise, his brother's schooner, *Elizabeth Rodway* tied up in Bridgetown. He rowed to her side and climbed aboard to shake hands with his brother in joyful reunion. *Elizabeth Rodway* left Spain bound for Marystown with a load of salt, sailed through the same storm that destroyed *Parks* and was forced to put into Barbados.

One of the crew on *Lowell F. Parks* was Thomas Fraize, a seaman from Carbonear, who had one of the most adventurous and perilous of lives. On that occasion he spent five days in a small open boat, with practically nothing to eat and only rain water to drink, and there was very little of that.

He was a member of the *Oleanda* when she was lost in 1926 and was on the little schooner *Princess* when she was wrecked and lost. On the 22nd of January, 1928, he was on the S.S. *Sagua La Grande* when she left Philadelphia and disappeared. Her story is found in Chapter Four, Story Eight.

Miraculous Escape

For two and a half days in August of 1927 — from the 24th to the 27th — one of the most memorable "August Gales" to ravage the southern part of Newfoundland struck with destructive and deadly results. Many small Placentia Bay craft and larger schooners were on the fishing grounds; several were lost with crew including *Hilda Gertrude* of Rushoon; *Effie May*, Rencontre West; *John Loughlin*, Red Harbour; *Annie Healey*, Fox Harbour and others. This story is not about one of these disappearances, but of survivors who escaped unscathed — well almost.

One vessel caught in the storm went through a tough time of it while sailing on the western side of Placentia Bay on August 24, the day the devastating hurricane howled through. The name of the schooner is not recorded although it is known she was carrying lumber and other supplies to Placentia Bay ports. Deeply laden with lumber below and stacked on deck and facing one of the worst gales in decades, the schooner had been "making very bad weather" for several hours.

To ease the strain on the main boom, the skipper took the end of a twenty fathom length of rope, clove-hitched it around the boom and set it taut to the end of one of the timbers in the deck load. This took about six fathoms of the rope and the remaining end the captain coiled up and threw in between the timber ends. The skipper, seeing his vessel was doing relatively well in the face of a gale, went below for some well-deserved rest.

The man at the wheel, not liking the look of things — the high seas breaking on the side of the vessel and a part of unused rope lying about — took the loose end and passed two turns about his waist. He then tied the loose end around another end of lumber. This was the same rope the skipper had used to secure the boom.

A short while after, a tremendous sea swept the deck of the schooner throwing her down on her beam ends, or side. Her mast heads were in the water and stayed there for a minute or so. This same sea carried most of the deck load of lumber overboard. But more serious, one of the crew working on deck was carried over the side with the loose lumber.

This man kept his wits about him for he succeeded in getting to the crosstrees at the mainmast head, and held on. A second wave followed across the partly-submerged deck. This cleared the deck of any remaining lumber and also carried away an iron-bound keg of molasses which had been tied or strapped to the deck.

The keg, with considerable force, struck the man hanging onto the crosstrees in the head and neck. He could have been killed outright, but escaped with serious injuries — a broken jaw and collarbone and the chime (iron rim) of the keg inflicted a jagged cut across his forehead. He was only partly conscious and may have lost his grip on the rigging, but a third sea, cold and hard, brought him fully conscious. The same sea completely carried the debris of the deck load clear of the hull and the schooner slowly uprighted.

The remaining two or three crew were below deck when this happened; all told that only one or two minutes had elapsed. As the vessel came back on an even keel, they rushed topside to inspect the damage. To their surprise, the deck was bare of cargo and all moveable equipment had been washed away as well. Worse, two men, the guy working on deck and the helmsman, were nowhere to be seen. It was quickly surmised they were washed overboard and gone. Eyes scanned the choppy ocean immediately for some sign of them.

Then a blood-curdling scream and shriek could be heard over the roar of the gale and it came from above. It was a crew mate hailing them from aloft and a ghastly object he was. Drenched in blood pouring down over his face, with his jaw slack, and head and shoulder held at one side from his injuries, he was trying to get down the main shrouds.

When he reached the rail or deck, one man helped him below as carefully as circumstances permitted while the other two scanned the ocean for the helmsman. The skipper walked back toward the cabin and noticed a rope hanging over the taffrail which he soon realized was the same one he made fast to the boom and lumber some time before.

As he examined it he thought there was something attached to the end. As soon as he had all three able hands mustered on deck, they pulled in the rope. Presently they saw it was a man and a length of lumber tied to the rope. And more wonderful yet, it was the helmsman, still alive despite his horrific experience!

The schooner had continued forging ahead at a good clip which kept the rope tight. This, coupled with the fact that a piece of lumber was still attached to the rope, kept the man's head and shoulders above water. Seas passed over him, but quickly, and he was not submerged long enough to drown, although helpless to shout or to pull himself aboard.

Quite often such incidents at sea resulted in a man or two lost and the schooner sailed to the nearest port with a flag at half mast to indicate death. Often the exact circumstances of how a man was washed overboard was never known.

But, in the August Gale of 1927, two men survived to tell the tale. Perhaps there is no other record chronicling two such marvelous escapes of two men on the same craft at the same time.

Armed Insurrection in Placentia Bay

As told around the kitchen tables and fishing sheds of Placentia Bay, there is an oral account of an armed insurrection of Placentia Bay fishermen. In 1928 the government decided to move the fog alarm built on Jude Island, Placentia Bay.

The horn had been put there in the mid-1920s, but in an attempt to garner votes in Fortune Bay, the bureaucrats in St. John's planned to move it to St. Jacques Island, Fortune Bay. On the day of the planned relocation, scores of Placentia Bay fishermen, armed with muskets, sticks, axes and pitchforks, assembled near the horn house on Jude Island.

Lying twelve kilometers east of the town of Red Harbour, Placentia Bay, Jude Island appeared as Cape Judas on several maps of the seventeenth and eighteenth centuries. The island, about five kilometers long and four kilometers wide, had only one sizable permanent settlement, Hay Cove. This community was first recorded in the 1891 *Census* for the Burin district, with eighty-six Methodist inhabitants.

Jude Island was near a productive fishing ground for cod and prospered throughout the late nineteenth and early twentieth centuries, with the family names Dicks, Keeping, Miller, Peach and Senior being recorded there during these years. By 1921 there were only sixty-eight people living in the community, the number had dropped to nine by 1956 and by the 1960s the community had been abandoned.

Those early pioneers were not about to let bureaucracy and vote mongering affect their way of life. In due course, the Reid Newfoundland

> **Song of Insurrection**
>
> They lowered their boats,
> cops came on shore,
> One man stepped out
> but not no more;
> For if these had,
> I feel quite sure,
> There would be
> strife on Jude.
>
> But very soon
> we were surprised,
> We scarcely could
> believe our eyes,
> Fore they were gone
> to Paradise,
> Not venturing
> back to Jude.
>
> Now what relief
> whether night or day,
> When the fog is thick
> and you run the Bay,
> For the watch
> to come below and say,
> "I hear the horn
> on Jude."

steamer *Argyle* arrived with thirty carpenters and an escort of Newfoundland constabulary commanded by Sergeant Simmons. While the carpenters waited on *Argyle* for word to begin dismantling the structure, one policeman was sent ashore to Jude Island to negotiate with the determined mob of gathered men. After a discussion, the policeman went back aboard the S.S. *Argyle* to report, no doubt, of the fierce determination of the Placentia Bay fishermen incensed over the possible loss of the fog horn station. Within hours the steamer left and the crisis was over. The horn on Jude stayed.

According to local history, a key defender of the horn was a tall fisherman from St. Joseph's who was a fine specimen of a fighting man. He didn't mince any words when describing who would end up headfirst in a blubber barrel. Another spokesperson for the enraged fishermen let it be known there would be bloodshed. The local song-writer/poet was quick to describe the incident, part of which is given on the previous page.

Swimming in the Middle of Nowhere

An unusual article appears in the *Daily News* for August 12, 1935. A local schooner came upon a man swimming in the Atlantic, the nearest land 160 miles away! He was identified as Walter Robolek of Nova Scotia and had been employed on the vessel *Notre Dame*. The article did not say who rescued him, why he was in the ocean or what happened to him after. He was dressed in a white sweater and pants and was taken by an American plane from the fishing vessel that found him. The man mumbled incoherently, but was expected to tell his tale when he recovered from exhaustion, hunger and derangement.

A similar story comes out of Elliston, Trinity Bay. A man named William Pearce of Elliston was a member of a banking vessel out of Catalina. While crossing Trinity Bay one stormy night in the 1890s, Pearce was knocked overboard by a swinging boom.

He was not missed at first and general work on deck and below continued. It was only when his friends realized Pearce was gone, they presumed he had fallen overboard and drowned.

Meanwhile William Pearce was in the water and saw his schooner sailing on without him. Realizing his crew didn't know he had fallen overboard, he kicked off his sea boots and started to swim. Purposeful swimming to get to land was really not his intention at first, but he concentrated on keeping afloat and on fending off the cold seeping into his bones.

The Daily News

ST. JOHN'S, NEWFOUNDLAND,   MONDAY, AUGUST 12, 1935

FIND FISHERMEN SWIMMING 160 MILES AT SEA

Plane Takes Man From Fishing Vessel That Rescued Him—Is Apparently Insane

Boston, Aug. 11, (C.P. Copyright) —A fisherman, believed to be a Nova Scotian, found alive swimming, but apparently insane, 160 miles at sea, was brought to land to-day by a United States coast-guard plane. The plane picked him up from a fishing vessel whose crew had hauled him from the ocean a few hour earlier The rugged figure was in a white sweater and slacks and he told the aviators his name was Walter Robolek of the fishing craft Notre Dame. He mumbled incoherently and the identification is incomplete pending his recovery from exhaustion, hunger and derangement. He declined to talk to the hospital attendants but prayed audibly on his knees at his bedside. Captain Soreson of the Boston trawler Ripple said he had to lock him in the mate's quarters because of violence after he was rescued.

Newfoundland Lady Dead At Sydney

North Sydney, N.S., Aug. 11, (C.P. Copyright) — Mrs. George Strickland, aged twenty-eight, of Port aux Basques, who entered Hamilton Hospital here three weeks ago for treatment, died there on Saturday night. Besides her hus-

The story of a man found swimming in the middle of the Atlantic hits the local press.

Pearce knew the cold water would bring hypothermia; thus he didn't expect to survive any more than a half hour or so. Yet amazingly he lasted all night and was still swimming when another vessel saw him just after daylight. He was picked up seven hours after he fell into the water, none the worse for his experience!

A Debt Repaid, Forty Years Later

When another ship is in trouble on the sea, other vessels nearby rush to the scene. And the crew's greatest wish is to get there in time for rescue. There's an unwritten tenet that bonds those who ply the treacherous oceans of the world — if a ship needs help you give it. Sailors and fishermen, realizing all too well the demands and claims of the relentless ocean, believe a rescue favour will someday be returned. In this true story of the sea, a debt of rescue was repaid after forty years — such a time had passed that the son of the original rescuer was the recipient.

George Hampton was the second engineer of the Newfoundland coastal freighter *National IV*. He described, in the November 1946 issue of *Atlantic Guardian*, a true story based on his diary he kept of the incident.

It was October 16, 1936. The ocean, as it does more often than not, was acting up. High winds churned up whitecaps and the winds soon turned to hurricane force. Captain Kenneth Barbour was homeward bound from the Labrador coast in the *National IV*; his vessel was deep with a load of codfish and cod oil for owners Lewis Dawe of Bay Roberts.

For two days Barbour and his crew of five fought a losing battle with the fall hurricane. Seas were whipped up into mountains — each mountain threatened to fall over on them to engulf ship and men. Worse, the seas had pounded the propeller, broken the shaft and forced the blades back upon the rudder rendering the rudder useless as well.

Engineer Hampton described the elements that day:

> Between waves that broke like snow drifts across the vessel, [we] had managed to drop over the side most of the 50 casks of cod oil carried on deck. The spreading oil helped somewhat to keep the seas down, but it didn't prevent one huge wave from rolling down the deck and smashing the only dory to pieces.

Hostile seas, no rudder for steerage, no propeller for power and no lifeboat! Odds were stacked against the six men struggling on the ocean. Cold, wet and almost blinded by ocean spray, they had retreated to the pilot house as darkness settled over the ocean on a second night of hardship. To compound their troubles, food supplies ran low; all that was available was a quarter of a bag of hard bread. There was no butter and no drinking water.

Earlier in the day three steamers had passed, but were too far away to see distress signals sent up from *National IV*. As engineer George Hampton recalled:

> About 7 o'clock the lights of another steamer appeared to the southeast. Frantically [we] sent up flares from the exhaust pipe on the pilot house. With grateful hearts [we] watched the lights draw near. The steamer circled our drifting vessel, finally sent a lifeboat over with a tow rope.

Captain Barbour went aboard the rescue ship while the steamer, which was not identified, towed *National IV* to St. Anthony. During the long haul to port, Captain

Barbour talked with the steamer captain, John Mitchell, an English merchant mariner who, on this particular trip, was bound to Canada.

In the course of conversation of ships, storms and wrecks, Kenneth Barbour told Mitchell that forty years previously, his father, William Barbour, was sailing northward on a sailing vessel. He came upon an ocean-going steamer that had been crushed in the ice and was sinking. Captain William rescued the grateful crew. The captain was John Mitchell (Senior), the father of Captain Ken Barbour's rescuer.

It took forty years, but a debt was repaid and an acquaintance renewed by the sons of two captains.

Photo courtesy of Hubert Hall

The 100 ton *National IV* (above), was one of four boats once owned by National Fish, Halifax, who sold her to Lewis Dawe, Bay Roberts. In 1938 her skipper was Eli Davis of Bay Roberts.

Eventually *National IV* was sold to Clifford Shirley and Sons of English Harbour West. She was lost on October 25, 1961, when she stranded in the entrance to Point Enragee Harbour (Point Rosie), Fortune Bay. Captain Charles Holley, Point Rosie, mate Ernest John Walters, Garnish, engineer Philip Power of English Harbour West and the other crew escaped safely.

Struck by Lightning

A nother case of the unusual on the sea happened in September 1938. While the schooner *Nyoda* of Gloucester was fishing on George's Bank during a severe storm, Captain Steven Fudge was struck by lightning and killed instantly, but strangely, there was no damage done to the schooner. In the rain and electrical storm, he had gone aloft to the masthead to secure the sail. Captain Fudge, born in Belleoram, had been a resident of Gloucester for seventeen years. News of the unfortunate accident was sent to his brother Captain Edward Owen Fudge.

Photo courtesy of John Drake

Bait vessel *Malakoff* (above at Belleoram) delivered bait around Newfoundland. Built in 1918, she was sold privately in the 1950s, renamed *Arctica*, then *Illex*. In 1935 she was commanded by Captain Burgess.

Of the fifty terms co-jointly signed between Newfoundland and Canada in December 1948 (and which came into effect March 31, 1949) when Newfoundland prepared to join Canada, two were unusual. Term 33 gave Canada property like the Newfoundland railway, its coastal shipping and Gander airport. It also names a ship, the *Malakoff*, the only ship mentioned in the lengthy agreement. This vessel collected bait, such as herring and caplin, and brought it to storage units around the coast. According to the Terms of Union, the federal government was required to own and to operate Newfoundland's *Malakoff*.

As stipulated in the Terms of Union between Newfoundland and Canada, Solo Margarine was produced by The Newfoundland Margarine Company Ltd. prior to the "Good Luck" label. It also allowed Newfoundland to continue manufacturing and selling margarine (or oleomargarine) around the province. Everywhere in Canada, its sale — in direct competition with dairy butter — was restricted. Margarine was a popular, cheap substitute for butter which was not readily available from small Newfoundland dairy farms.

Despite competition from large manufacturers on mainland, the Newfoundland Margarine Company produced margarine before and after Confederation with Canada. Later brand names changed from Solo, Golden Spread, Silver Spread, and Green Label to Good Luck and Eversweet.

A radio ditty claimed, "Solo Butter, So high in quality, So low in price."

Chapter Two

Wreck

Stories of wreck and ruin have been the fodder of Newfoundland folk tales and songs for many generations. Along the 6000 miles of the island's coastline, it has been estimated there have been 10,000 wrecks. Only a fraction of these are documented in books, ships' lists or newspaper accounts.

Here are eight previously untold stories of the sea — all true as verified by archival sources and the people involved.

Wrecking of S.S. *Calitro*

W hile there is not much evidence of deliberately luring a ship ashore in Newfoundland, ship "wracking" or illegally taking goods from grounded ships and wrecks was a more common crime. Judge D.W. Prowse presided over the trial of three men accused of wracking the vessel *Adonis* in 1877, and later killing the crew. All three were released due to lack of evidence. In August 1888, Judge Prowse tried and convicted three men of Placentia for their role in boarding and stealing coal from a wrecked collier from Nova Scotia. The *Morna* had gone ashore near Placentia with no loss of life, but men from the area ignored the entreaties of the captain and took the coal illegally (See Chapter One, Story Two).

Between 1869 and 1898, D.W. (Daniel Woodley) Prowse was a Police Magistrate, a Justice of the Peace, and Newfoundland's Circuit Judge. As circuit judge he travelled throughout Newfoundland holding court and trying lawbreakers. In addition to his efforts to reduce poaching, there was one other criminal activity that Prowse wished to curb: illegal hoarding of goods from wrecked ships. He became a connoisseur of the ways of wrackers of abandoned vessels and their cargoes on the long stretches of the island's rocky coast.

Every year the toll of wrecks and incidents of salvage, legal and illegal, was high. Through a series of arrests, trials and convictions, Judge Prowse sent a strong message to outlying towns that this criminal activity would be punished severely.

One of Prowse's most celebrated cases came from the wreck of the S.S. *Calitro* which went ashore at Horse Fire (or Hoss Fire) Rocks, near Red Head, close to the town of Grate's Cove, in the night of May 18, 1894. *Calitro* (often locally pronounced Caliko) sailed from Sunderland,

England, to Baltimore with a cargo of cement and general merchandise. She was a large vessel at nearly 3000 ton and 320 foot long.

Off Newfoundland she steamed through dense fog. Officers believed the ship was running between Cape Race and Ferryland Head; actually they were nearly 100 miles further north. One of the crew later stated:

> There was a big shock to the ship and consternation among the crew. All around was darkness, fog, massive rocks, surging waves, a sad sea moaning and a piercing wind. Where had the ship struck? Nobody aboard knew. Water began to flow into the ship and she began to settle; her hull heaved over.
>
> Three boats were launched; five in one and the remainder in the other two. Four hours of dangerous time and terrible suspense passed in the boats; not knowing whether there was safety or human habitations near. Eventually a landing was effected and some of the crew travelled along and reached Grates Cove.

Captain Storm, his wife and twenty-six of his crew barely escaped with their lives. They walked into Grate's Cove at dawn, May 19. Mrs. Storm, dressed only in her nightgown, was weak and barely able to walk. People of Grate's Cove, in a show of generosity typical of Newfoundland towns, immediately opened their doors and hearts to the strangers who appeared on their doorstep. The captain and his wife, for example, stayed at Jonah Avery's home.

However upon hearing the news of a "ship ashore" several men jumped in their boats and hastened to the wreck. William Henry Meadus and his son William John were first to the scene, followed by a boat belonging to Stephen Martin. In Martin's boat were Robert Avery, William John Avery and his son, Thomas. The men in this boat were the first up over the side of the stranded steamer. As well, Eli Avery went to the site with Josiah Avery in Josiah's boat.

To save goods from a wreck was viewed as a commendable act and was well within Newfoundland law. To compensate salvors, the law also stipulated that a portion of the value of the goods be given to the salvors. All items taken from a wreck must be declared and this is where the men of Grate's Cove slipped up. Much of *Calitro's* silverware was taken and hidden. Items included the ship's navigational instruments, clothing, especially Mrs. Storm's fine garments such as her fur boa or throat wrap, a silk cape and other items.

Captain Storm's wife had no extra clothing, so the next day the captain went to William Henry Meadus, who was the poverty commissioner for the area, and pleaded with him for assistance in the form of medical help and clothing (in fact her own clothes, now hidden in the town). William Henry did get the medical help, but gave not the slightest hint he knew anything about salvaged clothes.

Reverend George Bolt, the resident clergy in Bay de Verde, came to Grate's Cove and spoke to the congregation, but no one was willing to admit there was any salvage, much less say the goods were concealed under rocks and fish flakes. The only clothes forthcoming was the fur boa and silk cape which no one had much use for anyway. Just before Mrs. Storm left for St. John's on the tug *D.P. Ingraham*, she had to buy a dress from the woman she stayed with, Mrs. Jonah Avery.

Within a few days Sergeant Williams and Constable Butler arrived at the wreck site to secure it from further boarding. They begged the men to give up the hidden material. Thomas and William John Avery promised to deliver all, but produced only a small amount, about one-twentieth. Another policeman, Sergeant Dawe, managed to retrieve much of Robert Avery's stashed silver which was hidden under a flake.

Several men were arrested and were brought to St. John's before Judge Prowse, known to be especially tough on salvage offenders. Prowse explained that there was no public premise in Grate's Cove suitable to hold court and that the defendants would get better legal assistance in St. John's. Mr. Carty argued for the prosecution; Mr. Green, Q.C. defended William John Meadus, Mr. Knight for Thomas and Eli Avery. The other salvors present may not have had the benefit of a lawyer.

By June 6, 1894, Prowse had heard all the evidence, delivered his judgement and concluded:

> Even after our (Prowse and Sergeant Dawe) arrival it was only through the most unwearied exertions on the part of the constables that a considerable portion of the property was obtained, and even now a large quantity of goods belonging to the steamer, including the chronometer, are still concealed in the Grates.

The law gave Prowse authority to award maximum punishment: Eli Avery was given six months imprisonment and a four hundred dollar fine. William John Meadus was sentenced to six months. The other men were given three to four months in prison.

In conclusion, Prowse said he had punished the actual predators, "hoping it will be a warning to all that in the future not to bring a disgrace on the Colony by acting dishonestly at wrecks."

"Belles" of the Ocean

The word "belle" comes from the French language and generally means pretty. From the French, the word migrated into English where its connotation changed slightly to mean pretty woman as in the phrase "belle of the ball." No doubt the sight of the sleek and handsome lines of a schooner on the stocks or at full sail showed they were indeed beautiful ladies of the Atlantic. When one scans lists of schooners built or owned in Newfoundland, it can be seen that several vessels were named "Belle": *Village Belle, Neva Belle, Virgin Belle, Fanny Belle, Orissa Belle, Pubnico Belle, Belle Haddon, Cledda Belle, Belle of Burgeo, Belle of the Exe* and so on.

Yet many sailing Belles met with untimely or tragic ends; of those above the *Belle of Burgeo* was found capsized on September 6, 1918, with a loss of five crew and *Pubnico Belle* wrecked at Baccalieu Tickle on July 8, 1891. Two women and five children drowned. *Belle Haddon* was found bottom up near Twillingate in November 1890 and all three crew — Joseph Wellon, Ladle Cove, Simeon Bemister and Percy Mutch, both of Ragged Harbour — were lost.

Although there was no loss of life, the crew of eight on board the forty-four ton *Souris Belle* had a trying and unique experience. The schooner left Western Bay, Bay de Verde, on June 1, 1909, headed for St. John's. Her crew was Captain and owner Joseph Bishop, James Kennedy, J.M. Crawley, Levi King, Samuel Cooper, Clayton Crawley, J.J. Percy and Joseph Whalen, a young boy.

Everything went well until *Souris Belle* reached the Narrows at four or five A.M. June 2. Although it was June, slob ice and small ice pans covered the sea off the Northern Avalon Peninsula. In punching her way through, the schooner was caught in the ice and drifted out into Freshwater Bay. To Captain Bishop it seemed certain *Souris Belle* would be on the rocks in the rising winds. He put a flag in the rigging to indicate distress and let the two anchors down. The anchors dragged and had no effect.

When the schooner heeled over, the skipper gave the word to launch the two boats and to try to get to land if possible over or through the pounding ice floes. No sooner were the boats out, when a heavy sea swept in, turned the two boats over and threw the schooner on her beam ends.

E and S Barbour's business of Newtown owned a schooner called *Belle* which was built on Cobbler's Island, Bonavista Bay. Today only the name board resides at Benjamin Barbour House Museum in Newtown, Bonavista Bay. Queen Victoria and Prince Albert also hold a place of honour on the wall.
 Cobbler's Island, occupied from 1836 to 1869 with a peak population of ninety-seven, is where the Barbour shipowner/merchants originated.

Kennedy and the boy Whalen clambered onto a pan of ice and watched the boat they had just abandoned being broken to pieces. The larger boat turned bottom up in the tossing ice and Captain Bishop and the other five men had to jump on the pans to save their lives. Although the boat was broken and leaky, the men turned it over and got in, although they expected at any moment the ice pans would punch through the planking.

In the early morning dawn they saw their two companions, Kennedy and Whalen, several yards away and, hearing their shouts, made an attempt to get to them.

They threw a rope but it didn't reach the two on the drifting ice pan. When a ground swell broke under the boat, Bishop and his group figured they had to reach the safety of the shore to save their own lives.

Indeed it took all their strength and determination. When the ice would come together, they hauled the boat over it; when the ice receded with the sea and opened up, they jumped into the boat to save their lives. In this manner, they managed to reach the shore completely exhausted. Some of the men had cuts on their legs, arms and hands from the jagged ice.

Meanwhile, the other two were well offshore on a rectangular pan of ice measuring about twelve by six feet. Every few minutes a wave would wash over it as they drifted out toward Cape Spear. They saw *Souris Belle* capsize and finally sink.

The boy Whalen collapsed and was about to lie down in despair on the ice to die, but James Kennedy would have nothing of this. He kept telling him they would be seen from Cape Spear. Someone would telephone the harbour authority from the cape and a boat would be sent to rescue them.

And Kennedy was right. They had been on the pan of ice for two hours when the harbour tug *D.P. Ingraham* ploughed through the ice about eight A.M. and headed toward them. Once on land the two castaways were taken to the store of Jesse Whiteway who gave them dry clothing from head to foot. Whiteway also gave clothing to the other six men as they too had saved nothing but the wet clothes they stood in.

The six who were stranded on the shoreline had been picked up in a boat and landed at Maddox Cove in Petty Harbour Bay. Exhausted and destitute, they had to be housed and fed until the government provided means for them to get home.

These eight men of *Souris Belle* escaped with their

lives, but in the next tale another "Belle" was not so fortunate and this ship carried more than twice as many crew.

The Brigus schooner *Village Belle* left that port in March of 1872 in search of seals in the Gulf of St. Lawrence. *Village Belle* never reported and supposedly went down during a gale on March 17-18, 1872, with eighteen men. Seven were from Brigus — Captain John Antle, William Mayden, John Newell, Abraham and John Jaynes (Janes), William Roberts and John Martin.

Nine belonged to Bull Cove, a town now abandoned and located about two and a half kilometres east of Brigus. Its highest population was twenty-two and tradition claims that the loss of so many breadwinners in the tragedy contributed to the decline and eventual abandonment of the town. Bull Cove men lost on *Village Belle* were Philip, Henry, and John Youden; Ambrose, Thomas, and Jordan Sparkes; Robert and John Penney; and Henry Weeks. Francis Driscoll belonged to Harbour Main and Richard Power to Turk's Cove, Trinity Bay.

American Racer On Whale's Back

I n the era of the fast and able banking schooners, much was written and recorded about these ships south of the border — along the New England coast — of the exploits of schooner racing. Over the years, the stories of contests between the Canadian *Bluenose* and her American competitors were common. What is not so well known are the tales of the untimely ends of the larger schooners — driven on rocks and sand bars or those abandoned in the vast expanses of the Atlantic. This is a tale of one racer.

During a typical bout of stormy weather, the Gloucester schooner *Henry Ford* ran aground on the eastern end of the Whale's Back, a mile-long reef lying off

Martin's Point, north of Rocky Harbour. Two hours after she was stranded, a strong westerly wind with heavy sea forced the crew to abandon ship. *Henry Ford* left Cow Head on Friday and was making her last set for fish on Saturday at ten A.M. when, in thick cloud, she struck on the Whale's Back. The crew, after making several fruitless attempts to pull her off the reef, abandoned ship in the afternoon.

On Saturday morning June 16, 1928, she pounded on the rocks. This ripped out the bottom planks and put her on the bottom in eleven fathoms of water. For awhile only the mastheads showed above water. Captain Clayton Morrisey and his crew of twenty-five men launched their dories and rowed in safely at Gull Marsh, near where the S.S. *Ethie* was lost in December 1919 (See Chapter One, Story Five).

Captain Morrisey and his crew of twenty-five arrived at Bonne Bay on Monday. Nothing was saved from *Henry Ford* except the men's clothing. Farquhar's steamer *Skipper* went to the wreck early Sunday morning, but could do nothing in the heavy sea.

Morrisey and his crew left for Curling by S.S. *Sagona* to proceed to their homes by Friday's express. Local fishermen believed the masts of *Henry Ford* would be a navigational hazard and asked to have them removed. On her return voyage, *Sagona* hooked on to the masts and pulled them out.

One of Gloucester's most famous schooners, *Henry Ford* was built in Essex in 1922 and sailed out of Gloucester. She competed in the 1922 International Fisherman's Races, losing to the legendary *Bluenose*. After Gloucester's initial win of the trophy in 1920 (*Esperanto* over *Delawana*), Lunenburg built the *Bluenose*. The Nova Scotian crushed each of the four Gloucester challengers over the next seventeen years — *Elsie* 1921, *Henry Ford* 1922, *Columbia* 1923, *Gertrude L. Thebaud* 1931 and

1938. Only a single race win by *Henry Ford* prevented a total clean sweep.

Fortune Seamen Stranded

B y the 1940s, with the downturn in markets for salt cod, large banking schooners were becoming obsolete and were fast disappearing from Newfoundland harbours. In the off season from fishing, late fall and winter, bankers became coasting schooners and brought supplies from larger ports of Canada to Newfoundland communities. In time, businessmen and shop owners found smaller engine-powered freighting vessels and the "coaster" became more commonplace.

On the coastal run, these vessels with their hard working, experienced captains and crews, did yeomen service often under trying conditions. Voyages around the coast and across the treacherous Gulf of St. Lawrence to obtain coal, potatoes and other produce were made in the off-season when fall storms and unforgiving seas were prevalent. By the 1940s to mid-60s, when a completed Trans Canada Highway replaced sea trade, there were scores of ships "in the coasting trade" around Newfoundland; inevitably many were wrecked. The next story, while not a dramatic tale of wreck and rescue, nevertheless illustrates the end of one such vessel.

A coaster that appeared for a brief period in Newfoundland waters was *Nauphila*, a ninety-five foot pilot boat which once serviced Halifax harbour and guided ocean-going liners into that busy harbour. In 1946, she was sold to John King of Fortune, Newfoundland, and for two years plied the Newfoundland-Nova Scotia coastal run.

The vessel had been built in Mahone Bay in 1925; at

the end of her life — December 14, 1948 — the vessel was twenty-three years old. However, the end of her career was not in the safe and relatively calm confines of Halifax harbour, but in the open ocean between Nova Scotia and Newfoundland.

Nauphila left Fortune bound for Halifax on Friday December 10, but met a typical winter northeasterly gale. She lay to until Sunday before continuing her slow labour toward Nova Scotia. On Tuesday night, in a blinding snow-storm while heavy seas pounded *Nauphila*, the helmsman mistook the Whitehead light for Scaterie light.

Photo courtesy National Film Board of Canada

Fortune in the 1950s. Two men dump a handbar load of salt fish in the hold of the Portuguese steamer *Rio Alberto*. Other workers (bottom) stack the fish in the hold. The schooner (left) is *Mary Ruth*; in the background is the schooner *Vera B. Humby* while the masts of *Helen G. McLean* are barely visible.

When the freighter struck the rocks, she began to break up quickly. The crew — Captain George "Nick" Collier, owner John King, seaman Chris Hepditch, all of Fortune; Maxwell Collins, Lamaline and John H. Ayres, Point Crew — tried to launch a dory but it was swept away. Fortunately, there was a second one aboard. Captain

Collier was injured and had to be thrown into the dory from *Nauphila*'s deck when waves prevented him from being lowered over the side.

Waves swept the fragile craft onto an unfamiliar shore. In the darkness and against the protection of a cliff they crouched, huddled against the wind and blizzard. Finally they found and entered an abandoned fisherman's shack and lit a fire.

Twenty-seven hours after they jumped from the wrecked *Nauphila* the storm abated. Seas on that lonely isolated beach finally subsided. They launched their life dory and pulled into Whitehead on Wednesday morning, December 15.

Black Joe and the Isle of Demons

There is no shortage of legends about Belle Isle, situated at the northern end of Newfoundland, at the Atlantic entrance to the Strait of Belle Isle. Once known as Isle of Demons to early navigators, the island is approximately thirty-nine square kilometers (fifteen square miles) in area and has little vegetation. There are only two safe harbours: Lark Tickle and Black Joke or "Black Joe" as it was commonly called. The latter is only sixty yards wide and 300 yards long.

Belle Isle was also given the name Isle of Bad Fortune by the King of Portugal because, he believed, one of his ships was lost in the Strait of Belle Isle about 1503.

The first French woman to set foot on Newfoundland was believed to have landed on Belle Isle. Legend has it that Marguerite de la Rocque was put off on Belle Isle in 1542 while traveling on a ship with her uncle, Jean Francois de la Rocque, Sieur de Roberval. When he learned his niece was misbehaving with a young man on board the ship, he became very upset and they were both landed on Belle Isle. Marguerite's lover is said to have gone mad but she survived and was rescued by French fishermen.

But the lure of the rich grounds and valuable fishery in the surrounding waters drew ships; first from the extensive French enterprise, later the Newfoundland fishery. With the ships came wrecks.

In 1867 the French steamer *Napoleon*, which visited Belle Isle in the spring and fall to bring supplies to the lighthouse keepers, brought ten men and materials to build a house for ship-wrecked people. The shores surrounding Belle Isle were recorded as being unsafe with no secure anchorage. Many ships were lost there and those who travelled to Belle Isle were thankful if they made a safe return without loss of life and property. In 1902 seven vessels were lost in a storm: the crews had been fishing at Belle Isle. No lives were lost but fish and cargoes were.

In the fall of 1949, *M. & G. Fowlow* owned by Pierce Blackmore of Pilley's Island, became one of the last wrecks recorded on the island. All summer ten fishermen employed under Frank Roebothan worked on the rich fishing grounds in the Strait of Belle Isle. They had caught and salted 1200 quintals and *M.& G. Fowlow* was chartered to pick up the men and the fish. She left Pilley's Island, Notre Dame Bay on September 24, 1949, headed for Black Joe, Belle Isle.

The trip north was not easy since *M. & G. Fowlow* was "bubble light" with only two cord of firewood as ballast. Normally, little ships on this mission hugged the shoreline and carefully crossed the bays headland to headland. But in the gale the six crew — Captain Wesley Pittman, engineer Fred Locke, cook Selby Oke, all of Pilley's Island, Simeon Colbourne, Lush's Bight and two other deckhands — had to steer a course farther out to sea to avoid the shoreline reefs and rocks.

Late the next day, September 25, they anchored safely at Lark Tickle at Belle Isle and heavy weather forced them to stay there until September 30. Finally, *M. & G. Fowlow* moved to Black Joe. In the next three days of foggy weather, the crews loaded the catch as well as twenty-seven casks of cod oil. On October 4, all the salt fish, the fishing gear and the ten men were aboard and in the evening the final task of hoisting the skiffs aboard began.

By now it was blowing "half a hurricane", and an easterly wind right into the face of Black Joe. The men made no attempt to get out of the tortuous narrow cove. Seaman Simeon Colbourne recorded the events which lead to the wreck of *M. & G. Fowlow*:

> I was asleep in my bunk when I was awakened by our fishing skipper who said it was getting very rough. I got up and called the men in the forecastle saying, 'Boys we will have to leave her, I expect.'
>
> The schooner was by this time rolling very heavily. The other men and I got our clothes and bedding bundled up. At dawn the sea was still rising and breaking completely over the point which had given temporary shelter to our moored schooner.

Skipper Roebotham (foreman of the shore-based fishermen) and two others launched the boat on the stern of the schooner and Colbourne went with them as they rowed ashore in the heaving turmoil of the cove to the government wharf.

After several trips back and forth to what appeared to be a doomed vessel, all sixteen men were landed on the shore. Colbourne watched *M. & G. Fowlow* from the shore and saw her final moments. It was Thursday, October 6:

> By the time this was completed the schooner was rolling bulwarks in and riding heavily on

the anchor chains and shore lines. We were all wet through and cold and someone offered to get a fire going. The skipper checked this at once and ordered the boats hauled up out of reach of the heavy surf pounding the shoreline.

When we finished this task we climbed up a hill to see how the schooner was faring. All her starboard bulwarks were stove in and she was listing heavily to the port.

By this time the cook had a fire going and made coffee. [We] changed into dry clothes. A little later Skipper Pittman went up to see the schooner. He reported her "Gone!" and that only the crosstrees were sticking out of water. The white capped combers soon reduced the wooden schooner to debris along the rocks.

Now stranded on a barren island, *M. & G. Fowlow's* crew were safe, but all supplies had been lost in the wreck and food was in short supply. They could only await rescue. On Saturday October 8, a message went to Captain Martin G. Dalton, the Marine Superintendent of the Railway, asking him if any government steamers were in the vicinity. After Dalton replied there was no ship, authorities asked the Grenfell Association in St. Anthony to send a ship, but a message stated their hospital ship *Maravel* was stormbound in Forteau, a considerable distance away.

Finally Crosbie and Company sent the whaler *Olaf Olsen*, stationed at Williamsport, White Bay, to Belle Isle. When *Olaf Olsen* arrived on Sunday, a message to St. John's said there had been a second shipwreck on Belle Isle during the storm. It read:

> "Schooner *Scarlet Knight* lost during the night of October 6 in severe storm at Black Joe, northeast Belle Isle, all crew safe ashore. Schooner (thought to be out of Green Bay) was fishing here during the summer."

It was the second time in two years the whaler *Olaf Olsen* had plucked shipwrecked crews off an uninhabited island. On November 15, 1947, residents of Ship's Cove, near the tip of the Great Northern Peninsula, saw flares coming from the barren, windswept Sacred Island. In the heavy seas and winds no small ship could reach the island. It was eventually learned the wrecked ship was the British steamer *Langlee Crag*. Her forty crew were stranded for four days until *Olaf Olsen* arrived.

Rum Runner – Rum Chaser

In 1950 the rum runner, come rum chaser, *Shulamite* was rebuilt in Garnish. Her deck had been level and the Garnish shipwrights built bulwarks on the side so the vessel could carry deck cargo — legal cargo. Once back in the water and renamed *Norsya*, (a derivative of Nor - North, Sy - Sydney, A - Agencies) her duties changed.

Norsya, owned by the Norsya Steamship Company of North Sydney, of whom one of the founders was her captain Thomas Myles, was 105 feet long and powered by two 210-horsepower Fairbanks-Morris engines. She was a wooden ship built at Mahone Bay, Nova Scotia, in 1930 as a rum-runner. When the American Prohibition ended, she was purchased by the Newfoundland government as a "rum-chaser" to apprehend smugglers. With her two crude oil engines she had a cruising speed of about sixteen miles per hour. During World War II she was a navy examination vessel at St. John's and, after the war, was purchased by Captain Thomas Myles.

Now she carried freight from Sydney to Newfoundland and travelled northward to Corner Brook, St. Anthony, down to Notre Dame Bay and Bonavista Bay. Along the coast and at St. John's, she would load scrap iron. At

Bonavista she frequently picked up berries — usually partridge berries in ten gallon containers — and carried her cargo to Sydney.

Before she sank in 1953 *Norsya* had two unusual incidents: at one time she "raced" the Gulf steamer *Baccalieu*. Both were leaving Port aux Basques for North Sydney and as the much larger steamer came abreast of *Norsya* someone on the latter ship held up a rope. This could only indicate one thing! *Baccalieu* was slow. Did it wish a tow by the smaller ship? Soon a race was on and white smoke poured from the great stacks on the steamer. *Baccalieu* was no match; *Norsya* arrived in North Sydney six miles ahead of the steamer.

But such frolics courted trouble. The throbbing of *Norsya*'s powerful engines shook her timbers. Should the propellers come out of water in the trough of high seas, the props would rotate or race at high speed causing the engines and vessel to vibrate dangerously.

On the night of December 24, 1950, *Norsya* was on St. Pierre Bank steaming to North Sydney loaded with scrap iron collected in Newfoundland. The seas were high, rough enough that the engineer at the time, Clem Miles, who could see the seas through the engine room companionway, slowed the engines when he saw a high wave approaching.

Miles knew that from the length of the voyage they should have reached the relatively calmer waters of Sydney Bight. He went to look at the compass and realized it was "off" by several degrees. The reading had been affected by some scrap iron resting on or near the binnacle or compass housing. First Miles discussed this with the mate; then both went to inform the captain. *Norsya* was indeed off course.

A check of charts showed *Norsya* near the dangerous shoals approaching Louisbourg, Nova Scotia. It took nearly a day extra on the voyage to get from Louisbourg to

North Sydney, the intended destination. If the vessel had continued the course and speed, no doubt it would have wrecked somewhere near Louisbourg.

Shulamite (above), later renamed *Norsya*, had a long and varied career in Newfoundland waters.

On September 19, 1953, the old freighter met her end. *Norsya* struck a submerged object and sank in two hours. She was ten miles north of Matane in the St. Lawrence River and headed to Forbisher Bay with a load of logs. Official sources say *Norsya* struck "an object" but there are many who suspect it was a dead whale or a log.

Her crew rowed into Baie des Sables, Quebec. They were: part owner and captain Wallace Thomas "Tom" Myles, age forty-six, born in Harbour Breton but living in North Sydney; chief engineer Garland Vallis, thirty-eight, Coomb's Cove; and five men from Harbour Breton, mate John Joe Stone, fifty-two; second engineer, James Skinner (son of Peter), thirty-four; cook Joseph Day, twenty-nine; seamen John Moore, eighteen; and Bud Skinner, age seventeen.

The crew stayed one night in a Montreal hotel and returned to North Sydney the next day.

On the Cliffs of Cappahayden

We were lucky to be alive for we were all non-swimmers and there was a heavy swell on. If the *Marvita* hadn't drifted in near a large rock we would have had to jump in the surf at the bottom of this cliff.

It was under these conditions described above that Captain Mike Macdonald and eight crew, including the storyteller Clyde Collins, escaped the wreck of the Custom's boat M.V. *Marvita*.

Thursday, July 15, 1954, was a grey foggy day off Cape Race and although *Marvita* was supposed to be five miles off land, she went aground about six P.M. "We saved some suitcases," recalled Collins, "a bit of clothes and the captain saved his log, but that was all. Yes, we were fortunate there was no loss of life and I'll tell you why."

Built in 1930 in Nova Scotia, *Marvita* was one of the "Banana Fleet" boats designed as a tanker to carry illegal liquor during the American Prohibition. She was one of several boats built in that era; designed with a low profile and given lots of speed. In a way they resembled a submarine or a banana; hence the name. The 190 ton *Marvita* was one of the most successful rum carriers stealthily running the triangular St. Pierre—New York—Nova Scotian routes.

When the ban against the importing or manufacturing of alcohol, commonly known as Prohibition or Volsted's Act, ended in the United States in 1933, *Marvita* was eventually sold to the Newfoundland government. Fred Hounsell was her first local captain. In Newfoundland waters her role reversed; she became a revenue cutter designated to reduce smuggling from St. Pierre to Newfoundland.

Cloying blankets of fog often enshroud the southeastern Avalon in mid-summer and *on Marvita's* final run in July 1954, it was a real "pea-souper." *Marvita's* duty was to carry the Custom's Inspector, Gus Gardiner, from Argentia to St. John's. Macdonald, an experienced and veteran captain, wisely kept his vessel about five miles off shore and set a course that would take *Marvita* safely around Cape Race. Over the years, the stretch of coastline between Cape Ballard and Cape Race had justly earned the dubious name, "Graveyard of Ships."

Marvita carried nine crew: Captain Macdonald, born in St. Mary's and a resident of St. John's; mate Maurice Murphy, Fox Harbour; chief engineer Boyd Duffett, Catalina; second engineer Martin Barron, St. John's; cook Patrick Barron, probably from Placentia; steward Frank Burry, Greenspond; and sailors George Collins, Lamaline; Larry Sheehan, Cappahayden and Clyde Collins, who lived in St. John's, but was born in Lamaline.

Many of the crew were ex-servicemen. Maurice Murphy had served in the Royal Navy, Larry Sheehan in the Newfoundland Regiment and Captain Macdonald had been in the navy as well.

Clyde Collins and mate Murphy, who both took watch at four P.M., sounded their fog horn every two minutes.

> Both the mate and I kept a sharp lookout, but the only indication of being close to the rocks we had was an echo. It seemed to bounce off a cliff and by the time we sounded a second blast, it was too late. We both saw white seas breaking and put *Marvita* in reverse. She had two Fairbanks Morris engines. There had to be time — from several seconds to a minute or two — for the engines to stop and then gear into reverse.

But it was too late! Apparently a strong inset of tide, or iron on the bottom from scores of other steamers and ships wrecks in the general area threw the compass variation out by a degree or two. *Marvita* slid upon a rock, one engine stopped and propeller blade went into the bottom of the vessel. There was no way to back off the ledge. Collins remembered:

> We had a lifeboat, but there was too much sea to get it off deck. The swell kept her on the ledge for twenty minutes, but she gradually moved closer to a large flat-topped rock near the base of the cliff. Seeing he could do no more, Captain Macdonald gave the order to "Abandon ship."
>
> Seas would take her in close to the rock; then she'd fall back. The mate and I stood outside the rail and when she was carried in closer to the rock, we jumped. We got a rope ashore and the guys left on *Marvita* kept pressure on the rope keeping her close to the rock.
>
> Each man jumped; the cook missed his footing and went into the water, but caught the rope. Last off was the second engineer who was probably getting some personal items before he jumped.
>
> We were lucky no one was drowned or injured. If we had to jump into the surf to reach the beach or the cliff, things might have turned out differently.

All nine men now stood on a rock barely above water at the base of a cliff somewhere near Cape Ballard. No one knew exactly where they were. Fortunately no one was hurt and, although they couldn't see the top of the cliff in the fog, it was not steep. Collins remembered the climb:

> We all helped each other up. Mr. Gardiner, the Custom's Officer, was a heavy-set man, about 250 pound and around sixty years old, and he couldn't scale the incline. George Collins and I went down to help him.
>
> At the top we tried to get our bearings, but

had no idea which way to walk. Before we grounded we heard the horn on Cape Race; so we knew we were near Cappahayden. We walked inland from the cliff for a good while, but went in a complete circle and arrived back at the cove where our ship was. By now *Marvita* was partially submerged; planks and wood drifted away from her.

Photo courtesy Maritime History Archives, MUN

On November 21, 1946, *Marvita* (above) towed the motor vessel *Granite*, owned by Earle and Son, Carbonear, from Prosser's Rock at the entrance to St. John's harbour. *Granite*, en route to Pacquet, White Bay, carried a full cargo of winter supplies and was aground all night. The Harbour Master at the time, Captain Newton Halfyard, reported the weather was civil and when the tide rose in the morning of November 22, the powerful *Marvita* had no difficulty dragging the stranded vessel from her perch.

Once again the nine men, who were getting tired after the efforts of self-rescue and the climb up the cliff, set out inland. They walked across a marsh and reached a patch of woods around dusk. They decided to stay there for the night; perhaps by morning the fog would lift. As it turned out, as Collins remembered, shipmate Larry Sheehan, a resident of Cappahayden, knew the lay of the land. He recalls:

In the fog and darkness we saw a stump, first it looked like a large tree cut off near the ground. Then Sheehan recognized it as part of the old telegraph pole line that ran into Cappahayden. Then he knew where we were located. We followed the old pole line right into Cappahayden reaching there about eleven or twelve in the night.

We found a place to stay in a club or motel which had several rooms. The next morning several men of Cappahayden took the captain and mate Murphy to the wreck site. *Marvita* was under water by that time. The rest of us took a taxi to St. John's.

Collins recalled his six years on *Marvita*: the smuggling patrol and in 1949 after Confederation when she carried the first RCMP officers to the south coast of Newfoundland to places like Burgeo, Harbour Breton, Grand Bank and Burin. In the weeks prior to the vote for Confederation she delivered the ballot boxes along the Labrador coast to the northern communities and to the "floater" fishermen of Conception Bay stationed on the Labrador coast.

After the loss of *Marvita*, Collins, a member of the Newfoundland regiment in World War Two, joined the Fisheries Patrol boat *Eastern Explorer*. He later worked in Bennett Brewery in St. John's until he retired. Today he enjoys reminiscing of his experiences on the sea.

Camperdown Goes Down

A veteran 'wooden wall' at the sealing front was old and tired and ready to give up the ghost. She was slowly sinking into a white grave. The twenty sealers aboard climbed out onto the ice and waited for the vessel's final throes.

It was the 145 ton *Camperdown*, owned and captained by Patrick Miller of Fogo. On March 30, 1960, while forty miles north of Belle Isle near the northern tip of Newfoundland, heavy ice opened seams. Water seeped in, slowly at first, but, within hours, increasingly more.

By the next day she lay on her side with a thirty to forty degree list. Knowing she could not be salvaged, the crew removed as much moveable gear — anchor and chains, deck engines, lifeboats — as possible to the ice floes. Yet *Camperdown*, partly submerged, refused to go willingly and quickly to the bottom.

Captain Miller had already called for help and the Canadian ice-breaker *Wolfe* responded. In the morning of April 1, when the crew and gear from the sealer had been rescued, *Wolfe* rammed the 145 ton *Camperdown* to

Photo courtesy of William Lockyer

Camperdown is down by the stern. Her lifeboats and other moveable gear are on the ice.

ensure the derelict would sink. However, the tough old sealer wouldn't go easily; the ice around her kept her afloat. *Wolfe* steamed up to ram the vessel and although *Camperdown* rolled down past her mastheads, she bobbed back up. Finally on the third or fourth attempt, *Camperdown* went to the bottom.

Wolfe landed the men at Lewisporte. Miller, in speaking to the media, said he hated to see his vessel go: "*Camperdown* was a good vessel and to replace her will cost at least $100,000. The crew had taken some seals when she took water after being trapped in the ice that kept a constant pressure on her. Finally the seams in the ship's stern opened and she had to be abandoned."

Photo courtesy of Newfoundland Tourist Development Office

Wooden sealer *Terra Nova*. Like the *Camperdown*, the wooden sealer *Terra Nova* died "in the ice." She was crushed by ice on March 21, 1964. Leaking, she was abandoned and set fire at latitude 50.18 North, longitude 55.07 West. Captain Saul White of Carbonear and his thirty-eight sealers escaped with their lives in the Gannett Island area. White said, "We were following a running joint or lead of water through the ice toward the seals. Then the ice cut in. Big sheets of it. It came against the ship and almost sliced it in two. It took the deck off the port side and the ship was splintered."

Terra Nova, a 138 ton ship, was several hours before it sank giving the men enough time to take personal effects and food off. All were transferred to sealer *Arctic Prowler* about a quarter mile away.

Camperdown, a former Halifax pilot boat built in 1944 at Shelburne, Nova Scotia, had been used by the Miller business of Fogo for eight years. Her crew was Captain Miller, Joseph Payne, George Payne, Raymond Bursey, George Warrick of Fogo; Raymond Heath, Deep Bay, Fogo Island; Gergus Penton, Brendan Emberley, Donald Decker, Joe Batt's Arm; George Snow, Chesley Snow, Noggin Cove; Maxwell Hoffe, Change Islands; engineer Everett Parsons, Carmanville; Joseph Sacrey, Woodstock, White Bay; Willis Bath and two other men hailed from Horse

Island, White Bay. Names of the first mate from Corner Brook and the two cooks who belonged to Carbonear are not recorded.

Camperdown was the third vessel the Miller business had lost in thirteen years. Eight died when their coaster *Francis P. Duke* struck the rocks off Pool's Island and Badger's Quay on December 16, 1947. Among the victims were two sons, William age thirty-four and captain of the vessel, and twenty-one year old Ignatius.

Prior to the loss of *Camperdown*, it had been several years since a sealing vessel had gone to the bottom. In 1954, three ships were lost within eighteen days: the *Newfoundland*, owned by Captain Johnny Blackmore or Port Union, was crushed by ice off Eddies Cove on March 17; *Truls*, registered in St. John's, went down on March 31. The third ship lost that spring was *James Spurrell*, a small sealer which stranded and sank off Cape Ray on April 4. There was no loss of life on either ship.

Coal in Trinity Harbour

The 277 ton M.V. *Fenmore* had been built in England as a mine sweeper during World War Two. She was later converted to a trawler. In 1956 Captain John Blackwood bought the ship to carry coal from North Sydney to Newfoundland. He had the hatch openings enlarged and the fish pounds removed. *Fenmore* had plenty of power with a 48 horsepower engine and could make a top speed of ten knots.

Blackwood left North Sydney on Thursday, October 13, 1960 with over 300 ton of coal destined for Trinity. He carried a Newfoundland crew: mate James Sturge from Gambo, chief engineer Roland Clarke, second engineer Fred May, both of Twillingate, cook Herbert Burrage, seamen Don Legge, Joe Clarke and Hedley Keats were from Dover, Bonavista Bay.

Weather on the way down was exceptionally fine. Making great time, they arrived off Trinity on Saturday, October 15 about nine P.M., steered toward the entrance between Skerwink and Admiral's Island and Captain Blackwood kept his vessel in the channel. It was a pitch black night with no moon or stars in the sky. Cruising ahead at about three knots, the engine was going dead slow.

Blackwood said afterward he felt a slight bump and the vessel struck a rock on the starboard bow. At the time, the radar showed the ship to be in the exact centre of the entrance. Blackwood said later, "I didn't think any damage had been done until one of the crew called out that the forecastle was filling with water."

The captain asked the engineer to stop the engine and immediately ordered the lifeboat lowered; by the time the lifeboat was in the water Fenmore's port side rail was awash. The captain recalled:

> She was settling heavily by the head. The crew and I just had time to push off from the vessel's side when her stern rose into the air and she slid under bow first. As we rowed away she went under, approximately half an hour after she struck. Very few personal belongings were saved as nobody had time to grab anything.

She went down in fifteen fathoms of water inside the protecting head of Skerwink. The eight men rowed ashore and were accommodated for the night at Trinity Cabins. For many years *Fenmore* lay intact and upright on the bottom and was visited regularly by divers.

Fenmore was the second vessel Captain Blackwood lost in five years. The 149 ton *Mont Murray* sank fifty-eight miles southwest of St. Pierre in September 1955. This vessel foundered at the onset of a hurricane. Blackwood and his crew were rescued by the trawler *Red Diamond* just before *Mont Murray* went under.

With the sinking of *Fenmore* in 1960 and the loss of M.V. *Marvid* in Trinity on February 8, 1957, that put 600 ton of coal on the bottom of Trinity harbour. These losses came at a time when many Newfoundlanders were becoming more dependant on coal and were cutting less wood for the winter.

Chapter Three

Fatalities

These eight stories of death on the sea range from the loss of one life to the great tragedies of many lives; geographic locations vary as do the circumstances. These are the stories of wrecks where someone survived to tell the tale. All happened many years ago in Newfoundland.

Only Two Came Home

I n October of 1874 the brigantine *Orient* left Carbonear for Chateau, a town located on the Labrador side of the Strait of Belle Isle. From there, the ship headed to Montreal to land her fish and to pick up a general cargo of flour, pork, butter, sugar and vegetables — especially onions, all destined for the dinner tables of Carbonear.

Orient, owned by the Joyce Brothers' business of Carbonear, had ten crew, all Carbonear seamen. She was commanded by Captain John Edgar Joyce, age twenty-seven, who had his brother Obadiah Gilbert Joyce as chief mate. The latter was also a qualified captain himself. Other crewmen were Joseph Taylor, twenty-five, Richard Taylor, nineteen, Stewart Taylor, seventeen, Thomas Fitzpatrick, forty-three, William Clark, twenty-one, Charles Henry, thirty-six, Ambrose Forward, twenty-six and seaman Eli Moores. Most were related to each other.

Orient arrived at Quebec City in mid-November; took on a river pilot and left on the seventeenth. When the worst of navigating the St. Lawrence River was over, Captain Joyce landed the pilot and sailed for Newfoundland.

The voyage into the Gulf was rough with easterly winds and fog for three days. On November 21, the wind chopped northwest, blowing a gale with snow and temperatures well below freezing. It was under these terrible weather conditions *Orient* grounded seven miles north of Cape West on Anticosti Island. It was four A.M. and pitch black. The southwest lighthouse was seven miles away but the crew couldn't see it through the snow squalls.

With no time to lose, they lowered the boat, but it was swamped on the side of *Orient* before they could manoeuver it away. The ten men were thrown into the icy water. Captain Edward Joyce and three others were drowned when the boat filled with water; six managed to cling to the rigging.

The lighthouse keeper on Anticosti Island at this time was J. Pope who had his assistants working at the light with him. In a letter written to a newspaper on May 5, 1875, Pope described his role in the wreck on that bitter day in November:

> As soon as we saw them my men went to the scene of the disaster and reached there with great difficulty because of the seas running up the cliffs, taking us off our feet several times. We were unable to render any assistance at the time as the sea was making a complete breach over the vessel.
>
> We picked up bodies that were washed on shore and laid them out some distance from the sea. Then we directed our attention to what remained of the spars and the boats.
>
> It was a sad duty for two of us to perform in the darkening of the late evening to carry the remains of so many fine stalwart men lacerated and bleeding. They were afterwards brought to the point and interred together in one common grave.

Some of *Orient*'s men clung to the rigging, but in the cold they perished one by one. Obadiah Joyce and Eli Moores clung to the masts which, like the rest of the wreck, was covered with ice formed from freezing spray. Joyce removed his mitts to get a firm grip on the rope and suffered severe frostbite; eventually all his fingernails fell off. Moores had both feet frozen.

All day the two clung to life as would-be rescuers could only watch from several feet away on shore. About seven o'clock, at low tide, Moores and Joyce left to walk ashore. Assisted by lightkeeper Pope, his assistants and family, both survivors walked the nine or ten miles around

South West Bay to the lighthouse residence. At times they were up to their waist in water or ploughed through high drifts with their clothes frozen on them.

Pope had a family of ten; each helped bring cold water to rub and massage the frozen limbs of the two survivors back to life. After weeks of careful nursing, Moores and Joyce were able to walk again. They stayed with the family all winter for treacherous waters or ice surrounded Anticosti and there was no communication or transportation to the island until spring.

Back in Carbonear, the relatives of the ten seamen knew some catastrophe had befallen the ship. It should have arrived by November or December. As the new year 1875 slipped into February and March, it was firmly believed *Orient* and her crew had been lost with no survivors.

But on Anticosti Island spring slowly broke the winter ice barrier. On the first of May a small boat of about twenty ton, came from Gaspe, Quebec, to West Point, Anticosti. It salvaged some flour from *Orient*'s wreckage and inquired at the lighthouse about the wreck. This little boat took Obadiah Joyce and Eli Moores to Gaspe where the two sent a telegram home. This was the first news of what had happened to *Orient* and her crew in six months.

From Gaspe the two survivors travelled to Montreal where they were treated by doctors. From Montreal they went to Portland, Maine, and then by steamer to Halifax. At Halifax they boarded the S.S. *Hibernian* for St. John's. When they arrived at Carbonear on the coastal mail packet *Lizzie*, they were viewed as men who had been resurrected from the legions of drowned mariners — the only two left from ten men who had left Carbonear in October.

From the day of the wreck in November to May, Joyce and Moores had no means of communication from icebound Anticosti. By late spring mail service resumed. They sent a letter to U.J. Gregory, Quebec's Marine and

Fisheries official which was published in the newspaper *Quebec Chronicle* on May 4, 1875.

Oddly, in one of the quirks of communication, the survivors were back home when their same letter (and another letter from lightkeeper Pope) was re-published in the *Harbour Grace Standard* on June 26, 1875. It read in part:

> ...We were very badly frozen and injured, not able to help ourselves for several weeks and through great skill and attendance we have been restored to health and the use of our limbs for which we cannot be sufficiently grateful. We are also thankful for the attention and respect shown to the remains of our unfortunate shipmates.

> (Signed) Obadiah Gilbert Joyce, C. Mate
> Eli Moores, Mariner

Ortolan: "Naufrage" is Shipwreck

St. Pierre has been dubbed, along with several other coastlines which share a like and dubious distinction, the "Graveyard of the Atlantic." A map of St. Pierre "naufrages" or shipwrecks shows the location of five or six hundred wrecks strewn around in every cape, corner and cove. There on the shipwreck map, squeezed in between the wreck of *Peneloy*, 1927, and *Southbourne*, 1881, is the tiny dot on the southwest corner of Langlade — *Ortolan* wrecked in 1877.

George Simms was the stipendiary magistrate of Grand Bank at this time and, as magistrate, Simms had the extra duties of Justice of the Peace and Wreck Commissioner for the coast. As Wreck Commissioner he reported on ship losses near his home and recently his account of *Ortolan*'s loss was located.

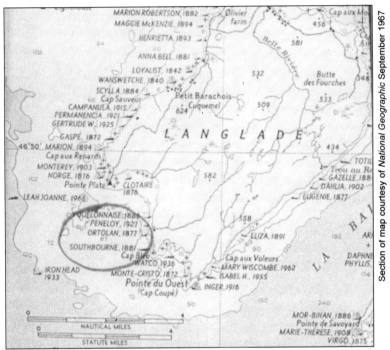

Section of map courtesy of National Geographic September 1967

Squeezed between the wreck of *Peneloy*, 1927, and *Southbourne*, 1881, this early map of shipwrecks "Naufrages du St. Pierre" shows the location of *Ortolan*, 1877.

Simms knew the vessel *Ortolan* for it had been built and owned in Grand Bank by George Bell. The vessel's unusual name refers to a small English bird. Bell sold it to Thomas Bond of Frenchman's Cove between 1872 and 1877. Stories of schooners out of Frenchman's Cove are rare although the town, located between Garnish and Grand Bank, has been involved in the fish trade since its earliest beginnings.

One creature of the sea not exploited there nor fished by Newfoundlanders in the 1870s was the lowly lobster, considered at that time a nuisance and fit only for fertilizer. But businessmen from Nova Scotia knew of their value and set up factories along Newfoundland's south coast to can the product for export.

They brought with them many single young men to

run and to work in the lobster canning factories. Many married local girls and the families later moved back to Nova Scotia. My great grandfather's sisters, Amelia Forsey married Clarence Estano of Halifax and Dinah Rose Forsey married Duncan Lamont of Dartmouth. One who stayed was William Fox, a tinsmith with Stainer's lobster factory in Grand Bank, who married Susan Francis.

Vessels like *Ortolan* carried the products to foreign ports. On October 5, 1877, she left Grand Bank bound for St. Pierre with Thomas Bond as master. In addition to her crew, those on board were some Nova Scotian passengers — Lawson Corkum, agent for Fortune Lobster Factory; Peter Bows of Dartmouth; John Mulcahy, Halifax; C.A. Hutchins, all connected with the Chebucto Lobster Packing Company. William Mitchell, agent for the Garnish Lobster Factory and one woman, Mrs. Corkum of Sambro, Nova Scotia, were also on the schooner.

Bond's crew came from nearby towns: Edward Follett, Grand Beach; George Reeves and Thomas Grandy of Garnish; William Reid and George Lahey, Frenchman's Cove. Lahey was probably employed in the Frenchman's Cove lobster factory, but wasn't born there. All told twelve people sailed on *Ortolan* on that windy Friday evening when she left on a relatively short run to the French Isles.

Evidently in the gale that followed, the schooner did not make St. Pierre harbour but was beaten to pieces near a high cliff between Point Platte and Cap Bleu, Langlade Island, northwest of St. Pierre. As *Ortolan* passed over a shoal before striking the cliff, a heavy sea swept across her deck and washed all twelve people over the side. A rebound of the same sea from the overhang of cliff pushed eight souls back unto the ship or near enough so they could grab lines or rigging. But four were not so fortunate and disappeared in the boiling surf — Mrs. Corkum, Bows, Mulcahy, and sailor George Lahey. Their bodies were never recovered.

Ortolan's fate was sealed; she broke up quickly. The survivors waited for a moment or two for a favourable position and then crawled out on the bowsprit one by one reaching the cliff before *Ortolan* was dashed to pieces. They now faced a formidable task of scaling an almost perpendicular rock face. Several hours later the whole group managed to reach the cliff top and waited till daylight, October sixth.

The survivors, except Hutchins who was too exhausted to move, set out for the nearest habitation. They figured, from the footpath and other signs, that a house or farm was not far away. But Hutchins refused to go. The others gave him strict orders to remain in that location so as he could be easily found later.

The seven who set out on foot found a house and help. Within a few hours a group of men from Langlade arrived at the place where Hutchins was last seen, but there was no sign of him. Apparently within an hour after his comrades left, his strength and determination returned and he set out to walk or to ramble himself.

Four days went by before a search party finally located him, again too exhausted and feeble to move. He had existed on partridgeberries and brook water during that time. Close to death, Hutchins could not be transported to the hospital on St. Pierre island. A few days later, a small steamer sailed to Langlade for him.

At this point, with the final recovery of C.A. Hutchins, the Nova Scotian agent for the Chebucto Lobster Packing Company, magistrate George Simms ended his tale of death and disaster on the rocky shores of the French Islands. Simms (1829-1893) opened a window into the past giving us, after all these years, a glimpse of a ship, a wreck, the extent of the lobster packing industry in Fortune Bay, and the travails of those who go down to the sea and work for a living.

The Great Tragedy of Coley's Point

The greatest sea tragedy for the people of Coley's Point happened many years ago. The schooner *Excel* was at Black Island, near Grady, Labrador finishing up the fall fishing in October 1885. Aboard were fishermen and their families, including several women and children.

Commanded by Captain George Morgan (father of John Morgan, Coley's Point), *Excel* was anchored outside Black Island on October 11 and waiting for the weather to settle. The long voyage home to Conception Bay would begin, but on Saturday night a gale came on continuing through Sunday.

At twelve o'clock Sunday night, the ship parted her chains and drifted near shore. Heavy seas swept over the decks and Captain Morgan ordered the spars cut away. When the foremast fell, it broke into three pieces; the top of the mainmast lodged for a while on the shore.

Miss Emma Jane Roach (afterwards Mrs. W.H. Littlejohn), the only female survivor, stood in the vessel's hatchway with several other women seeking shelter from the combers raging across *Excel*'s deck. Roach, looking for a way to save herself and others if possible, jumped on the spar and, using it as a crude bridge, reached the land.

Stephen Russell who had already struggled or swam to the shore, reached out for her as she clung to the rocks and kelp to keep from being dragged back into the boiling sea. Just as she reached the land with the help of Russell, the spar broke. But two men — William Batten and Abram Morgan — were on the spar attempting self-rescue by the slippery and narrow bridge. Both were swept away and never seen again. As well, Captain Morgan and several members of his family were lost.

In all, twenty-two men, women and children, perished. Many of the names were never recorded as they were passengers (freighters) from other places. Three or four bodies were recovered and brought to Coley's Point for burial; others were interred on Black Island. Some bodies were not recovered. In later years the disaster was called "The Great Tragedy of 1885."

Coley's Point, which became part of Bay Roberts in 1965, was settled before the 1820s with families like Snow, North, Fradsham, Bowering and Littlejohn. The first census in 1857 shows it as a separate town and population reached a peak of 1,334 in 1884. Early settlers depended on inshore fishing, but the seal hunt and Labrador fishery soon supplemented that.

By 1874, a few years before the "Great Tragedy" of *Excel*, there were as many as twenty-one vessels and 183 people engaged in the Labrador fishery. In 1896 a causeway, the Klondyke, across the harbour to Bay Roberts improved travel between the two busy towns. The first business of Coley's Point was owned by W.H. Greenland. Soon other families lived there like Parsons, French, Batten, Roach and Dawe.

Indeed it was a Dawe schooner, the *N.P. Christian*, that became the second great disaster of Coley's Point. After completing a fishing voyage to Labrador in the summer of 1894, the "Christian", as she was commonly called, was slated to sail from Bay Roberts to Sydney for coal.

N.P. Christian, owned by Captain John Dawe of Coley's Point, was built in Nova Scotia and netted about eighty ton. Her skipper was Captain Robert Parsons, brother of Captain Abram Parsons. Her crew was: Thomas Chard, John Roach, Robert Roach, Isaac Roach and Samuel Dawe.

On November 20, 1894, shortly after leaving Trepassey where she had stopped for supplies or minor repairs, *N.P. Christian* met a strong gale of southerly wind. She was then in company with several other ships all bound for Sydney to load the much needed coal for Conception Bay stoves.

N.P. Christian had a shallow draft and was heavily ballasted. The last time she was seen, the "Christian" was leaning out in a strong breeze under very little canvas. It was presumed the ballast, which was not secured or stored down, shifted thereby causing the ship to turn over. There were no survivors.

Other vessels in her company were larger or had the ballast well-secured. These, fortunately, survived the storm. One vessel among the contingent was the 120 ton *Hebe*, commanded by Captain Edward Mercer and owned by C. and A. Dawe of Bay Roberts. Captain Mercer's son was A.E. (Albert Edward) Mercer.

In the heavy seas of November 20, 1894, *Hebe* was thrown over on her beam ends, but the crew quickly went into the hold, shifted the ballast and the ship righted again. No less than three times *Hebe* leaned out her beam ends, very close to capsizing. Captain Mercer, who spent thirty-six hours at the wheel, decided that was enough. He returned to Trepassey; there the crew further secured the ballast, made necessary repairs and waited out the storm.

When *Hebe* eventually reached Sydney, the skipper enquired about *N.P. Christian*. The crew of *Hebe* — Mercer, mate Peter Keefe, cook Edward Wilcox, seamen John Samways, Albert French and Abram Parsons — realized their sister ship had been in jeopardy on the troubled ocean and they knew the crew personally. But nothing was ever heard from the "Christian" and Coley's Point went into mourning.

The *Hebe* remained a familiar sight in Bay Roberts and Coley's Point for years, and made several trips to Nova Scotia after 1894, but around 1909 she beached and her timbers rotted on the bottom of the harbour, a little east of Klondyke Bridge between Bay Roberts and Coley's Point. Today the ballast for *Hebe* (with an information panel nearby) can be seen at the end of a new finger pier constructed at the Veteran's Quay in Bay Roberts.

From an Island to an Island

The news of shipwreck was late getting from Brunette Island on Newfoundland's south coast to St. John's. The previous week's storm had downed telegraph wires near Harbour Breton and the message had to be taken to Burin by the Newfoundland steamship *Portia*. From there it was relayed to William Job's business at St. John's. According to the *Daily News* of April 13, 1907, the telegram from Captain Keeping read:

> *Jessie* total wreck on Brunette Island. Anchored in Saturday's storm (April 6). Wind chopped at 6 Sunday morning. Could not get away. Riding in sea all Sunday. Went on shore Sunday night. Rendell lost. Am sending by passing schooner to Harbour Breton.

A terse but poignant story buried in archival newspapers — the death of one man, Rendell, and the loss of the 143 ton schooner *Jessie*.

During Brunette Island's Come Home Year celebrations July 7-11, 1994, the wreck of *Jessie* was one of many tales told and retold as former residents strolled around the island reminiscing and reliving the past. Although Brunette, which had been a viable and proud community for generations, was finally abandoned by 1964 under the Government's Resettlement Program, the marble gravestone for Alfred Rendell of Fogo had survived the ravages of erosion as indicated in another island story.

Roughly triangular in shape, about nine miles long, Brunette Island bestrides Fortune Bay somewhat northeast of St. Pierre. Early settlers were attracted to the lure of cod, the teeming herring stocks, lobster and the availability of bait fish. They set up fishing stations occupying the most sheltered harbour, Mercer's Cove. Although lacking an adequate fresh water supply, the land was well-wooded with good soil and grazing ground for cattle and sheep. When the inshore fishermen secured and processed a catch, their products were sold or bartered at larger commercial centres on either side of Fortune Bay — Harbour Breton, ten miles seaward to the north, Grand Bank and Fortune to the south.

By 1907, the year of the loss of the St. John's schooner, Brunette Island had been occupied for well over 100 years. Because of French presence in the area, it is likely that some type of settlement existed on the island from the early 1700s, but it was not until 1836 the town first appeared in Newfoundland census records. Brunette, a French word for "brownish in colour", then had a population of 103.

By 1935, population peaked at 223 and that year also marks the name change of the largest community from Brunette to Mercer's Cove. Located across the isthmus from Mercer's Cove was a second settlement, Forward's Cove, with only three or four families. Unselfish actions of people from these towns averted what may have been the loss of an entire ship's crew.

On March 22, 1907, *Jessie* left Barbados for Harbour Breton laden with a cargo of molasses. Built in Lunenburg, Nova Scotia, in 1901, Job's had purchased the schooner from Lunenburg three years previously. On Saturday, April 6th, Captain Keeping and *Jessie* entered Fortune Bay, passed St. Pierre with the islands of Brunette looming ahead. A southeast wind accompanied by heavy snow steadily increased in strength.

Rather than continue his journey to Harbour Breton, Captain Keeping decided to take shelter on the northwest side of Brunette Island, near Little Cape. There the vessel was sheltered from the southeast gale.

Between midnight and six A.M. Sunday, the wind veered around northwest exposing *Jessie* to the brunt of a windstorm, now approaching hurricane force. With both anchors down, the schooner rode out the storm. By daylight the wind increased and it was evident to Captain Keeping and his four or five crew that *Jessie* was doomed.

Rather than wait until the schooner was pushed on the rocks, the crew launched a dory in the hope of breaching the wild combers of Back Cove Beach, a narrow cobblestone strand now lashed with rolling breakers and exposed to a bone-chilling snowstorm. Just as they pulled away, the dory upset and all were thrown into the water. Somehow, through some miracle which the men could not explain, they were thrown onto the beach and each man assisted the other as best they could. Lying on a snow-swept beach, cold, wet and exhausted, *Jessie*'s crew took stock of their situation. One shipmate did not make it — Alfred Rendell. He removed his life jacket in order to put on his oil skins underneath, about the same time the boat upset.

Unless help came soon the survivors, wet, cold and exhausted, knew they would perish. Someone on Brunette had witnessed the feeble efforts of *Jessie*'s crew. Reports of shipwreck quickly circulated around the tightly-knit community. Residents of the island bearing namesakes of those who had settled there many years before — Hillier, Thornhill, Douglas, Price, Miller, Cooper, Banfield — rushed to the assistance of strangers on their shore, now nearly dead from fatigue and exposure. The shipwrecked mariners were taken into warm island homes and comforted in every way. By this time *Jessie* had grounded and was fast breaking up on the shore.

On Monday, April 8, Captain Albert Dyett, bound from Gloucester to his home in St. Jacques, saw the wreck and sent a boat ashore to ask if the crew wished transportation to Harbour Breton. All went except Captain Keeping who remained by the wrecked *Jessie*, but sent a message to Mr. Elliott, Job's agent at Harbour Breton. Elliott went to

Brunette hoping to salvage as much cargo and gear as possible.

LOSS OF THE SCHR. JESSY.

Boat Upsets and Men Fight For Their Lives.

Severe Storm Raged at the Time.

Local papers commented on the tragedy on Brunette Island.

Jessie carried a full load of molasses in puncheons and no doubt some of the salvage, as was so often the case along Newfoundland's shores, ended up in local homes. Today, according to local knowledge, the inlet where the schooner broke up is called Lassie (molasses) Cove.

Victim Alfred Rendell was buried in St. Stephen's Church of England graveyard, his final place of rest overlooking the little pond near the Brunette church. Alfred Rendell, born at Fogo, Notre Dame Bay, resided on Goodview Street, St. John's with his wife Mary (Russell) and one child, William. Another son, Alfred, was born five days after his father's death.

Some months following the death of her husband,

Mary Rendell had no choice but to commit her two children to an orphanage. To become financially independent, she moved to Massachusetts, studied and graduated as a licensed practical nurse, married one of her patients and then sent for her two sons to join her.

Every shipwreck brings with it its own footnotes of tragedy and hardship; like so with *Jessie*: eighteen year old William John Douglas, during his part in the rescue of *Jessie*'s crew, was struck in the leg by a piece of debris. Tuberculosis, a dreaded killer in Newfoundland's early years and called in those days 'galloping consumption,' set in. Almost within twelve months of the wreck he too was buried next to Rendell. Today, on Brunette Island, both stones stand adjacent, each as if in quiet tribute to the other.

Photo courtesy Phyllis (Rendell) Steiner

(Above) Amid the island wild flowers, near the concrete foundations of the church stands the headstone to Rendell. To prevent desecration and vandalism, the church was dismantled in the 1970s. Tents of returnees colour the background.

In the summer of 1994, colourful tents, flags, and booths dotted Brunette Island for the Come Home Year reunion (appropriately given the slogan "Back to Yesterday"). Still visible are the silent sentinels of the past:

Alfred Rendell

remains of abandoned homes and root cellars, grassed over potato gardens, a peaceful cemetery, concrete foundations of the church and the rusted remnants of Brunette's old lighthouse.

Many former residents and visitors returned to the deserted island; most to revisit yesterday's homestead; some to view natural beauty; others to observe the varied forms of wildlife — birds, Arctic hare, a small caribou herd or the lone survivor of a prairie buffalo herd. But those who know Brunette Island best lingered for a moment longer to pay tribute at the silent stones of island pioneers.

Brunette's last home crumbles. One of the most memorable events in Mercer's Cove was the offloading of twenty-four buffalo brought from Elks Island Park, Alberta, in 1964. Although the island had about 155 acres of semi-cultivated grassland, buffalo mortality rate due to internal parasites, accidents and disease was high.

Unlucky 13 in St. Lawrence Harbour

Did two thirteens — March 13, 1913 — have anything to do with a disaster in St. Lawrence harbour? Probably not. Our hardy pioneers of the sea, those born on the edge of the ocean, believed in hard work, skill and determination. They had no control over rocks and weather and that's what caused the demise of a good ship and three seamen.

At ninety-seven ton and eighty-five feet overall length, *Lucy House*, a relatively large schooner, was built at Grand Bank. Most schooners on the blocks there averaged only forty or fifty ton (except for tern schooners built in later years). *Lucy House*, a two-masted schooner built for John Smith's business of Harbour Breton, was slated for the foreign-going trade and was not a banker. At her launching in 1911, she fell over on her side and lay beached for some time in Grand Bank harbour. Before she could be uprighted weeks later, the schooner had already cost the owner unnecessary embarrassment and money.

A bad beginning? A forewarning of trouble? — It came only two years later. The story of her loss comes from a letter from St. Lawrence which details the misfortune. The writer says how lamentable it was that:

> The ship went down just when a friendly port was reached, and doubly so that she carried three brave men with her. It only revives the truth of the saying: 'In the midst of life we are in death.'

Captain Robert Courtney and his crew of five had taken *Lucy House* to Oporto with a load of fish and taken on a load of salt at Portugal. Now on February 13, 1913, they were approaching St. Lawrence. In that era, St. Lawrence had a vigorous offshore bank fishery enterprise and the salt was to be discharged there. Only two crewmen beside Courtney, who belonged to Grand Bank and age twenty-six, are known: cook Joseph Melloy, age twenty-five of St. Lawrence and Timothy McCarthy. McCarthy's home is given as Fortune Bay, but he likely belonged to Terrenceville.

Lucy House had been forty-eight days on the westward journey and had battled bad weather and adverse winds all the way. At one A.M. in a blinding snowstorm, which reduced visibility to nil, she veered off course and struck the Blue Beach sunkers. The schooner lay on the rocks for about two hours pounding and grinding. A plank and pieces of board floated up from her side after she struck.

Courtney and his crew were in trouble. Their dory had been smashed by waves on the journey, distress signals, or flags, were useless in the night and a bitter winter storm raged. When the blizzard abated the people of Herring Cove, alerted by the repeated sound of a schooner's horn, saw the vessel or her sidelights on an offshore ledge. To further compound the problems, the cove was full of ice and the men of Herring Cove had difficulty getting a dory through it.

But this did not stop the determined rescuers. William Pike and Samuel Reeves ran to St. Lawrence harbour, roused other people and were soon joined by William Kelly and William Lake. The four manned a dory and went to the rescue. They had not gone far when it could be seen, as it was now breaking daylight, that the schooner had drifted from the rocks. Rising tide and Courtney's crew, after several hours at the pumps, lifted *Lucy House* free of the ledge.

By the time the four men in the dory reached the vessel, she was 300 yards from land and had drifted further out of the harbour. Courtney asked that he and the other five be taken off and this was done without delay. The dory would have had ten men aboard and been overfilled — seven was her capacity. Joseph Melloy wished to get in the dory, but seeing it full, said, "Never mind, boys, I'll go the next time." Courtney and McCarthy stayed behind as well.

The dory — with four St. Lawrence men and three from the sinking schooner — now had about a thousand yards to go to reach a safe landing spot. As the dory pulled away from *Lucy House*, William Kelly spoke to Captain Courtney:

"Captain, lower your jumbo (sail) and drop the anchor because if the vessel drifts outside Calapouse Head, it will be impossible for us to help you."

Courtney lowered his sail but, perhaps through misunderstanding or judgment, did not drop anchor. And that cost him his life and the lives of the other two — Melloy and McCarthy. *Lucy House* was fast settling in the water. Kelly, Lake, Reeves and Pike landed their human cargo at Doctor's Cove and made every effort to get back in time to take the remaining three from the schooner. While the dory was a little distance off shore, *Lucy House* went down. Winds, seas and distance had hindered the rescue. Captain Courtney was seen jumping off the stern of his ship along with Melloy and McCarthy. All three lost their lives on that February 13 day.

The derelict schooner, awash and drifting, eventually grounded near shore. When the weather settled and the salt in her hold melted, the schooner was refloated and towed into St. Lawrence by a group of men using Victor Turpin's boat. In March, *Lucy House* was taken to the St. Pierre slip, repaired and lived to resume her overseas voyages. On

SCHOONER WRECKED

Entering St. Lawrence Harbor

THREE MEN DROWNED

Letters from St. Lawrence give lengthy details of the loss of the schr. Lucy House, of Harbor Breton, while entering the harbor of St. Lawrence on the 13th, by which disaster Capt. Courtenay and two men were drowned. She was on the way from Oporto, where she had gone with a cargo of fish, and was forty-eight days on the way, having had bad weather. It was sad that the ship went down just when a friendly port was reached, and doubly so that she should carry three brave men with her, but it only revives the truth of the saying "In the midst of life we are in death." In the morning of the 13th, entering St. Lawrence in a blinding snow storm, she struck on Blue Beach "sunkers" about one o'clock, lay on the rocks for about two hours and pounded badly, as many planks floated up shortly after she struck and she made much water fore and aft. The crew were in a bad plight, their boat having been smashed on the voyage and their distress signals being useless in the face of such a storm. Not until this abated could the people of Herring Cove, attracted by the sound of the horn, discern the vessel on the reef, and, to make matters worse, this cove was full of ice at the time and no dory could be got out. William Pike and Samuel Reeves ran to the harbour and made an outcry, and being joined by William Kelly and William Lake, manned a boat and went to the rescue. They had not got far, however, when the vessel was seen to slide off the rocks and when they reached her was 300 yards from land, drifting out the harbour. The Captain asked to be taken off and this was done without delay, but when the mate and others were on board the dory, she was getting filled — seven men was considered quite enough for her in such a bad time. The cook tried to board the dory, but missed her, and when told to — on, said, "Never mind, boys I'll go next time." The dory had to row a thousand yards before they could land and William Kelly advised th captain, as left the vessel, to lower the jumbo and drop the anchor "because," he said, "it the vessel drifts outside that head," meaning Calypoose, "it will be impossible for us to help you." The captain heard the first order but ignored the second which cost him his life and that of the two other men. As the craft was fast settling down in the water, the dory men made every haste to get back in time to take off the three still aboard but they only reached her in time to see her go under with her three men

The letter describing the loss of *Lucy House* appeared in a Newfoundland newspaper under the headlines above.

March 13, 1917, the unlucky schooner was stopped by an enemy submarine and sent to the bottom. This time, however, her crew reached Gibraltar and safety.

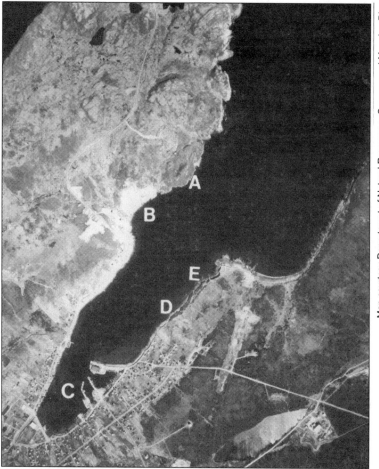

Ariel Map of St. Lawrence showing Calapouse (A), Herring Cove (B), St. Lawrence (C), Doctor's Cove (D), and Blue Beach (E).

Map courtesy Department of Natural Resources, Surveys and Mapping Div.

The loss of schooner *Lucy House* was surely a tragic drama played out on the treacherous sea on that February 1913 day where the men of St. Lawrence, both the victims and the heroes, played a role.

The body of Robert Courtney, a member of the Grand

Bank Orange Lodge, was recovered ten days later. Fellow lodge members, Philip Keating and his brother Eunice Keating, Edward Riggs, James Warren and George Handrigan, volunteered to travel overland — each man with his horse and sleigh — to try find his remains. They left, carrying grapnel hooks, lines, vital supplies and tents for the horses on Thursday morning, February 20. The men stayed with George Lambert.

They first searched the area where *Lucy House* sank. At eleven A.M. Friday the first body, Joseph Melloy, was found and before Friday night McCarthy was recovered. By late Sunday evening the searchers were about to call off the search and return home. It was decided to continue after dark on Sunday night February 23; it was then Courtney's body was found and taken to his hometown for burial.

𝒥atally Rammed

A s if seeing two friends and crewmen washed overboard was not enough trauma and hardship to bear, the remaining sailors on *Artizan* were witnesses to a collision — on their own schooner. That final cross put their vessel to the bottom and took their captain with it.

Artizan, commanded by Newfoundland seamen, left St. John's December 26, 1916, with a cargo of salt fish for Gibraltar. Right from the beginning, Captain Jeremiah Callahan and his crew — mate Matthew Shannahan, cook Herbert Score of St. John's, deckhands Martin Best, William Kelly and Joseph Aspell — began a fight for their lives. A typical winter gale with snow besieged their schooner. High seas lashed the decks fore and aft doing considerable damage. On December 27, two days out of port, the high winds intensified to a northwest hurricane.

Artizan ploughed along under "bare poles," in other words with all canvas lashed down to prevent it from being blown away. About twelve noon a high sea washed across the deck. Seaman Joseph Aspell, who was at the wheel, was washed overboard. Aspell, who belonged to Cape Broyle, was never seen again. It was useless to try and get a boat off the deck to attempt rescue, even if they had seen him going over the side.

Much shaken by the death of their friend, the remaining five took stock of the damage the wave had inflicted. Practically everything movable on deck was gone, the cabin skylight was smashed and part of *Artizan*'s railing was torn away. There wasn't much they could do above deck to make effective repairs as white combers broke on deck almost without letup. The cabin and forecastle partially filled with water, but that was only the beginning of a series of disasters.

On December 28, Herbert Score, who like the others attempted to work around on deck, was washed off the after deck and drowned. Seeing two shipmates snatched from them in two days, the others then took no risks about deck, fearing a similar fate. Although melancholy and heart sick, they still had to work around the clock to keep *Artizan*'s head into the wind. Fortunately the next morning the high winds subsided.

Now seriously shorthanded, Callahan asked his men to do their best and to straighten away for Gibraltar. Under favourable winds, *Artizan* reached there on January 13. The captain, Shannahan, Best and Kelly were so fatigued they were hardly able to stand up. They had lost two of their crew and had to take double watches. From Gibraltar, *Artizan* sailed for Alicante on Spain's Mediterranean coast, discharged the fish, and then went to Santa Pola for salt.

On February 17, she left Santa Pola and headed out of the Mediterranean. On the night of February 20, *Artizan* was sailing off Malaga under conditions the survivors of *Artizan* described as "pitch black" darkness. A Spanish freighter, the *Espanolito*, suddenly loomed off *Artizan* amidships and rammed the luckless Newfoundland schooner. *Artizan* was nearly severed in two parts and the impact was so great that Shannahan and Kelly, who stood watch, were thrown overboard. They reached the rigging of their doomed schooner and held on for dear life.

Meanwhile, as Shannahan and Kelly were attempting to climb onto the freighter, Captain Callahan and Best came up from below. They had been asleep at the time of the collision and ran on deck. The bow of *Espanolito* was almost through *Artizan*, but the schooner stayed afloat for about five minutes.

Best and Callahan had enough time to get aboard the freighter, but Callahan went back below to *Artizan*'s cabin. It is thought he attempted to get his ship's log and papers. While he was below *Artizan* sank and the captain went down with his ship. Shannahan, Kelly and Best climbed aboard the freighter and were taken to Malaga.

The British Consul in Spain cared for the luckless St. John's seamen and arranged for them to get to Gibraltar. On one of the many ships headed west, they found a passage to Newfoundland. When they finally reached St. John's, it was March 22, 1917; there they had to relate the sad tale of the ill-fated *Artizan* and the deaths of their three shipmates.

The Long Walk

At one period in its history the Union Trading Company owned thirty schooners and three steamers. Founded in 1911 by William Coaker as the commercial branch of the FPU (Fishermen's Protective

Union), the headquarters for the Trading Company was Port Union, Bonavista Bay.

By 1926, the Union Trading Company was the largest commercial enterprise in Newfoundland. Like most fishing/exporting companies, it had its share of losses at sea. One of the most traumatic was the wreck of the tern schooner *President Coaker* in 1924 and the death of her six crew.

Port Union in the early 1940s about fifteen years after the loss of the FPU schooner *Hillcrest*.

Two years after that loss, disaster struck the Union Trading Company schooner *Hillcrest*. On February 26, 1926, she sailed from Lunenburg, Nova Scotia, headed for St. John's. With Captain Rideout were a crew of five; mostly from the Port Union-Catalina area: mate William Edgecombe, sailors Cecil Quinton, John King, Alex Russell and cook Fred Russell, the youngest aboard at age nineteen and on his first trip at sea.

Two days later, March 1, about four P.M. the men of *Hillcrest* sighted the coast of Newfoundland and, as a snow storm came on, checked their bearings. They were off Placentia Bay. The captain decided to seek shelter in either Burin or Marystown harbour, but when the wind changed to south southwest he and the crew knew they would not make those ports. It required all their skill to keep the vessel off the land.

After several hours battling winds, they were close enough to determine the cliffs ahead were on Long Island, Placentia Bay, but the wind, now at hurricane force accompanied by fog and rain, thwarted any hope of sailing into Harbour Buffett. About 6:30 P.M. March 3, *Hillcrest* smashed into ledges and breakers off Red Island, Placentia Bay.

The story of how they reached shore is best told by Captain Rideout:

> The first sea took boats and everything moveable on deck. Three of the seamen were swept to the forehead of the schooner. Myself and the cook, Frederick Russell, clung to the windward rigging. Another sea took Russell and carried him to the forehead. I tried to get up when another sea took me to the fore of the ship.
>
> I then decided to go out on the jibboom to see if it were possible to land on the beach for I could see the beach run dry at certain times. The crew and I cut a rope of ten fathoms from the halliards and we made it fast to the top of the jibboom.
>
> Seaman John King first went down on the rope and landed safely; after the rest landed, I was the last down. By this time the vessel was practically in splinters and the sea was sweeping over her continually.

Although they were off their schooner and standing at the head of a small cobblestone beach surrounded by high cliff, the men were still in great peril. As Rideout said later:

Viewing the position of the spars we had to move twenty or thirty feet from there, in case the spars should founder and crush us to death. By Divine Providence the spars fell in the opposite direction with a terrible crash. An hour later all the wreckage was piled up just below where we were standing.

Now the six shipwrecked men had to protect themselves against the elements of a cold March night. Someone had matches, but they were wet — there would be no fire to warm them. They surveyed the range of cliffs towering above; each seemed too high, steep and dangerous to climb. Dawn broke at five A.M. One face of rock seemed about 200 feet high and looked like solid rock, not quite perpendicular, with footholds rather than loose rubble. Each man slowly and singly made his way up. Rideout recalled what happened next:

We now started to walk to look for inhabitants. After an hour the cook Frederick Russell stated he was tired. Cecil Quinton had a sprained foot and found it hard to walk for his foot and leg were swollen tight to his boot.

Mate Edgecombe and two seamen stayed with these two and I walked a mile to the west side and found no inhabitants and then walked in the opposite direction for about an hour finding no one. I went back to the waiting crew.

Sheltered on a bank poor Russell, the cook, had given up to die. Then it was decided that Edgecombe and Alex Russell should walk in another direction to look for inhabitants. About twelve A.M. Fred Russell passed away from a period of thirteen hours exposed, having no oil clothes, no food and no fire.

At two P.M. it was thick with snow. King, Quinton and I sheltered ourselves in the woods to try to get through the night. Just as we had

boughs and wood to shelter us we heard the
sound of a gun. Inhabitants from the town of
Red Island came to our rescue and had brought
stimulants and food.

The rescue party took the corpse along with
them and at 4:30 P.M. we arrived at the houses
of Red Island harbour.

Rideout concluded his harrowing tale praising the hospitality of Red Island people especially a Mr. McCarthy, Mr. Ridley and Constable Ryan, the policeman stationed on the island. Ryan, in particular, took great care in preparing a casket in which to transport the body of Russell. Through the orders of a Mr. Brownrigg, *Hillcrest*'s crew received clothing.

The coastal steamer *Argyle* was sent to Red Island to take the men and the body to Placentia and the train station; from there they reached Clarenville and joined a branch train to Trinity Junction. The Union Trading Company had already dispatched the M.V. *Seneff* to Trinity; aboard was Hazen A. Russell, the Assistant Manager of the Trading Company. It was Russell's duty to question Rideout about the circumstances of the death and the loss of another of the Trading Company's fine vessels.

When they reached Trinity, Percie Barbour found food and shelter for the shipwrecked men. Captain Edward Blackwood loaned his horse to help Rideout and his men get the body from Trinity Junction to the *Seneff*.

As Rideout reported the details of the loss of *Hillcrest* to Russell, he finished his tale saying that "My hardest suffering was the necessity of calling at the house of Thomas C. Russell to inform him and his family that his son, Frederick, was a victim of this sad affair."

Collision off The Narrows

The danger of collision with transatlantic liners was an ever present threat to fishing schooners on the Grand Banks. For many years when the shipping routes were located further north, they cut directly across the prolific fishing grounds of the Grand Banks. In time, legislation directed the liners to take a more southerly track.

A 15,000 ton steamer would cut through a small schooner like a hot knife through butter. Even if the schooner saw a liner coming, it would practically be impossible to make enough noise to attract the attention of anyone on the larger ship. In the dense fog which often covers wide areas of the banks, fishing vessels, often at anchor on productive grounds, would be neither seen nor heard by steamers. Over the years, many relatives of sailors 'without a trace' swear their loved ones' ships were cut down and the accident never reported.

There was a story which circulated on the eastern seaboard of the United States about the steamer *City of Paris*. A passenger on this transatlantic liner claimed that one night as the ship was crossing the Grand Banks in a storm, watchmen on the bridge noticed something odd on the forecastle head. On close examination, it was discovered to be ten feet of a schooner's mast lying on the deck. This was reported to the captain who presumed that, in the storm, they had cut down a schooner and part of her mast had fallen on deck. Not one person had the slightest knowledge or had heard any noise to signal such a tragedy. The fate of the poor schooner's crew can only be imagined.

Of course not all collisions occurred in mid-ocean with large liners, but closer to home the dangers may have been just as great. In the high volume traffic entering and leaving major ports, ships large and small unfortunately ran into each other. About midnight on July 26, 1950, the little vessel *Annie L. Johnson*, Captain Clayton M. Johnson and his father Captain Eli Johnson, left St. John's. She carried a full load of general cargo destined for Catalina.

Forty minutes later while off Sugar Loaf, six miles from The Narrows, the motor vessel *Linda May* en route from St. John's to Harbour Grace, steamed directly for *Annie L. Johnson*. The night was clear with relatively calm seas.

Annie L. Johnson, a schooner of about sixty ton, was owned by the Johnson family of Catalina. On her last voyage, she carried three crew — Eli, Clayton, and Morrissey Johnson. Two boys were aboard: the captain's son Gerald Johnson, age twelve, and John Healey of St. John's going to Catalina for a holiday.

The helmsman on *Johnson* swung the wheel to avoid a collision, but *Linda May* sliced into the Catalina schooner. Immediately after impact, Captain Beaton Winsor of *Linda May* put out his dory and took the crew and the two boys from the rammed schooner. But Gerald Johnson, who was asleep in his father's berth when the collision occurred, suffered fatal injuries when the fluke of the anchor was driven in through the hull of the vessel.

At the launch of coasting vessel *Annie L. Johnson* in Catalina.

Photo courtesy Maxine (Johnson) Turner

Linda May bore for St. John's at full speed, and the young Johnson boy was rushed to the General Hospital, but he passed away before reaching there.

When *Linda May* left the scene of the accident, *Annie L. Johnson* was still afloat. At two A.M. Captain Winsor left St. John's again to try to locate *Annie L. Johnson* and to tow her to port if possible, but she had gone.

Photo courtesy Maxine (Johnson) Turner

Annie L. Johnson in St. John's Harbour. The Captain was treated for scalds he received when two kettles of hot water fell on him durning the collision.

Chapter Four

Disappearance

In Newfoundland maritime history, the tales of ships which left port and seemingly vanished in the vast expanses of the North Atlantic are numerous. Scores of ships, large and small, are entered in shipping lists as "Lost at Sea" or "Presumed Lost with Crew." In my hometown of Grand Bank for example there were twenty-five ships lost with crew in a one hundred year span. No one knows for sure what happened, exactly where or on what day they made their fatal plunge.

The stories and speculation of the probable fate of many ships have now passed into a realm where it is difficult to separate fact from legend. In each tale though there is truth, a whole bushel of truth. Sometimes a story may be dismissed by what pure historians perceive to be "a kernel of misinterpretation or hearsay" yet the event did happen or was reported in some form.

Here are twelve stories of ships that disappeared from human ken with no survivors to relate how, where and when the disaster occurred. All we have are brief written reports or stories passed on through family history.

ℐortune Seamen Lost at Sea

I n September 1874 a Fortune vessel, *Charles Pickles*, was lost at sea. It happened so long ago that very little of the details of the ship, her size, destination and cargo have been passed on in local oral history. Yet church records list the men who disappeared with her as Abraham Newell, age twenty-seven; Jasper Collier, twenty-one; John W. Collier, eighteen; Richard Spencer and Hezekiah Noseworthy. Newell moved to Fortune from Pouch Cove, married Grace Piercey and had four daughters.

Hezekiah Noseworthy's age, according to family tradition, was about twenty-two. He too had been born in Pouch Cove and lived with his father, Samuel. Another of Samuel's sons, Simon, lived in Grand Bank. As a young man Hezekiah was in bondage or servitude, perhaps through an unpaid debt, to the Hon. Edward White in St. John's. In 1871 he ran away from his master, but had to spend twenty-one days in jail.

To escape from his unpleasant experiences or more time in prison if apprehended, he fled to Grand Bank with his brother Simon. In time, Hezekiah went to sea on the schooner *Charles Pickles*, lost with crew in 1874.

Simon's son became a well-known seaman out of Fortune — Captain Hezekiah "Ki" Noseworthy called after his uncle. In later years Captain Noseworthy often went to Pouch Cove to visit his relatives. Simon Noseworthy moved from Grand Bank to Fortune and had a cobbler shop near Temple Street.

The Wesleyan/Methodist clergyman who served in the Fortune-Grand Bank circuit in 1874-75 was Rev. Charles Pickles; thus the ship was most likely named in his honour.

Not much has been recorded verbally or in print of this

disappearance; yet a list of victims in church records verify there is a kernel of truth to the story. Perhaps someday it will be fleshed out in more detail, but for today — another mystery of the sea.

Memories of Success

When kinfolk in Fortune Harbour, Notre Dame Bay, waved good-bye to their men on the schooner *Success* in October of 1880, little did they know it would be forever. But the ship sailed for St. John's, reached there safely and left for home on November 5. *Success*, with five Fortune Harbour men in her crew, disappeared sometime after that; today not much remains to prove the vessel ever existed, a brief newspaper clipping and a few memories passed on through family.

By 1875 the enterprising young men of Fortune Harbour — located at the tip of the New Bay Peninsula — were shipbuilding as well as fishing and sealing. Several schooners were constructed there. About 1910, with the decline of the Labrador fishery, shipbuilding phased out.

One of the larger schooners built at Fortune Harbour — in a cove called "Southeast" — was the fifty-four ton *Success*, with an overall length of sixty-four feet. The Carrolls built a number of schooners in Fortune Harbour. Today it is generally thought *Success* wa built for the Smith McKay business of St. John's. Smith McKay co-jointly owned and managed the mining ventures at Tilt Cove and that may account for the belief *Success* was carrying iron to or from the Tilt Cove mines when she disappeared.

Over a month passed before island newspapers first commented that *Success* was missing. "Two schooners", the reporter said, "*Success* of Fortune Harbour and *Maggie* of Fogo, the latter with a general cargo for J.B. Tobin of this town [Twillingate], left St. John's previous to the recent storms and have not been heard from."

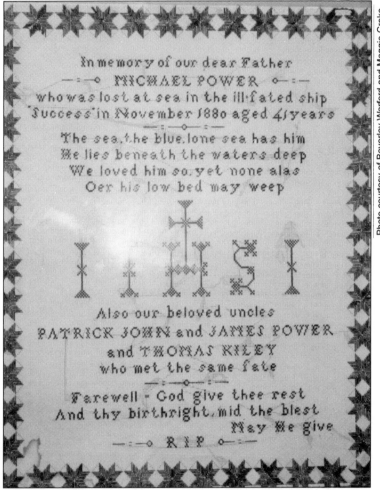

Photo of Memory done by Sarah (Power) Glavine, Fortune Harbour, after her father Michael Power was lost in 1880. It is now in possession of Maggie Croke, whose grandfather, Michael Power, was lost on *Success*.

A "Memory" is done by cross stitch much like a "sampler" on which young girls perfect various types of stitches. Unlike a sampler which usually gives birth dates and genealogical information, memories perpetuate the loss of loved ones particularly by sea.

This one reads, in part, "In memory of our dear father Michael Power who was lost at sea in the ill-fated ship "Success" in November 1880...Also our beloved uncles Patrick, John and James Power and Thomas Kiley who met the same fate..."

From that date, December 15, 1880, the papers are mysteriously silent on the disappearance of *Success*. The seas between St. John's and Notre Dame Bay were equally silent on her whereabouts as well. No wreckage was ever found; nor was she sighted by other ships.

Sailing on her were five Fortune Harbour men: Skipper John, Patrick, Michael, and James Power who were brothers, and Thomas Kiley. Kiley, known as a "winterman" and who worked for the Powers, replaced another Power brother for the voyage. Two or three of the crew were married including Michael Power, age forty-one. His wife, Sarah (Brien), was left with two small children, James and Sarah. Another son, Michael, was born the following April, 1881.

The sea is never far from the providence of towns like Fortune Harbour. On September 15, 1900, a violent wind storm nearly claimed another Fortune Harbour schooner when *Ocean Traveller* was wrecked while sailing home from the Labrador fishery. Her crew of Captain John Quirk, Dennis Dunn, Joseph Cook, Thomas Croke, Patrick Croke, Morris Quirk, William Quirk, Michael Burn, William Burn and Ellen Dunn were fortunate to sail once again.

On June 23, 1915, the town was involved in another sea drama. On that date the Department of Fishery and Marine in St. John's received a message from Fortune Harbour. It said that the schooner *Samoa*, while sailing off Fortune Harbour, struck a pan of ice at two A.M. and sank in three minutes. A Captain J.H. Young saved five men, but Nath Mason, age sixty-five, of Catalina went down with the vessel. Captain Young landed the survivors at Fortune Harbour.

Success was not the only Newfoundland ship to disappear that winter; on December 31, 1880, the brig *Cora*, Captain Richard Lynch and crew, left St. John's for Europe, but never reported.

Derelict Sighted Twice

In August 1887 the Carbonear schooner *Ocean Friend*, Captain Elward Penney, sailed for the fishing grounds with a banker's crew; fifteen men identified as "the most promising young men in the neighbourhood of Carbonear."

Built in the United States in 1881, the eighty ton *Ocean Friend* had been purchased by Duff and Balmer for the bank fishery. About the time she was due to report from the fishing grounds, there was no word of her whereabouts for some time. No one had seen her and no news of *Ocean Friend* had been received for several weeks. Those connected with the vessel began to feel uneasy for her safety. Then on September 15 a telegram from Burin arrived at the office of Duff and Balmer, Carbonear, who owned *Ocean Friend*, saying the vessel was lost with crew on the Grand Banks.

The brief bit of information in the telegram was followed up by a more detailed letter from Captain Brushett of Burin. On August 28, while fishing on the banks, (as Brushett

Crew of *Ocean Friend*, Lost 1887
Robert Wareham, Salmon Cove, leaving a wife and six children;
Simeon Luther, Carbonear, a wife and three children;
mate Robert Penny, Carbonear, a wife and five children;
Robert Penney a son, fourteen years of age;
Thomas Howell, Carbonear, a wife and two children;
Thomas Clarke, Carbonear, a wife and four children;
Reuben Pike, Carbonear, a wife and two children;
Jordan Pike, Carbonear, a wife and child;
Richard Penney, Carbonear, a wife and child;
William Penney, Carbonear, a wife;
Noah Hull, Trinity Bay, a wife;
Single men, all of Carbonear: Captain Elward Penney Reuben French Thomas Power Nehemiah Ash

wrote) he had been aboard a Lunenburg schooner exchanging information on fish, weather and general news.

The captain of the Lunenburg ship told him that the previous day they came upon a derelict schooner, full of water and lying on her side. Her masts, sails and rigging were lying over the side; the deckhouse, bulwarks, and stanchions on one side were splintered. One side of the schooner was smashed. One of the crew stood on the after rail of the derelict, which was a little above water, and he could see the bodies of two men in the cabin.

Brushett could not recall the schooner's name as the Lunenburg skipper related, but could remember her place of registry written on the stern name plate — Carbonear. The wreck was located in latitude 45.6 North, longitude 48.22 West.

In mid-September, Carbonear received more bad news. Captain Moore in the Heart's Content schooner *Lizzie* claimed he was on board the same wreck on September 6, but saw no bodies. Moore's sighting confirmed the loss of *Ocean Friend*; on September 26, 1887, her crew list was published.

Neither Brushett nor Moore speculated on what had happened to *Ocean Friend*. Others thought she may have been cut down by another ship or foundered in a storm. In summarizing the loss of so many men from Carbonear, one of the newspapers of the day *Twillingate Sun* in its October 1st issue said:

> It was a melancholy duty to break the mournful intelligence to the bereaved and the scene of poverty and destitution that met our gaze as we entered some of the homes was heartrending. By this sad calamity, ten poor women are now widows and twenty-four little ones are now fatherless — the eldest of these children is not more than twelve years of age. As the deceased were

young men, their families are unprovided for. Subscriptions are being taken up in St. John's, Harbour Grace and Carbonear on behalf of the destitute.

A Flat Island Letter

A few years ago, I wished to know more about the disappearance of the fishing schooner *Reason* and called Joseph Smith of Fortune, a former resident of Flat Island, to ask if he knew anything of the disappearance of the Flat Island, Placentia Bay schooner. *Reason* had left to fish off Cape St. Mary's in early August 1892 and had never reported. She probably went down in the August Gale that ravished the area about the middle of the month.

Smith, who seeks and treasures tales of the islands of Placentia Bay especially Flat Island, had the crew list. He had found them recorded in an old family Bible. At the time that was all the information I could gather on the loss of *Reason*. Newfoundland papers said very little about the disaster.

Several years later, while I searched for information in Nova Scotia on the disappearance of the Lunenburg fishing schooner *Cashier* in the same August Gale, I inadvertently located the following letter in the Nova Scotian newspaper *Halifax Herald*. The letter dated October 10, 1892, confirmed the disappearance of *Reason* and verified her crew list. The story of the disappearance is somewhat explained in the heart-rending letter dated September 10, 1892.

Dear Sir:

It is to be feared that another casualty must

be added to the list of disasters caused by the gale of 15th of August. The schooner *Reason* has been missing since that date. She was spoken to on the 14th somewhere about "Whale Deep." She had then 80 quintals of fish and intended leaving for home, as they were out of salt and provisions. So far nothing has been heard of her since. It has cast a gloom over the whole place as all her crew belonged here.

Their names are as follows: Captain Isaac Crann, his brother Abraham Crann, brothers Henry, John and Joseph Senior; Ephriam Collins; Nathaniel Collins, married and three children; Charles Senior; Albert Joyce; Charles Clarke, married last fall; The captain was married but had no children.

All of these were young men ranging in age from thirty-four down to twenty years and it is very sad. It is now currently reported that the schooner was not fit for the banks and the captain had said he knew it, but if she would carry them safe this year he would give her up in the fall.

They had done fairly well up to that fatal day; so the owners and suppliers will lose nothing as no doubt she was fully insured.

(Signed) A Flat Island correspondent

All in all, a tragic story. Mothers and relatives left behind had to raise a family as best they could. The descendants of men on the *Reason* are scattered across the globe today. They and the men lost were born and raised on the shores of the great Atlantic, the ocean which gave them life and employment, but such was the price paid.

Author standing by the Seamen's Memorial stones at Lunenburg, Nova Scotia. The marble columns list the ships lost with crew out of that port. *Cashier* lost in 1892 is listed at the top of the stone. *Reason* of Flat Island, Newfoundland, disappeared in the same storm that claimed *Cashier*.

Disappearance of *Phyllis*

Another mystery of the sea began in early December 1898 when the schooner *Phyllis* left St. John's. Under command of Captain John E. Davis, she left laden with salt fish for Spain, arrived there and discharged. At Oporto *Phyllis* and her crew of six or seven picked up a load of salt and by January 1899 left for Newfoundland.

Unfortunately *Phyllis* never reported at any port, presumably lost with crew. Local papers are strangely silent for she was not listed as missing. No mention is made of lost men: Captain Davis of St. John's and, as is thought by descendants, Cornelius Murphy. Murphy, born in 1844, lived at 150 Signal Hill Road in a home he built himself after being burned out in the Great Fire of 1892. A white marble monument was erected to Davis' memory in the Belvedere cemetery in St. John's.

Phyllis was built in 1892 at Gander Bay by shipwright J. Dalton for Robert K. Bishop, partner in Bishop and Monroe's business. *Phyllis'* movements around Newfoundland are clear for two years prior to her disappearance. Her life was stricken from the Registry of Shipping in June 1899 with the words "presumed lost with all hands" — her full crew list, the time or day and cause of the disaster are unknown.

One short note appeared in the *Evening Herald* June 12, 1899, bearing the ominous heading **Sighted a Wreck.** It says:

> The English schooner *Rosie*, Captain Deadwith, arrived at Rendell's premises (St. John's) Saturday evening, salt laden 33 days from Cadiz. On the voyage, she met a large red buoy adrift.
>
> On her outward trip on March 10th, she ran dangerously near a vessel bottom up. The copper was new and the sea had washed off sheets of it, some of which was adhering to the hull. There was not a sign of life on board; her three top masts were gone, and her sails, some of which were set, streamed in fragments to the breeze.
>
> A large English barque came near the stern of the derelict and floated signals, but received no answer whereupon she resumed her course and was lost with the derelict in the gloom of a stormy evening. The first vessel, the crew believed, might have been the *Owney Bell* or the *Phyllis* and the latter might have been abandoned days before.

Phyllis left Oporto about the end of January, 1899 so the date the *Rosie* sighted the wreck in March coincides with *Phyllis'* appearance off Newfoundland.

The Winter of Discontent

I n the spring of 1912, shipping officials and ship owners gave a sigh of relief that the long winter was finally over. Officially, winter lasts from Dec 22 to March 21 — but heavy losses on the sea began with the autumn gales of September 1911 and lasted through to the winter winds of March. William Shakespeare (*King Richard III*, Act 1, Scene I) wrote, "Now is the Winter of our Discontent"; for Newfoundland it was a winter of tragedy and sadness. Seven ships disappeared on Atlantic crossings taking over seventy men; several other lives were lost on vessels stranded on hostile rocks and reefs.

A virtual litany of losses began in September 1911. One of the luckier crews survived the sinking of *Lady Napier*. But for the timely arrival of another ship, her six sailors may have been posted "Lost at Sea." The story of how *Lady Napier* sank and her men lived is dealt with in more detail in a subsequent story. Crosbie and Company's *Nina L* was abandoned in mid-ocean in October while coming from Oporto to St. John's. That same month Bishop and Company lost *Golden Hind* which sank at sea while coming from Brazil, they also lost the westbound *Aureola*. The barquentine left Troon, Scotland, on November 22, 1911, with coal, but fought a succession of gales for weeks. On January 27, the Norwegian steamer *Marie* came by, picked up Captain Christopher Olsen, eight crew and a passenger — a twelve year old boy named McKinley. They were rescued and taken back to England. The two hundred forty ton *Aureola*, built at Bradford in 1873, was set afire before the captain left her so as she would not become a navigation hazard.

In January 1912, Goodridge and Company lost *Bella Rosa*, Captain Newhook, while she was on the way from Oporto and the same month, *Maggie*, owned by Baird's of

St. John's went down, also coming from Oporto. In February, Job's *Hispaniola* was also stranded at St. Jacques with total loss. Of those three, only one life was lost — a sailor from the *Maggie*.

A visible reminder of the devastation of dark winters like those of 1911-12 when many ships disappeared. This gravestone inscription relates a story of loss: Samson John...Hiscock Aged 29 years who was lost on the ill-fated sch. *Dorothy Louise* which left Oporto in Nov. 1911 and was never since reported.

In all of these, there was little loss of life (except for the unusual circumstances of *Aureola*.) By mid-January, just as the new year began, reports of overdue ships and missing men increased. On January 10, the schooner *John Harvey* was stranded at Gabarus, Nova Scotia and two young men — John Keeping of Lally Cove and John Foote of Rencontre

— both died of exposure. *Coronation*, abandoned off Spain while en route to Newfoundland from Cadiz, lost a man.

In January other Newfoundland ships went down with no loss of life: McRae's firm of Harbour Grace lost *Clara* in mid-ocean and the Ryans in Trinity-Bonavista lost *Virginia* the same way. One of the first appalling disappearances was the vessel *Reliance*, owned by Templeman and Company of Bonavista. This one hundred ton schooner, built in 1904, was headed to Newfoundland from Naples. She never reported in any port and was eventually posted as "Lost at Sea." Some of *Reliance* six crew members are known. It is thought she was commanded by a Captain Brown and that seaman Alexander Martin Lawrence, about fourteen years old and the son of John Withers Lawrence, was aboard.

Schooner *Arkansas*, owned by Samuel Harris' firm of Grand Bank, was bound from the south coast to Gibraltar with fish but simply disappeared with her six crew. Likewise, Harris' tern schooner *Dorothy Louise* with six men including Captain Samson Hiscock, mate Jacob Hickman, bound from Oporto with salt went down with full crew. Another Grand Bank schooner Samuel Piercey's *Margharita*, a ninety-eight ton vessel built in 1904, was wrecked in the Bay of Fundy in January 1912. Fortunately there was no loss of life.

The winter of tragedy wound down with three more ships missing: Rorke and Company's *Beatrice*, Goodridge's *Grace* and a new steamer making her first trip to Newfoundland, the *Erna* with fifty-one men aboard, most of them from St. John's. Ironically, the crew of *Aureola*, which had been rescued in mid-ocean and taken to London, were aboard *Erna*. Five Carbonear men were on *Beatrice* — Capt. Tom Fitzgerald, Tom McCarthy, Herbert Homer, Noah Murray and M. Maddock, while Captain William Fitzgerald and five men were lost on the brig *Grace*, most were from Carbonear. Some years before William Fitzgerald had been honoured for bravery at sea as recorded in James Murphy's book *Newfoundland Heroes of the Sea*:

> In April 1895 a gold watch, richly embossed and with the German Emperor's face carved on the back was presented to Captain William Fitzgerald. It was presented by Governor O'Brien at Government House as a reward for heroic rescue work done by Fitzgerald for saving the crew of the German steamship *Cassandra* in mid-ocean, on June 6, 1894.
>
> Capt. Fitzgerald, of the ill-fated schooner *Grace*, and his younger brother, Captain Thomas Fitzgerald, of the ill-fated brigantine *Beatrice*, were both lost during the never forgotten year of marine disasters, 1912. (page 10)

The "never forgotten" year took staggering total of seventy-four lives on seven ships that never reported, plus four other seamen lost when their schooners were wrecked or abandoned.

On June 18, 1911, a Marine Disasters Fund, convened by the Newfoundland Board of Trade and chaired by Governor Ralph Champneys Williams, was set up to provide monetary relief to stricken towns and widows.

This appeal for help appeared in four Newfoundland publications of the day. This one is taken from *The Newfoundland Quarterly*.

Erna: In the Days of the *Titanic*

In mid-April 1912, news of the unsinkable *Titanic* coincided with a local tragedy: the disappearance S.S. *Erna.* *Titanic's* story, as related by survivors, rescuers and the information on wireless messages sent before she went down on the night of April 14-15, 1912, was well-publicized. But the 3000 ton sealer *Erna* disappeared sometime in February-March, 1912, without a trace; there were no survivors to tell her story.

In fact by the last week of April 1912, the tragedy of the White Star liner *Titanic* practically pushed details of the St. John's based vessel *Erna* off the front page of local papers. The main players in the *Titanic* drama — Captain Edward Smith and his officers, the rich and famous passengers, the survivors and those lost — became household names across North America and in Europe.

The questions about the crew of *Erna* and the concern for the families of the victims were equally tragic, but were voiced mainly in St. John's and Conception Bay.

Exactly when did *Erna* leave Greenock, Scotland? And when was she due back in Newfoundland? How many crewmembers did she have and who were they? Who had relatives on the S.S. *Erna*? When the St. John's-based ship had been missing for five weeks these were the questions that surfaced. Didn't the *Erna* also have on board the survivors of the wrecked and abandoned *Aureola* of Harbour Grace?

As far as owners were able to determine, *Erna* left Scotland on February 26, 1912, bound for St. John's. On board were Captain Thomas Linklater, his wife and nine year old son, Captain Jacob Winsor and thirty crewmen who were mostly from St. John's.

Captain Linklater purchased *Erna*, had repairs made, installed a new device for ice breaking, and added other improvements to the wooden ship, built in Scotland. Linklater, born in Scotland and who had a career with the Gulf Line steamers, had lived in St. John's for ten years. He was not going to the seal fishery himself, but had hired Captain Jacob Winsor of Wesleyville to take command of *Erna*.

By May 1912, several Newfoundland towns reported foreign-going vessels which had disappeared while crossing the Atlantic that winter. In addition to *Erna*, the *Reliance*, *Grace*, *Aureola*, and *Beatrice*, belonging to Conception Bay ports and St. John's, the schooners *Dorothy Louise* and *Arkansas* both of Grand Bank, disappeared on Atlantic crossings.

An editorial in the April 23 paper said,

> ...the fate of the *Erna* and of certain long-overdue vessels, has been constantly before the vision. It is accentuated the general sympathy with the survivors of the *Titanic* and of the sorrow for the international loss of life. There has been silence because, until the actual fate of *Erna* is known, there is always hope from the sea.

Name	Residence	Martial Status
Captain Linklater	Scotland/St. John's	wife, one child
Capt. Chris Olsen	St. John's	a daughter
Capt. George Jackman	St. John's	wife, 2 children
Capt. Jacob Winsor	Wesleyville	wife, 4 children
steward Joseph House	St. John's	wife, 2 daughters
cook H. Whitten	St. John's	?
bosun Peter Jackman	St. John's	wife, 5 children
engineer John Leary	St. John's	wife, 5 children
stoker John Grouchy	St. John's	wife, 2 children
stoker Bernard May	St. John's	wife, 2 children
stoker John Byrne	St. John's	wife
stoker John Collins	St. John's	single
stoker John Locke	St. John's	single
stoker John Connolly	St. John's	single
stoker Joseph Joyce	St. John's	single

stoker Joseph Jackman	St. John's	single
seaman Gerald Graham	St. John's	?
seaman M. Palfrey	St. John's	single
seaman James Murphy	St. John's	single
seaman Albert Howell	St. John's	wife
seaman John Finn	St. John's	single
seaman Caleb Winsor	Wesleyville	wife, one child
seaman Silas French	Carbonear	?
seaman James Penney	Brigus?	?
seaman Harold Fifield	?, Newfoundland	?
seaman Peter Wills	?, Newfoundland	?
seaman Herb Balsam	?, Newfoundland	?
seaman F. Lucas	England	?

Two or three engineers from England whose names were not reported.

Erna carried five passengers — Mrs. Linklater and her son; Miss Oakes, Scotland; another unidentified woman and William Atfield, age twenty-five of St. John's who was a naval reservist sailing out of England. He took a westward passage on *Aureola* which was wrecked in mid-ocean. Her crew and Atfield were brought to England and once more they faced, for the last time, the treacherous Atlantic on the ill-fated *Erna*.

There is a family anecdote connected with Bernard May, aged about twenty-four and stoker on the missing ship. He was married to Mary Frances Mallard (1884?-1961) and probably resided in Quidi Vidi. In later years Mary married John R. Bennett and she became a singer of the 1930s and 40s. Using the stage name "Biddy O'Toole" she sang on the radio and on the Old Barn Dance and was performing when the Knights of Columbus Hostel burned on December 1942. Ninety-nine people died; Biddy O'Toole survived.

Sagua La Grande Disappears

On January 22, 1928, *Sagua La Grande* steamed out of Philadelphia and sailed straight into the teeth of a hurricane. Owned by the Hawke's Bay Trading Company of St. John's, the steamer headed for Halifax, but never made it to any port. Ordinarily the 450-ton ship required a crew of eighteen; she was short by four men when she sailed. It seems as if two or three men escaped death for they were hospitalized in Barbados (from the sailor's social disease, it is said) and one man, John McGrath of 246 Hamilton Street, St. John's, did not report for duty when *Sagua La Grande* left Philadelphia.

Sagua La Grande was built at Hamburg in 1921 and was 191 feet long. Named after a river in Cuba where the ship was first registered, it had two masts and could carry a heavy cargo — mainly coal as was her cargo when she left Philadelphia. The soft coal was destined for Samuel Cunard & Company in Halifax.

The ship and crew, who were nearly all Newfoundlanders, never reached port — one of the worst hurricanes of many years saw to that. Her course lay through the strife of mountainous seas and raging winds. Proud ocean liners twice her size were slowed to a crawl; other staunch craft were disabled. The Nova Scotian schooner *Mayotte* was abandoned at sea after one man was washed from the deck to his death and the vessel threatened to go down at any time. *Sagua La Grande*, top heavy with coal, didn't last long, nor could any lifeboat be put over her side in the tossing ocean. It is likely the coal shifted and she rolled over.

Captain Olsen, a Swede, hired the crew. His job was to find sailors for Marine Agencies of St. John's. Captain Samuel T. Jones, born in Little Bay Islands, resided at 73 New Gower Street. Jones was one of twelve children born to James Jones who became a well-known shipwright in Port Union. Mate George Berg, age fifty-four, lived in Chamberlains, but was born in Latvia. He had married Sarah Anthony of Brazil Square. Frank Hollett of Great Burin, son of Captain Fred Hollett, was a qualified captain himself, but signed on *Sagua La Grande* as second mate.

Several other seamen were from St. John's: John McGrath, 37 Lime Street; W. Doyle, 139 Duckworth Street; James Duffett, 41 Feild Street; Jose Bidal, 489 Water Street; Albert Bragg, Buchanan Street; Frank Spencer, 8 Fergus Place and Ralph Snelgrove of 99 Aldershot Street. Thomas Fraize lived in Carbonear; Richard Sutton and C.M. Sheppard, Port Union. Chief Engineer Rowland belonged to England.

In mid-February, twenty days after leaving port, Captain Olsen reluctantly expressed his regret to the media saying "I have very little hope for the ship" and with that her story, like the ship itself, faded from public knowledge.

In early October of that year another, a much smaller, Newfoundland vessel slipped into oblivion: the *Lucy Ann Cox* of Wreck Cove, Fortune Bay. Owner John Cox and Philip Cox left Wreck Cove for Bay d'Espoir, but first sailed into Harbour Breton to wait out a strong southerly wind. After a day or so, Cox took her out to sea and once again returned to Harbour Breton. On the third attempt the skipper was determined not to let the wind stop him. The little vessel did not put back in Harbour Breton, nor did she reach Bay d'Espoir.

By late October a search along the coast was concluded. Inspector Dee, a policeman stationed on the coast, found the vessel's small fog horn and pieces of her hull east of Hermitage. Magistrate W.E. Parsons of Harbour Breton notified the Minister of Marine and the final words "All Hope Abandoned" appeared in the magazine *Family Fireside*, November 1928.

Marine Agencies Ltd.

S.S. Sagua La Grande

Sailing from Halifax, N.S., January 28th for St. John's, Nfld.

We respectfully solicit the patronage of the Trade for the above sailing.

For further particulars apply to

MARINE AGENCIES, LIMITED, ST. JOHN'S, NFLD.
NEWFOUNDLAND-CANADA TRADERS LIMITED,
HALIFAX, N.S.

jan19,71

No photo of *Sagua La Grande* could be located; today the only evidence she ever existed lies in a few obscure newspaper "schooner" obituaries and ads for her services as
placed in local papers.

Vanished

The first public report that something was wrong
appeared in a local paper on January 28, 1929, a couple of days after the steamer *George B. Cochrane* was
due to arrive in port. There was no great concern at first.
The story with its headline "No Report Yet of S.S. *George
B. Cochrane*" indicated the overdue vessel was probably
stuck in ice and would soon be arriving in St. John's.
Assumptions and speculations were wrong.

Headings in bold print appeared on the middle pages
(yet no front page headlines) of *The Telegram* and *Daily*

News until February 4. Then, a brief story of a man who did not sail on the steamer was published. Strangely, and perhaps because her crew did not sign on at St. John's, her roster and details of her voyage were more difficult to locate.

However, the weekly paper of Port Union-Catalina, the *Fisherman's Advocate*, was very concerned over the ship's whereabouts and carried specifics. Six of her eight crew belonged to those towns.

The S.S. *George B. Cochrane*, built at Beverley, Massachusetts, in 1918, had an iron hull and was 294 gross ton with a length of 125 feet and a width of twenty-three feet. A few months prior to January 1929, the Hudson's Bay Company purchased the steamer and she was then chartered by Job's business of St. John's to bring coal from Sydney. Captain George Bragg of Port Union went to the mainland with a skeleton crew to bring the ship and coal to Newfoundland.

Now in the dead of winter and with a treacherous Gulf of St. Lawrence to face, *George B. Cochrane*, laden with 270 ton of coal for St. John's, left Sydney. It was Sunday morning, January 20. A winter storm had subsided and the barometer was rising. But on Monday at three A.M. another northwesterly storm blew up. Seas and ice in the Gulf would play havoc with shipping.

Friends and relatives knew Captain George Bragg, married with three children, would not have a smooth voyage. He had an experienced and veteran seamen with him. Ron White, wife and one child; Harold Clouter, wife, three children; Richard Mason, wife, five children; Ansel King, single, and Samuel Carter. All belonged to Catalina. Two were from St. John's: chief engineer John Hart and William Collins. Collins, age around forty, was originally from Newtown, Bonavista Bay. He had a wife and six children; three boys and three girls.

Samuel Carter, age eighteen, left Catalina on January 9

with the others for Sydney to bring down the *Cochrane*. His family believed he was probably lost on January 20th or 21st. He had two brothers, Fred and John, two sisters, Gertie and Mrs. C.W. Bartlett who resided in Trinity. Carter was eighteen and unmarried.

Public concern increased when the Shipping and Transportation section of the January 28 *Daily News* said "No Report Yet of S.S. *George Cochrane*." Newfoundland's Minister of Marine and Fisheries telegraphed key Atlantic ports asking for any news of the missing ship. The Minister stated he thought the steamer was stuck in ice and would arrive in due course.

By January 31 reports were more ominous. Captain D. Brenton of the S.S. *Kyle*, which had been diverted from her usual coastal run to search, sent a private message to Herbert J. Russell, manager of the Newfoundland railway. Brenton said he left Ramea, searched a wide area of the Gulf to within five miles of Scaterie Island off Nova Scotia, then returned to Port aux Basques. He said there was loose slob ice, a strong ocean swell in those areas and visibility was poor. He sailed north to a position five miles from Flint Island and saw nothing but ice.

Brenton spoke to the S.S. *Montcalm* which had been out searching for a schooner and assisting the S.S. *Sambro* through the ice. Personnel of *Montcalm* had not seen the missing *George B. Cochrane*. In St. John's, Captain Brenton's report appeared in *The Telegram* of January 31 stating: "S.S. *Kyle* Made Fruitless Search for Missing Steamer." The Gulf passenger ferry *Caribou* and all ships in the immediate area had been radio telegraphed to keep a lookout.

By February 2nd there was still no trace of the small steamer; she had seemingly been swallowed up by the sea and ice. In St. John's, although two city seamen were lost, there was also a sense of relief when it was learned another person had had a narrow escape from *George B.*

Cochrane. Harbour pilot Lewis had been in Sydney looking for a passage to St. John's and would have joined the
steamer, but he didn't know the departure hour and
missed a free ride. He travelled on the S.S. *Beothic* a day
later.

The words appearing in Port Union's paper
Fisherman's Advocate were more traumatic. The feature **It
Looks Like a Tragedy** said, "Worst fears are entertained for
George B. Cochrane...There is always hope from the sea,
but grave doubts are now felt for the little
steamer...Eighteen children are now fatherless."

In a move toward emotional and financial support, the
public gathered in Port Union's Church of England Parish
Hall on Friday, February 8. Peter Coleridge presided over
the gathering which selected a committee from the four
towns of Port Union, Catalina, Little Catalina and Melrose.
Led by chairman Sam Mifflin with V.J. Guy, Secretary and
assisted by Rev. G.L. Mercer and Dr. Baggs, the group can-
vassed door to door for help.

Although shipping lists and official documentation of
vessels that are "Lost at Sea" often omit the vanished
George B. Cochrane, descendants of the missing men
remember all too well. As an author's note: in 1999 I
became aware of her disappearance when Walter, the
youngest son of William Collins (of the missing steamer),
asked me if I had ever read anything of the "Cochrane." I
had not, but since that time some details of her loss have
come to light.

William Collins once owned a schooner in Newtown,
Bonavista Bay, but Mrs. Collins and the family, now left
with no source of income, were forced to sell the vessel to
make ends meet. Another organization, the Marine
Disasters Committee, did provide some limited financial
help.

December Storms

In mid-December 1951 an intense wind and snow storm put several south coast schooners in danger. Most made it into a harbour, but only in the nick of time — storm battered and leaking. One small schooner was not so fortunate: Walter Bond's motor vessel *Barbara and Ronnie*. Bond and his crew left Nova Scotia on December 18, but failed to make it into home port of Petites.

Built in 1944 at North Bay near LaPoile by Edward and Ernest Farrell, *Barbara and Ronnie* was about eighteen net ton and forty-six feet long. She was a small craft, perhaps too small to battle the tremendous seas that lashed the Gulf of St. Lawrence in December.

Captain Walter Bond, often called "Bonnie" by many seamen, purchased *Barbara and Ronnie* in 1949. In the summer of 1951, she fished out of Glace Bay for the firm P.J. Caddigan Ltd. and in the fall went coasting to bring food and supplies to Newfoundland from Nova Scotia.

In December 1951, she carried a small cargo of general freight and Christmas goods for merchant Robert Newman (Newman Brothers), Petites. The storm lasted several days and when Captain Bond failed to appear in Petites or any south coast port, it was at first thought he had taken refuge somewhere else, perhaps in a Nova Scotia harbour. Or maybe the *Barbara and Ronnie* had grounded somewhere. Others believed she may have been pushed out to sea and her crew picked up by a Spanish or French trawler.

Heavy weather slowed search planes and ships when *Barbara and Ronnie* was first posted as missing. By December 26, planes from Greenwood, Nova Scotia, and Torbay, Newfoundland, scoured the Gulf of St. Lawrence. Most local people believed she went down in the night of December 18-19.

With Captain Bond, who was thirty-seven years old, were five crew and a passenger: Charles Courtney, age nineteen; Thomas Bennett, thirty-three; Ward Mauger, twenty-four; and Richard Gosse, eighteen, all of Petites. Russell Billard belonged to Grand Bruit. The latter was a single man, the twenty-two year old son of Wallace and Mary (Harris) Billard. Passenger Kenneth Courtney, who hitched a passage from Glace Bay, was twenty-five and single. No wreckage, debris, or bodies were ever located.

The same storm forced the schooner *Mary Ruth*, Captain Pomeroy, back to her home port of Brigus. Her bows, rigging and fore hatches were coated with ice inches thick from the freezing spray sweeping the schooner. Several Grand Bank schooners were in storm trouble; one put into Burgeo with all canvas gone, leaking, dories smashed and her deck load of coal washed overboard. The crew had pumped for thirty-six hours without letup.

Captain Thomas Hardy, owner and master of *Mary Pauline* of Jersey Harbour, Fortune Bay, left Sydney for Harbour Breton approximately the same time as the missing *Barbara and Ronnie*. He and his crew of six, which included his son Alex Hardy, had a difficult time in the southeasterly gale.

The final ship reported in trouble was the S.S. *Mayfall* which had been adrift off Newfoundland for seven days. Captain John Rose, a resident of Jersey Harbour and the son of Richard Rose, and his crew of twelve, told of hardships and privations suffered on their disabled ship.

Seven miles off St. John's her fuel pump gave out and she began to drift. *Mayfall* had no means of communication, such as wireless or radio telephone on board and the crew had to resort to flares and distress rockets. For a week she was at the mercy of the sea. Food and water ran short; the only fire on board was in the galley stove and it was there the distressed crew huddled.

Eventually, as *Mayfall* drifted 170 miles southeast of St.

John's, the Swedish passenger liner *Anna Salen* found the ship and attempted to tow her to St. John's. Off St. John's, the M.V. *Algerine* finished the tow. *Mayfall's* crew were mostly south coast seamen: Captain Rose, Ben Thorne, Arthur Herridge, Arch Cluett, Russell Ashford, William Wheatley, William Sheppard (of Conception Bay), Clayton Hynes, Charlie Curnew, John Howse and Aurello Torres of Cuba.

Mayfall, (above) a 521 ton steamer owned by Flordia interests, was under charter to North Sydney Agencies to carry Sydney coal to Bonavista. Enroute from Bonavista to St. John's, mechanical difficulties and weather nearly claimed her.

The onset of fall and winter storms usually claimed its victims from the Newfoundland fleet of wooden schooners. By 1951 their era was fast coming to an end and most vessels lost were not replaced. Gradually each disappeared from our coasts. News reports for November to December 1951 documented the loss of several Newfoundland schooners.

On November 3, *E.M.A. Frampton* was wrecked. On December 10, 1951, the rocks of Lumsden claimed the historic schooner *Sea Bird*. Built in England in 1878 as a racing yacht, she had teak decks and polished brass. In the early 1900s she was purchased by E.S. Barbour of Newtown, Bonavista Bay and put into the coasting trade. For fifty years she ploughed the ocean around Newfoundland, but while loading fish at Lumsden and under the command of Captain G.T. Furlong, a December gale pushed her on the rocks to total loss.

Two days later the coal-laden *A and R Martin* drifted onto a shoal off Lamaline. Her crew — Captain Ben Snook, Ambrose Murphy, Maurice Snook, Frank Barnes, cook Charlie Fizzard and passenger Clyde Warren — abandoned ship. The schooner was never refloated.

The Old "Swile", Gone But Not Forgotten

Today it is a rare occurrence for a well-built modern vessel, fully equipped with up-to-date navigational aids, to disappear at sea during a voyage. In the days of sail, however, ships reported 'lost with crew' or 'missing without a trace' were, unfortunately, more common. Most small towns which had a fishing or sealing fleet experienced the loss of a vessel with all crew without ever knowing the day or hour of her fatal plunge or any word on the circumstances of her loss.

About twenty-five years ago a local schooner, the motor vessel *Swile*, although fitted with many modern navigational aids — wireless or ship-to-shore, radar and other equipment — disappeared. For many years I looked in vain for documentation on the *Swile*. Several people knew vaguely of the demise of this small schooner for she was a familiar sight all over Newfoundland's northeast coast as she nosed into ports on a regular basis.

She had been built by shipwright Captain Jim Jones in the Port Union Shipping Company yards in 1928 and was used primarily as a sealer and in the coasting trade.

Indeed, her name "Swile" is synonymous, especially along the northeast coast, with the word, seal. The 111 ton M.V. *Swile*, considered a sister ship to the *Young Harp* and the *Young Hood*, was commanded for many years by Captain Gottfred "Fred" Tulk with Ned Mason as his engineer. Mason began work on *Swile* in 1945 and went "to the ice" in the spring of 1946 and 1947; the latter year may have been her last fling at sealing.

Photo courtesy of Canadian National Railway and Lance Blackmore

The old *Swile* in better days docked at St. John's with Signal Hill in the background. A few years after this photo was taken, she disappeared somewhere between Newfoundland and the eastern seaboard of the United States. In the spring of 1929 Captain Charlie Blackwood had command of *Swile*; his cooks were Thomas and Samuel Lodge. In 1930 Captain Malcolm Rogers took her to the front.

Recently a section of engineer Mason's log book became available. It consists mainly of times the engine was started or stopped and how long the engine ran during the winter of 1947. From the log it can be seen *Young Hood* was at the front as well for *Swile* transferred supplies to her on April 24, 1947. *Swile* left the ice in company with S.S. *Eagle* on April 26.

By May, *Swile* went on the coasting run (i.e. carrying supplies along the northeast coast). A look at a portion of the engineer's log for 1947 shows a busy schedule:

Partial Log of *Swile*, 1947
May 15, Start again on summer work, left Port Union at 12 midnight;
May 16, Arrived at Valleyfield at 8 am and left again at 12 noon, arrived Wesleyville at 12:30;
May 17, Left Wesleyville at 11 am, arrived Greenspond 12 noon and left again at 8 pm;
May 18, Arrived Port Union at 2 am;
And an excerpt from 1948 shows her visits to the islands of Bonavista Bay:
August 10, Left Port Union 7:30 pm, arrived Flat Island 1:30,
August 12, Left Flat Island, 3:45 pm and arrived Gooseberry Island, 12:10 pm;
August 13, Left Gooseberry Island 11:30 am, arrived Deer Island at 3 pm.

In fact her summer runs show many ports of call from St. John's in the east to the more northerly LaScie: Cottles Island, Cape Island, Seldom, Tilting, Joe Batt's Arm, Trinity, Fair Island, Doting Cove, Ladle Cove, Nipper's Harbour and Harbour Grace.

According to some sources, Captain Tulk passed away at Valleyfield while he was in charge of *Swile*. Mate Willis "Pikey" Pike skippered her for several years after. While other crewmen were laid off in the fall, engineer Mason worked all winter while *Swile* was tied on at the FPU wharf, stripping down and tuning up the engine and painting the engine room. Every evening Mason would pump out the leaky old schooner. When Ned Mason moved to permanent work ashore, Calvin Diamond replaced him as engineer.

In the heyday of sealing, the Port Union fleet was admired without a doubt. In 1930 a poem was penned called "The Port Union Sealing Fleet." It affectionately lists some sea dogs of the historic town.

Port Union Sealing Fleet

...Of steel ships there's one going out,
Of auxiliaries there are three.
Now the name of these auxiliaries
Are the *Young Harp, Hood* and *Swile*
And the men who will command them
I'll tell you with a smile.

George Norman in the *Young Harp*
It's his first year in command
...Malcolm Rogers takes the *Swile*
With Ned Quinton in the *Young Hood*
He's the youngest of the band.

The *Sagona* will be here the fifth
And here's the latest news
Ezra Welshire is going out store boss
And her cook is Jimmy Cooze.

Charlie Blackwood will be in command
We'll meet him with a smile,
Although we'd rather see him
Commander of the *Kyle*...

By the 1970s the *Swile*, one of a few Newfoundland schooners still afloat, attracted the interest of foreign buyers. Sometime perhaps in the late 1970s, *Swile* was sold to American interests. A captain from the United States (probably Florida) accompanied by his teenage son, came to Port Union to pick up the vessel. It is believed the schooner, upon its arrival in the United States, would be converted into a pleasure craft.

Three or four Newfoundland seamen helped sail her

from Port Union to St. John's, but on that short voyage the local sailors realized *Swile*, by then over forty years old, was unseaworthy. Captain Reuben Carpenter of Port Union, master shipbuilder in the era of wooden vessels, had surveyed the leaky schooner and deemed her unsafe and unfit to sail anywhere.

Wisely, the Newfoundlanders signed off at St. John's but not before advising and warning the owners to repair the vessel as soon as possible. The American captain and his son managed to get the *Swile* to the United States naval base in Argentia where she was temporarily repaired or patched up.

In time the little schooner, manned by father and son, departed Argentia for the United States. According to those who knew about the *Swile*, after she left Newfoundland waters she did not reach any American port and was never heard from again. Her official registry closed in 1972, but the exact date, her crew, and the circumstances of her loss remain unclear.

Photo courtesy of Maritime History Archives, MUN

In the late 1940s, the S.S. *Eagle*, at one time a veteran sealer like *Swile*, was deemed unfit for further use. In 1950 (above) she was towed out of St. John's harbour to be scuttled.

What Happened to *Port Kerwin*?

When the search for the thirty-eight foot longliner *Port Kerwin* ended, it had covered 85,000 square miles and had consumed a total of 174 flying hours by planes and helicopters. The search area centred on the seas near Sugar Loaf outside St. John's, but extended a hundred miles out to sea and down to Cape Race and had even touched into Trinity and Conception Bay.

Jake Hillier, age fifty, and his son Perry, sixteen, left their home on Southside Road, St. John's on a Sunday morning, January 11, 1976, to shoot turrs off Petty Harbour. Their eight-year-old vessel, *Port Kerwin*, was in good condition and carried a hundred gallons of fuel. Sunday's weather was relatively clear and the seas calm. Jake Hillier assured his wife, Olive, he would be back by dinner time. By Sunday evening their family, worried when the two didn't return when expected, contacted the RCMP. It was late Sunday night before any vessel prepared to search and by early Monday morning, various ships and planes scoured the seas off St. John's and vicinity.

The shorelines revealed no signs of debris; the two men had not put into another port; repeated ship-to-shore calls to *Port Kerwin* went unanswered; no signs of the missing longliner could be seen at sea. She may have lost power and drifted many miles to the southeast of the Avalon on Sunday evening and night, but the search proved fruitless.

By Wednesday, January 13, high winds hampered the search and on Friday, five days after *Port Kerwin* and the two men were reported missing, the official search was scaled down. It officially ended nineteen days after initial "missing" reports. The Hilliers had well-prepared their boat, although they had no food aboard for they intended to be on the water only a couple of hours. It had plenty of fuel, a Coleman stove, drinking water and navigational aids.

Also on board were two dozen forty-inch orange float balloons, some done in fluorescent paint visible at night. These floats were practically unsinkable. But none of them, nor any other sign that *Port Kerwin*, (painted blue with a white engine house), had been seen. Newspapers of the day as well as family members thought that it had taken too long for search efforts to get underway believing that coastguard ships should have gone out Sunday night.

Jake Hillier, born in the town of Brunette on Brunette Island, Fortune Bay, was a veteran of the sea. At age fourteen he had fished out of dories and eventually joined longliners, bankers and deep sea draggers. In the early seventies, he had been asked to skipper the Government-owned schooner *Norma and Gladys*, but refused since it would take him away from home for long periods. Married for nearly twenty-five years, Jake Hillier left behind a wife and nine children.

Nothing since *Port Kerwin* disappeared in January 1976 gave any indication of what happened. A spokesman for the air-sea rescue team concluded, as did others, "It's a mystery of the sea."

A vessel similar to *Port Kerwin* with large orange floats aboard.

Chapter Five

Debris

Perhaps this section could have been included in the previous chapter, for in essence, the ships in these stories were lost at sea as well. But in these five tales of ship losses, wreckage, flotsam, or pieces of mute evidence, drifted to shore and indicated a tragedy had occurred. Even then, as others picked through sparse debris, there was confusion and speculation as to the identity of the ship lost.

Double Tragedy at Cape Race

I t was a tragedy duplicated. The double loss of two sister ships of the Cromwell Line, sailing nearly an identical route from port to port and within a fortnight of each other, is one of the strangest occurrences in the annals of the sea. And both — *George Washington* and *George Cromwell* — were lost in nearly the same location on Newfoundland's southeastern tip and both ships had no survivors.

Over the years, Cape Race and environs had been the scene of many tragic shipwrecks; however none was more disastrous than the above. Cape Race has thick fog and, according to meteorological data, the coasts are shrouded for an average of 158 days a year. Added to this is the danger of icebergs in spring and a strong inset of tide which tends to pull ships toward the rocky coast.

Several large oceanic steamers travelling from Europe to North America have been wrecked in that vicinity; some with the loss of entire crews. Brig *Florence* wrecked at Cape Race in August 1840 with the loss of fifty immigrants voyaging to New York. American steamer *Britannia*, on a voyage from Liverpool, England to New York, struck land at Cape Ballard. All 200 passengers were saved.

Two of the most publicized wrecks were the *Harpooner* and *Anglo Saxon*. British transport ship *Harpooner* carrying 380 men, women and children, struck rocks off St. Shotts on November 10, 1816. About thirty survived. On April 27, 1863 *Anglo Saxon*, sailing from Liverpool to the United States, struck the rocks at Clam Cove, near Cape Race with 238 lives lost.

The two sister ships *George Washington* and *George Cromwell* disappeared in early 1877 near Cape Race. On January 20th S.S. *George Washington*, plying between Halifax and St. John's, was lost with all crew and passengers a half mile west of Mistaken Point. She carried eight passengers, twenty-three crew and a full load of barrels of flour, pork and general merchandise.

When the wreck was discovered by fishermen on the 25th at Bristow Cove, Trepassey Bay, only scattered debris remained. Several men were sent to retrieve bodies — Patrick Coombs, William Kennedy, John Neal and Thomas and Edward Malloy. Using a rope, the latter four lowered Coombs down over a 200 foot cliff and in this dangerous situation they recovered fourteen bodies and pieces of other victims. Some wreckage and bodies were brought ashore at Drook and Long Beach.

John Myrick, a longtime keeper of lighthouse at Cape Race, helped recover bodies and said that he and others "recovered about twenty bodies that drifted in one small crevice in the cliff. These were interred near the wreck scene." One man had the letters R.K. tattooed on his arm. He was later identified as Richard Keef of Ferryland who travelled on *George Washington* as passenger or crew.

Compared to *George Washington,* relatively little was recorded about the disappearance of the second Cromwell ship, *George Cromwell,* although this steamer had a closer connection with Newfoundland. She left Halifax for St. John's on January 31, 1877, and seemingly vanished. It was a week or so before the managing owners, Clark and Seaman, sent out a general alarm and serious inquiries as to her whereabouts. They knew *George Cromwell* had met with heavy weather and thought the delay had been caused by an engine failure or that she had blown off course.

George Cromwell, built in 1862 at New York, was a wooden screw-propelled steamer of 972 ton and measured 181 feet long. Like her sister ship *George Washington,* she carried a full cargo as well as mail from Canada and the United States. Her crew, except one — William Cavanagh, a boy from Newfoundland who worked in the galley with the cook — hailed from the eastern U.S. As well she had seven passengers: F.H. Jordan, E. Kent, John Dooling, William Skinner and Charles E. Tyler of the Halifax Brush Company.

The New-York Times.

NEW-YORK, SATURDAY, FEBRUARY 17, 1877.—WITH SUPPLEMENT.

LOSS OF THE GEORGE CROMWELL.

SHE IS DASHED UPON THE ROCKS ON THE COAST OF NEWFOUNDLAND—ALL HANDS SUPPOSED TO HAVE PERISHED—THE VESSEL AND HER OFFICERS.

The steamer George Cromwell, of the Cromwell Line, from New-York to Halifax and St. John's, left this City on the 21st of December, 1876. She reached Halifax safely in the usual time, and left Halifax for St. John's on the 31 of January. Nothing had since been heard of her until last night, when a telegraphic dispatch was received from St. John's, conveying the news that a life-buoy marked "George Cromwell" had been picked up in Placentia Bay. Soon after the receipt of this dispatch another was received by Clark & Seaman, the agents of the line in this city, also dated St. John's, Feb. 16, and signed by Harvey & Co., repeating the announcement about the finding of the life buoy.

Later on, further dispatches said that quantities of wreckage began to come ashore about the 11th instant seven miles south of Placentia, among the articles being tubs of butter, a cabin door, a life-buoy, and a case of geese. The impression among seamen at St. John's was said to be that the George Cromwell had been driven ashore on the night of the 5th of January, two days after leaving Halifax, and that she had struck on Cape St. Mary's. This cape is 25 miles east of Cape Race, on which the George Washington was wrecked nearly a month later, and the shore is of the same character as that of Mistaken Point — high, rugged, and dangerous, and so wild as to be seldom approached by the dwellers along the coast. There is no doubt that all hands on board were lost.

The George Cromwell was a wooden-screw steamship of about 1,000 tons burden, and was built in this City, in 1866, by Westervelt & Co., to run with the George Washington, on the Cromwell Line, between this City and New-Orleans. She was 184 feet in length, 30 feet breadth, of beam, and 18½ feet depth of hold. Until 15 months ago she was employed on the Southern Line, when larger vessels being required for the Halifax and St. John's trade, they were placed on that line. She was considered to be a staunch vessel, and had passed an examination in 1872. Her cargo was a general one, principally provisions, and was insured by the shippers. The vessel was partly insured, but the exact amount could not be ascertained. The number of persons all told, the crew being principally from this City. The passengers and officers are as follows:

From New-York, St. John.

Headlines for February 17, 1877 *New York Times*. Commentary from the *Times* states: "Seamen of St. John's say two days after leaving Halifax she struck on Cape St. Mary's. This cape is twenty-five miles west of Cape Race on which the *George Washington* was wrecked and the shore is of the same character as that of Mistaken Point — high, rugged, and dangerous and so wild as to be seldom approached by the dwellers along the coast. There is no doubt that all hands on board were lost."

Two passengers were from Newfoundland. Francis Aspell, age twenty-four, was a machinist from Brooklyn,

New York. He had been away for twelve years and was returning to visit his father, Peter Aspell of St. John's. William Henry Roper was one of three brothers born in Bonavista. Joseph Roper owned a successful watch and chronometer repair business in St. John's. John Roper was a magistrate in Bonavista.

In February, after weeks of speculation, the newspaper *Morning Chronicle* declared the S.S. *George Cromwell* "Lost with Crew," speculating she had met her end on Cape St. Mary's Keys or the Main Keys. Eventually some wreckage drifted ashore. On February 14th and 15th a lifebuoy marked "George Cromwell," a cabin door, some flour and butter were found on the beach at Golden Bay.

One source of information came from Joseph McGrath, the postmaster at Cuslet, a small town near Cape St. Mary's. He kept a diary of local events for forty years and wrote that in February 1877, a box containing dressed (prepared for cooking) geese was found on the strand a few miles northeast of Cuslet. This debris, wrote McGrath, was wreckage supposedly from *George Cromwell*.

Gradually the news of two devastating shipwrecks both occurring in January 1877, both owned by Cromwell line and both lost with entire crew near Cape Race dwindled. The final piece of information on *George Washington* which met the same fate as *George Cromwell*, comes from an extract of a letter written by a resident of Chance Cove, north of Cape Race:

> The late accounts received respecting the loss of the two Steamers of the unfortunate Cromwell Line are very sad to relate. No part of the cargo appears to have been saved with the exception of some scattered pieces of pork and hides of leather, which are much burnt.
>
> It seems to be very probably that on striking the rock, the boilers must have exploded, as the

bodies, or rather parts of bodies, picked up along the shore are much disfigured and mutilated and also denude of clothing. (Other sections of the letter sent to the newspaper *Newfoundlander* describing mutilation in graphic detail have been omitted.)

The Seaman's Trunk

It is said that any town which sends a fleet of vessels to the sea pays a price in lost and missing ships and men. Carbonear, Harbour Grace and Spaniard's Bay in Conception Bay have a long maritime connection, and with that liaison come the tales of hardship, tragedy and heroism. The disappearance of *Ocean Friend* in 1887 (see Chapter Four, Story Three) is one of many. Seven years after the tragedy of *Ocean Friend*, a ship owned by John Rorke sailed out of Carbonear; in time, only a dead seaman's trunk from the ship returned.

Inside the chest were the usual items: clothes, personal effects and papers. Examination of the contents identified the owner as George Penney and the ship he sailed on was *Snowbird*. The tale of the ship and the trunk begins in Carbonear.

John Rorke and Son's vessel, the seventy-three ton *Snowbird*, left Conception Bay on April 26, 1894, headed for LaHave, Nova Scotia for lumber. The crew of veteran sailors and young seamen were well-known in their hometown Carbonear — Captain Samuel Carswell Rumson, married with two children; mate John Clarke, married, one child; George Penney, married, two children; Allan Penney, George Taylor and Hayward Osmond were single. *Snowbird* was built in Liverpool, Nova Scotia in 1878 for Rorke of Carbonear.

By late June she should have been in Newfoundland

waters, but it soon became evident in Carbonear something was wrong. *Snowbird* was long overdue. Eventually, contact with Nova Scotia showed the ship left LaHave on June 4th with her cargo of lumber. Built in 1878, the vessel was relatively old as sailing ships go, but the owners proclaimed *Snowbird* as sound and in good sailing condition. Relatives of the missing crew discussed recent weather conditions.

On Friday, June 15th an intense gale roared through the Maritimes and pounced on unsuspecting schooners. By Sunday, damage reports came in from Placentia Bay saying that the schooner *Edith Annie*, anchored at Placentia Roads (the seaway off Placentia Harbour), had all dories and movable gear swept from her deck. Another schooner broke both anchors riding out the storm. The Harbour Buffett schooner *Shooting Star* reported seeing a schooner bottom up off Cape Pine. Her Captain Brinton reported this as a dangerous navigational threat as it lay in the shipping track. The skipper ventured near and retrieved the main gaff with the canvas still attached. Another schooner, *Grace Carter*, saw the same hulk about eight miles west southwest from Cape Pine.

Seas were too rough to determine the name of the derelict for only a small portion of her keel was visible above water. On Monday, June 18, *Shooting Star* attached a line and towed the wreckage into Riverhead, St. Mary's Bay. By June 27th news reached Carbonear — the vessel was *Snowbird*.

The derelict hulk rested at Riverhead. After she was pumped out and uprighted, the vessel was sold and her cargo of lumber still stored in the holds, was auctioned off.

It was thought at first bodies would be found in the cabin, but this was not so. One item recovered from *Snowbird* was a sea chest. The clothes and personal effects in it indicated the chest belonged to George Penney. In time this was returned to Rorkes' business and eventually presented to the Penney family. The owner and relatives concluded that *Snowbird* must have come to grief on St. Mary's Keys, a treacherous navigational hazard for ships sailing past the southern Avalon Peninsula, and no one survived to tell the tale.

GOLD SEAL FLOUR

FOR SALE BY ——

CLIFT, WOOD & CO.

ily9

FOR SALE.

AT **Riverhead, St. Mary's, on** Wednesday next, 11th inst., at noon, the hull of wrecked schooner " Snow Bird," as she now lies, after which her cargo, l'consisting of Assorted Lumber, which will be sold for the benefit of whom it may concern.

july9,2i **A. LARDER, Agent.**

TOTAL ABSTINENCE *HALL.*

Ad for the sale of derelict *Snowbird* advertised in the July 10, 1894 *Daily News*: For Sale at Riverhead, St. Mary's, on Wednesday next, 11th inst., at noon, the hull of wrecked schooner "Snowbird" as she now lies, after which her cargo, consisting of Assorted Lumber, which will be sold for the benefit of whom it may concern. A. Larder, Agent.

In Carbonear, the loss reminded everyone of the story of the Welsh brigantine *Resolven*. In August 1884, she sailed on a beautiful summer afternoon from Harbour Grace bound for the Labrador. Shortly after, the derelict was picked up and towed into Catalina with her Welsh crew and passengers missing. They were never to be found despite an intensive search. The four passengers were Thomas and George Colford and Douglas Taylor of Carbonear and Edward J. O'Keefe of Harbour Grace.

The *Lady Glover* brought the ship to Harbour Grace where she was sold in public auction to Munn's business. *Resolven* sailed again out of Harbour Grace. Both the *Resolven* and *Snowbird*'s mystery prompted this editorial in the July 9, 1894, edition of the *Daily News*:

> *Snowbird*'s story is a sad one, the vessel returned, the crew gone. Carbonear has suffered at times from maritime disasters. The *Ocean Friend* and *Orient*, and other vessels whose names we cannot recall left bitter and painful memories...
>
> And now the *Snowbird*, whose crew has disappeared, is to be sold, and she may yet again walk the waters, but those who, full of life and energy, passed her decks are gone from this world.

A Puzzling Wreck

It was about a hundred years ago when a fair amount of controversy and discussion centered on wreckage brought to the St. John's harbour front. What ship was it? From what wreck could the debris have come? Rumours were flying. S.S *Lucerne*, Harvey and Company's vessel! One man argued the debris matched this steamer; another authority countered it didn't.

When the tug *D.P. Ingraham* arrived in St. John's with the bits and pieces, practically the whole of the city turned out to view it. From February 15 to the 19, 1901 local papers ran several long columns on the mystery. One article said:

> The wharf was black with citizens as the *D.P. Ingraham*, Captain Lewis Young, hauled in and hundreds visited her to view the articles she brought back.

The first reports of wreckage came February 3 from Lead Cove, Trinity Bay: a white spar, parts of a steamer's bridge, and pine planks. Five days later the Government sent Captain Young on the *Ingraham* to collect evidence and bring it to St. John's for identification. The search began at Baccalieu Island where the lighthouse attendant Frank Ryan reported that he had seen no wreckage nor a steamer.

There was such a sea raging at the Grates and Lead Cove, Young could not land. People on shore signalled that the best place to land was at Big Brook. There Young found wreckage: three large angle irons with no planks attached. The eight planks had been removed by salvagers. *Ingraham* went on to Hant's Harbour where Young and Constable Dwyer of Bay de Verde, who accompanied him, drove by carriage along the shore northward to Old Perlican searching every cove as they went.

At Russell's Cove, they found a piece of teak about seven feet long. From a man named Abraham Button at Lead Cove, Captain Young obtained a piece of plank and a fine moulding that came from a wreck. At Lance Cove he took a piece of ship's rail from a resident. Other people said tubs of butter had washed in at the next cove, but that had long since been eaten. At Adam's Cove some men tried to salvage a red sea chest drifting off shore, but were not successful. This chest was later thought to belong to seaman Eugene Sheppard of Harbour Grace, who sailed on S.S. *Lucerne*.

Abraham Button did not tell Captain Young about an interesting piece of machinery he had found on the shoreline. Word about this came to St. John's after *D.P. Ingraham* left the area. Button had found a lamp-wick roller. This device, made of wire, had been fashioned by James Rooney, one of *Lucerne*'s crew. Before his ship left port, Rooney had shown it to several people on the waterfront and he prided himself on his invention. It was so unique it would have positively identified *Lucerne*. A telegraph was sent to Button asking him to send it to St. John's immediately; yet it never was sent.

A painting of S.S. *Lucerne* inside a lifebuoy with "Lucerne" written on top and "St. John's, NF" below, the Red Ensign, left and Harvey and Company's house flag, right. This commemorative lifebuoy measures about six by six inches and was probably given to each family by Harvey's management. For years the one above hung in Charles Augustus (Jr.) Winsor's home on Hamilton Avenue, St. John's.

On February 15, Captain Young and *D.P. Ingraham* steamed back into St. John's. Those who looked at the pitiful remains of some splendid ship could not positively identify the vessel. Controversial headlines appeared in the local papers: February 16 — "Marine Tragedy Remains Unsolved"; and two days later, "Nothing Found to Identify *Lucerne*." Captain Young saw no name board, lifeboats, or any clear evidence to identify the ship as the S.S. *Lucerne*.

Laden with coal *Lucerne* left Ardrossan, Scotland, on January 23, 1901, and was expected to arrive in St. John's by February 5th or 6th. The steamer was a frequent visitor; seemingly everyone in the city knew or was related to someone in her crew. Men who worked in the coastal boat premises had a first-hand knowledge of her fittings and wood work. According to reports, hundreds of St. John's people visited *Ingraham* to pass some opinion on the evidence gathered.

The Evening Telegram, ◆ ◆ ◆ ◆

THE "INGRAHAM'S" REPORT

FROM SCENE OF WRECK.

What Capt. Young Says About the Wreckage He Saw--No Name or Anything Else to Identify the Ill-Fated Ship With the "Lucerne."

THE D. P. *Ingraham*, Capt. Lewis Young, returned from the scene of the wreckage along the South Shore of Trinity Bay at 11.30 yesterday forenoon. Leaving here at 2.30 Friday morning, Capt. Young went first to Baccalieu. The sea ran high, and the captain with great risk and difficulty effected a landing at the Light House at 7.15 in the morning. The light before returning, and steamed out around that way. Nothing in the way of wreckage was seen or found. A large crowd of people boarded the *Ingraham* yesterday on her return, amongst which were many friends and relatives of the *Lucerne's* crew. Two pieces of wreckage found were shown to everybody who wished to examine them. Amongst those present

Controversy was stirred up when St. John's harbour tug *D.P. Ingraham* came back from the wreck scene as *The Evening Telegram* of February 15, 1901, reports. Mr. E. Wills, a seaman who spent more time on *Lucerne* than anyone else, confidently stated the remains belonged to *Lucerne*. But Captain Couch, who was at one time mate on the steamer, had an entirely different opinion.

Questions arose. If the wood brought to port was pine, weren't the deck and wood fittings of *Lucerne* teak? How could the steamer have arrived a week earlier than expected? Most confusing was the location of the wreckage. If she was due to make port at St. John's, why was debris located along the south shore of Trinity Bay? Had she steamed past the Avalon Peninsula in the night and attempted to enter Trinity Bay?

Owners A.J. Harvey and Company posted *Lucerne's* crewlist. Seaman Whitemarsh was first identified as William, but it later changed to Walter Whitemarsh, son of Robert Whitemarsh of Greenspond.

Some months after it was learned that Captain Golder had signed on in Scotland as *Lucerne's* second mate. He and his crew of Newfoundland sailors had been rescued from the brig *Emulator* a month before, were carried to Scotland, but only Golder left on *Lucerne*. The others, for some unknown reason, did not sail on the steamer. Golder lost his life while *Emulator's* crew arrived safely in St. John's on one of the Allan line steamers.

The trail of reports and evidence tapers off after February 19th. The harbour tug went back a week later, but found less wreckage than before. Despite the controversy S.S. *Lucerne* never did arrive in any port and it was finally concluded she had met her end near Grate's Cove or on the western extremity of Baccalieu Island. Other the-

---

Crew of *Lucerne*, missing January, 1901

ST. JOHN'S
Capt. Henry T. Reed, age 31
first mate Charles Augustus Winsor, 30
cook Daniel Voisey, 39
second engineer James Rooney, 35
third engineer James Vey, 28
donkeyman Matthew Moore, 48
fireman Michael Larkin, 24
fireman Thomas Hepditch, 32
fireman Joseph Molloy, 23
fireman Thomas Power, 27

HARBOUR GRACE
second mate (Capt.) Y. W. Golder, 31
seaman Eugene Sheppard, 25

BRIGUS
steward William J. Sparkes, 45

GREENSPOND
seaman Harry White, 19
seaman Walter Whitemarsh, 25

LOGY BAY
seaman John Vickers, 24
seaman Pat O'Donnel, 23

TWILLINGATE
steward Arch Whitehorn, 29

Three crew were from Europe

---

ories, albeit inconclusive, claim her boilers exploded and she probably caught fire. That would account for the fact that only broken and charred woodwork could be found and that not one of *Lucerne's* crew survived.

Photo of courtesy Hubert Hall, SHIPSEARCH Marine

Lucerne (above) was built in 1879 at Birkenhead, England, for J. and A. Allan of Glasgow. Lloyd's *Register* of 1899-1900 shows she was sold to A. Harvey and Company. In this photo her bow and name can be seen.

It is one of those odd and inexplicable connections that brought to light some knowledge of James Rooney, one of *Lucerne's* crew whose name is mentioned specifically in reports of the day. Carolyn Cockerline wrote in December 2000 and alerted me to the basic details of the steamer's loss. She is a direct descendant of the Rooneys and now lives in Ontario. James Rooney, one of nine children, was the son of James and Elizabeth (Bartlett) Rooney of St. John's. James the father was a gas pipefitter and later became the superintendent of the St. John's gas works. James, the young man lost on *Lucerne*, had an older sister Margaret who was married to Rev. J. Pincock, minister of the Alexander Street Methodist Church in 1901.

All in all, an unheralded tale of the disappearance of a Newfoundland-owned ship and her crew.

A Trinity Bay Mystery

For many years the disappearance of a schooner from Winterton was the topic of conversation for the people of Trinity Bay. Today the story is still remembered, but mostly by descendants of those who disappeared with the ship. *George May*, like many schooners of her time, carried fall and winter supplies from St. John's to the outports — those smaller towns serviced by St. John's.

Captain Arthur John Downey left St. John's on Saturday, October 12, 1912. On the following Thursday, this message appeared in local papers:

> Schooner *George May*, of Winterton, John Downey master, left St. John's in company with another schooner, *Ethie*. She has not yet arrived here, nor is there any report of her. Schooner *Ethie* did not see or hear anything of her.

The bearer of the bad news telegram was the Justice of Peace of Winterton, E.J. Sansom, who had wired the Colonial Secretary in St. John's. *George May*, carrying six people, was last seen rounding Baccalieu Island. Sansom finished his message with an urgent plea to officials: "Will you please make inquiries from all telegraph offices. All other schooners that left St. John's at the same time are here since Monday morning."

Newfoundland's Colonial Secretary at this time was Robert Watson, born in Hant's Harbour, a town located a few miles northeast of Winterton. Watson, who knew the people reportedly on *George May*, immediately arranged to have news of the schooner's arrival at any harbour relayed to him at once.

This ominous telegram from Winterton was followed by another, yet more foreboding:

Telegram from Winterton
"What time was wreckage seen? Her crew consisted of five men and one boy. Two of the men are married and three are single. Kindly wire if anything further."

Colonial Secretary Watson sent this telegram to Sansom:

> Sub-Collector at Catalina wires me that schooner *Rosie*, Captain Alfred Paul, reports seeing wreck ten miles N.E. of Baccalieu; spars and canvas only to be seen; schooner about forty ton; main boom painted pink; canvas (sails) patched. Please wire me whether this description corresponds with that of missing schooner.

Within hours, the telegram office at Catalina informed St. John's that the schooner *George May* had not arrived at Catalina, but a wreck was located near Baccalieu. One schooner tried to take the derelict in tow, but debris had tangled underneath. The name of the wreck could not be seen, but the description fitted the missing *George May*.

In the fall, ocean travel through Baccalieu Tickle, the

stretch of water separating the tip of Bay de Verde Peninsula and Baccalieu Island, was relatively heavy. Scores of ships traversed this passage to shorten travel distance between St. John's and northern ports.

At least two other schooners passing the island reported seeing the wreck: *Gower S*, Captain Joseph Reid, arrived at St. John's and reported a derelict apparently anchored at the northern end of Baccalieu. Likewise ,Captain Charles Chalk in *Reliance* arrived in St. John's from Clode Sound and reported a schooner partly under water near Baccalieu. His crew examined the wreck, but could not ascertain the name.

Grieving relatives retraced the last hours of the missing *George May*: she had left St. John's with a small cargo and most likely met the heavy southwest gale which came up Saturday night. Captain House of the *Mary Winnifred*, who was out in the storm while on the way to St. John's from Bonaventure, Trinity Bay, stated he had a trying time in the storm. Several other schooners which left Trinity Bay were forced to shelter in Catalina for Saturday night. It was also thought that Captain Downey intended stopping at Baccalieu to take a number of men on board who wished a ride to Winterton.

One of the final messages sent to St. John's gave the details of her crew:

> Captain John Downey, thirty-six years old, leaving a wife and four children, oldest nine years, youngest two; Charles Coates, single, age twenty-three; Martin Downey, single, nineteen; Ralph Greene, a boy of twelve; all of these belonged to Winterton. Absalom White, married with a wife and one child; Jesse White, single, age seventeen, both belonged to New Perlican.
>
> We suggest a steamer be sent to search around the vicinity where wreckage was seen.

At five A.M. on Saturday, October 19, 1912, one week after *George May* was lost the tug *D.P. Ingraham* under Captain Marmaduke Rose left St. John's to search for her. Aboard was the Minister of Marine and Fisheries, Archibald Piccott. About three in the evening, *D.P. Ingraham* came upon the south end of Baccalieu. Piccott signalled the lighthouse keeper and then proceeded to ask about wreckage. However, the lightkeeper had no sightings nor any knowledge there had been a wreck.

While the tug was in the area the weather was fine and it was possible to see twenty miles in any direction. There was no sign of the missing schooner.

Older seamen, who had sailed through Baccalieu Tickle on stormy nights, recalled other shipwrecks of a similar nature. In October 1877 the provision-laden *Mary Brown* left St. John's for Plate Cove, Bonavista Bay with five crew and a passenger, Miss Chevers (or Jeffers). The provision-laden schooner went ashore on the north end of Baccalieu; two crew and the young woman were drowned. The remaining three were able to get up unto a cliff where they stayed until rescued the next day.

Another schooner, the *Pubnico Belle*, en route to St. John's from Bonavista Bay on July 7, 1891, stopped in Catalina to pick up passengers; five women and five children. During a storm the next night, the old schooner struck rocks at the south head of Baccalieu. William Rose jumped ashore followed by another sailor. Both held a rope to help Captain Samuel Butt and other crew to safety. Apparently the women and children were not informed of danger and were requested to remain below deck until danger passed. Three women — Mrs. Rachel Burton, Miss Julia Burton and Miss Selina Wells — survived while Miss Caroline Higgins, Mrs. Freeman and five unfortunate children drowned.

Now in 1912 Baccalieu claimed another victim. Captain John Downey's widow later married Eleazer

Bishop of Heart's Delight. Descendant Everett Bishop of Grand Falls recalled stories passed on in family history and believes that there were six to eight people on this schooner including Arthur John Downey's wife and two children. *George May* left Winterton for St. John's with salt cod on her last trip for the year. She loaded supplies and left. The one ship behind her saw her lights at Baccalieu, but from that point on neither *George May* nor any of her wreckage was ever seen again.

Bonnie Lass – Stranded on the Bar

The first word to the rest of Newfoundland that lives had been lost in a September 1916 storm came from the Member of the House of Assembly for Placentia–St. Mary's, Trepassey-born, Richard. J. Devereaux. On September 27 he sent a message to St. John's:

> The hull of schooner *Bonnie Lass* on her beam ends and is submerged foul of the bottom just outside Waddleton's Point, Trepassey.

By that time, several men of the area had already been out to the wreck and towed the mainmast ashore. Others searched the area looking for survivors. Follow-up messages from Devereaux stated that there was no sign of the crew.

Veteran fishermen thought *Bonnie Lass* swamped coming in over the bar off Trepassey while beating in from St. Mary's fishing banks. Certainly she was caught by a sudden and intense September Gale but no one knew if the crew had gotten away in a dory; if there were some alive or dead in the hull of the wreck, or if all had perished at sea.

In the storm, which had its onset on the 25th and battered the southeastern corner of the Avalon Peninsula severely, seven fishing boats were pushed ashore and five fish stores in Trepassey were blown down. Other schooners were not yet reported. It was described as the worst storm damage in that area for years.

Viola May, a schooner commanded by Captain Petite of English Harbour West, was fourteen days coming from Cadiz, Spain — an excellent run across — but had met the storm head on off Cape Race. Petite dropped anchor to ride out the weather, but not before the foresail was torn away and other canvas shredded.

On September 28, other evidence indicated the seven men aboard *Bonnie Lass*, owned by Michael McDonald of Newbridge, Salmonier, were lost to the sea. People spoke of them in hushed voices: Captain John McCraith (probably today's McCrate), Peter McDonald of St. Mary's, three men from Salmonier — Richard McDonald, Michael Grace and Richard Grace. Harry Lewis and Edward Fagan were two others in her crew. All but Fagan and Richard Grace were married.

The hull was partly submerged with the bow up, although the bowsprit and foremast were intact. One anchor chain and cable hung from the bow. The double reefed foresail on the foremast was torn to pieces, mainmast unstepped (pulled out from the deck), but no one knew the condition of the schooner aft of the main hatch. That section was under water and sand.

Parts of her dories were located, broken and some in pieces, but with enough identifying marks to show they were from *Bonnie Lass*. It was thought the schooner did not run aground intact, but had swamped or capsized at sea.

In the final few days of September, motor boats were at the scene trying to tow the hull to land. Finally on October 2, the derelict was pulled in and examined, but there were no bodies. Loved ones and relatives had to face the terrible reality that the crew would not be seen again.

On the other side of Newfoundland, another vessel went missing in the same storm. By September 30, public concern surfaced about a schooner owned by James Morris of Trinity, the H.V. *Morris* (or *Harry D. M.* as she is referred in another source), had not been seen since before storm pounced. Aboard were James Morris, Robert Guy, Adam Lucas, James Locke, Ephriam Hiscock and Charles Hiscock. There is an ominous silence on the final status of this schooner, but it is known that on February 6, 1917, the Trinity Benefit Club sent notes of condolences to Robert Guy's wife and children and to Adam Lucas' wife and father.

Photo courtesy of Royal Canadian Air Force

Trepassey in the 1930s. *Bonnie Lass* was lost near Waddleton's Point, Trepassey. On April 29, 1931, another disaster happened near Trepassey when the coasting schooner *L & H McDonald* went ashore at Freshwater Point. Captain Michael McDonald of Newbridge/St. Joseph's lost his life; his two sons, Jerome and Frederick, as well as crewman James Allison survived by clinging to a spar. The forty ton *L & H McDonald* was built in 1928. Captain McDonald left a wife and twenty-two children.

Chapter Six

Survival

Most stories in this volume are titbits of material that I collected over the years; many were short but usable. Much I wrote as notes while researching in provincial libraries and archives. It was in going back over my files that I realized much information was not only unusual and unique, but may be useful or may shed some light on our colourful history.

Subsequent research and information from families or newspapers fleshed out the tales in more detail; others stories remain relatively short. Several years ago in another book, *Toll of the Sea* I briefly told the story of the ordeal of Michael Dormidy. In this volume the story is more detailed; also several errors in names and places have been corrected.

Don't Give up Hope

On November 30, 1881, the schooner *Hope* left Old Perlican to sail across Trinity Bay with a full load of railway sleepers for Foster's Point, a town on Random Island in Northwest Arm, Trinity Bay. The cargo was to be discharged at Theophilus Hart's business at Lady Cove, Random Island. Foster's Point (since renamed Weybridge) had sawmills and logging operations frequented by men from Old Perlican and Hant's Harbour.

Hope, a new schooner and well supplied with ship's necessities, carried a crew who hailed from Old Perlican: brothers James, age forty-eight, Henry and Nehemiah Strong; Samuel Strong, son of James; James Churley, Elias Churley and John Collins.

With the freight unloaded the crew decided to spend Sunday with the Adeys in Lee Bight (today called Adeytown). The canvas was hoisted again and the *Hope*, now empty and lightly ballasted, moved up the arm with a north west wind filling her sails.

As she passed the cape, Foster's Point, she was struck by a sudden squall of wind and fell over on her side. The crew, who were all on deck

Loss of the *Hope*
Oh, think of young Samuel, who rode out the storm,   A day and a night he drove down the arm.   His courage was brave and his flesh was like brass,   But, God in his mercy had saved him at last.
Oh, think of John Collins, who clung to the mast,   He went there for safety, but died there at last.   Oh, think of the prayers and hymns he had sung,   and think of the sorrow when he was brought home.

at the time managing the sails, were thrown into the icy water among the rigging and canvas. They scrambled up to the side of the boat and hung on to the stays during the cold November evening.

All night they drifted down the arm with the bitter north west wind biting through their soaking wet clothing.

When the sun came up next morning only two men were still alive and clinging to the wreckage.

The three Strong brothers died of exposure during the night and their bodies washed away from the wreckage. One brother was the father of Captain Thomas Strong of Old Perlican.

When the people from Hickman's Harbour arrived on the scene later in the evening, eighteen-year-old Samuel Strong was the only crew member alive. John Collins had tied himself to the mast, but died of exposure in the morning. *Hope* was towed into Hickman's Harbour where scores of local people came to view the melancholy scene and to speculate on the loss of six men.

Older persons of Old Perlican recall two verses of a song written at the time to record the event.

Terrible Disaster in Trinity Bay.

THE SCHOONER "HOPE" CAPSIZED AND FIVE OF HER CREW DROWNED.

News of a terrible disaster has just reached us from Trinity. It seems that on Tuesday evening last while the schooner *Hope*, belonging to Old Perlican, was proceeding from the latter place to Random for a cargo of Railway sleepers, she experienced a very severe breeze; but, as the craft

St. John's paper on December 1, 1881, carried headlines of the wreck of schooner *Hope* of Old Perlican.

The Hiss of Death

It has been said that "...men who would go dory fishing for a living would go to hell for a pastime." This view indicates to some extent the many dangers and hardships our pioneer fishermen experienced. It is probably impossible to say who the first offshore dory fishermen were or who was the first to perish in a banking dory. From the town of Grand Bank for example, it is documented that the first schooner to chase cod on the Grand Banks was the *Emily Harris*, owned by Samuel Harris. The year was 1881.

Six years later came a report of men adrift; dorymen unable to find their mother ship, and a near-death experience from exposure and hunger on the Grand Banks. It was August 1887. Richard Noseworthy and Esau Piercy fished from another of Harris' bankers, the *Mary F. Harris*, Captain Robert Rose.

Mary F. Harris, built in Grand Bank, was one of the early large deep sea banking schooners. In 1892 she was commanded by Captain James Forsey. *Mary F.* appears in the fishing statistics of 1898 under Captain Sam Piercy as having secured 1500 quintals for her voyages. Early fishing vessels were six to eight dory-bankers and Noseworthy and Piercy manned one of the dories. Noseworthy, born in Pouch Cove, moved to Grand Bank and married Fanny Rose. He had at least seven children. Piercy's home is not given, but he probably came from St. Jacques where there were families of that name.

Mary F. Harris had been anchored on the banks for two or three days when the two men set out in the afternoon to take fish from their trawls. Light fog settled heavier and by the time they had rowed to where the trawl was supposed to be, they missed the buoy or marker indicating its location.

It was about four or five o'clock and they fruitlessly rowed around searching for it. Had they found the trawl, they would have stayed moored to it in that location until Captain Rose sailed near it.

Now there was only one thing left to do — find *Mary F. Harris*. Before it turned dark, they turned their attention to that task. Alas they had probably rowed away aimlessly from their hope of salvation. Carefully they listened to the sound of the small cannon or gun (often called a "swivel") fired to give dorymen an indication of where the ship lay. Noseworthy and Piercy heard nothing.

Now they realized they were in a fight for their lives — at the mercy of the waves in a cockleshell of a boat. No doubt men who followed the dangerous occupation of dory fishing on the high seas had thought and discussed with others what to do in such emergencies. First they made a drag (or drogue) out of a bait tub, for a bitter wind was rising. It increased in intensity as the night dragged on. Throughout that first night, they fought the elements with the desperation of men who had the greatest stake to give in such situations — their own lives!

Two dorymen adrift. One man keeps the head of the staunch little craft to the wind; the other scans the horizon for help while signalling with his light. Noseworthy and Piercy did not even have the advantage of a light or flare. Sketch adapted from Murphy's *Newfoundland Heroes of the Sea*, 1923.

Thoughts of loved ones, wives, children, parents waiting at home filled their minds. No doubt within a day or so, Captain Rose would have no choice only sail on in *Mary F. Harris*. Perhaps he left for home to inform others that two men were missing and presumably lost forever.

Meanwhile two men faced the vast expanse of unfriendly water. At midnight a squall of rain hissed on the choppy sea. Rain, in low mutterings, seemed to foretell a grim prospect. Black, maddened water boiled over into their dory. No doubt, Noseworthy and Piercy thought the dory was staunch, but it was no match for the stormy Atlantic.

The contest was becoming unequal. But, if they were to perish, both agreed to do it manfully at the oars and fighting for life. "Perhaps," they said, "at daylight we'll see a sail." Before daylight, a wave swept the oars from Esau Piercy's hands, but the other man redoubled his efforts and kept the head of the dory into the wind. Piercy bailed water.

So the first night passed and all the next day with no sign of help. Night came on again, but despondency was lightened by the fact that the wind was abating. With less wind and high seas, the second night out was not so difficult. Morning came with a calm and peaceful sea, but a new danger faced them. Richard Noseworthy and Esau Piercy had now been without food or water for over two days. The dory carried none. In later years each banking dory was equipped with a sealed can of water and emergency hard bread or tack. But the two men had none of that.

After dawn broke calm and clear, they saw in the distance a large ship which seemed to be drawing closer. When within hailing distance, the two castaways tied a handkerchief on the "rising stick" and waved it aloft. In a while the ship changed direction slightly and bore down toward them. The steamer proved to be a German freighter plying eastbound between New York and Bremerhaven, Germany. The captain, Fordmahn, treated Piercy and Noseworthy in the most kind and humane manner given all survivors on the sea. He supplied them with food, drink and warm clothing. Their dory, the haven on the sea for over two days, was hoisted aboard the freighter.

At Bremerhaven, the English consul stationed there

sent the two men to Leith, Scotland. The superintendent of the Leith Sailor's Home did all in his power to enable them to reach home. He published their story in the newspapers.

Fortunately in Newfoundland Walter Baine Grieve, a politician and manager of Baine Johnston Company, saw the story and intervened. Grieve, always compassionate of the plight of fishermen (he was later appointed by Government to improve the lot of Newfoundland fishermen), provided help and hoped for reimbursement later. He sent money for their fare to Leith. The money got Piercy and Noseworthy to Liverpool where they obtained a passage on the Allan liner to St. John's. At Bremerhaven, the English Consul sold the dory for twenty shillings (about five to ten dollars) and gave this money to the two castaways.

The story, as passed on by Noseworthy and Piercy, ends here. They do not give the reaction of overjoyed families when the two showed up in St. John's and Grand Bank in early October, 1887. They had been gone two months. No doubt they were perceived as heroes who now appeared in life as being resurrected from the dead.

EVENING)U1

The Evening Telegram

ST. JOHN'S, OCTOBER 7, 1887.

ADRIFT ON THE BANKS

Thrilling Experience of Richard Noseworthy and Esau Percy

PICKED UP BY A GERMAN STEAMER.

The Story as Told by Themselves

THE following particulars of the casting away on the Grand Bank of Richard Noseworthy and Esau Percy, and of their being picked up by a German steamer—as noted in

This is how the story appeared in the papers of 1887.

They went back to sea for that was the way of our hardy ancestors. Richard Noseworthy is listed in the 1898

Census as a fishermen of Grand Bank. As for the *Mary F. Harris* she was sold around 1915 to a business in Harbour Grace where Captain Brien took command. She was wrecked in 1919.

Rescued by S.S. Eagle

Two fishermen, William Russell of Harbour Grace and John Skanes of Colliers, stepped ashore in St. John's and then walked to lawyer Parsons' office to obtain help. The two men had gone astray from the three-dory fishing craft *Mary Joseph*, a small western boat, a style of craft distinctive to the Cape Shore and Placentia Bay.

Mary Joseph, which normally carried a crew of seven, a skipper and six men for the three dories, had fished all summer on the Grand Banks, but in August one dory crew finished work and left for home. The other five men which included Russell and Skanes continued to fish the grounds located about twenty-five miles off Cape St. Mary's.

Shipped on, or hired, under skipper Michael Hartigan of Placentia in the summer of 1888, the two men left on the morning of August 20th to check their trawls. Fog, the nemesis of dorymen, drifted over them and they couldn't find their way back to their mother ship.

All day Russell and Skanes tried to determine the location of *Mary Joseph*. Eventually in the late afternoon they heard the sound of a horn moaning regularly. Thinking it was Captain Hartigan signaling for them, they rowed toward it and in a short time the hull of a steamer (which proved to be the S.S. *Eagle*) loomed up above them through the gloom and mist.

To ocean castaways who are not yet severely exhausted or hungry, there must have been apprehension and some fear of the unknown when stepping aboard a foreign ocean liner. Would there be a language barrier? To what distant country was the vessel bound? How would they get home? What about extra clothing, supplies and lodging in a foreign port?

Both men discussed the size, shape and possible destination of the unknown steamer and soon agreed to board the vessel. Russell remarked to his companion, "Wherever this ship is going, to England, Ireland or Scotland, we'll stick with her for she's the means of saving our lives." It was now about five in the evening. Skies had an ugly look and it looked like a storm of wind was in the offing. The two men had no water nor food aboard the dory and it leaked.

It is not known how they signaled, but the large ship stopped. Once aboard the vessel, they soon discovered it was a Newfoundland ship bound to St. John's and commanded by Captain Jackman. He welcomed Russell and Skanes to the *Eagle* and hoisted in the dory. The steamer's crew agreed that the dory was in poor shape and cobbled up with leather and patches to keep it afloat. It would not have lasted long in the storm that came on in the evening.

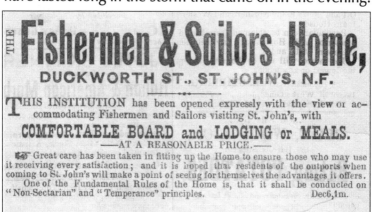

THE **Fishermen & Sailors Home,**
DUCKWORTH ST., ST. JOHN'S. N.F.

THIS INSTITUTION has been opened expressly with the view of accommodating Fishermen and Sailors visiting St. John's, with
COMFORTABLE BOARD and LODGING or MEALS.
——AT A REASONABLE PRICE.——
Great care has been taken in fitting up the Home to ensure those who may use it receiving every satisfaction; and it is hoped that residents of the outports when coming to St. John's will make a point of seeing for themselves the advantages it offers.
One of the Fundamental Rules of the Home is, that it shall be conducted on "Non-Sectarian" and "Temperance" principles.   Dec6,1m.

William Russell and John Skanes, two rescued fishermen, stayed in the St. John's Fishermen's Home or Institute.

Eagle arrived in St. John's at eight A.M. August 21st.

The two rescued fishermen went to the supplier for *Mary Joseph*, a Mr. Fox, and received a small amount of money to satisfy their immediate needs. They found accommodation in the Fishermen's Home and then, with financial help from lawyer Parsons, took the train to Placentia to join their vessel.

Captain Singleton, Sole Survivor

Captain Thomas Singleton of Salmonier-St. Joseph's in St. Mary's Bay considered his escape from the wreck of *Golden Arrow* nothing short of a miracle. When he learned the other five men who sailed with him were gone, he was speechless, in shock and was unable to give a full account of how he reached shore.

For the background to this epic tale of the sea, we have to go back to 1910 and two or three small towns in St. Mary's Bay — North Harbour, St. Joseph's and Holyrood. The latter is today called St. Vincent's and has a very long history. The location first appeared on Portuguese maps in 1519 and was known as Porta da Cruz. By 1693, it was known by sailors as Holyrode, a name which stuck for more than 200 years. Until 1910, when it was renamed St. Vincent's, it was called either Holyrood Pond or Holyrood South, to keep it distinct from the Holyrood in Conception Bay.

On Saturday, October 22, 1910, *Golden Arrow* left Holyrood, located at the western entrance to St. Mary's Bay, bound for St. John's with a full cargo of fish. The cargo belonged to J. Stamp of Holyrood. Singleton, in addition to his two seamen, had three passengers aboard. *Golden Arrow* had been built twenty-one years previously for the fishing and freighting trade.

On Saturday night the little vessel sailed in company

with other schooners, but as darkness closed in, they lost sight of them. The wind veered south-southeast with dense fog. Singleton was forced to reduce sail to keep the schooner away from the land. By noon Sunday wind increased to a gale and intensified to a hurricane that night.

Singleton, finding his vessel making bad weather and having lost some canvas, attempted to run to North Harbour, St. Mary's Bay. North Harbour, a fishing community located on both sides of a long, narrow inlet, was probably settled in the late 1700s or early 1800s by the Powers, who moved from St. Mary's. By the 1820s there were a few families settled on the west side of North Harbour: some at Patrick's Point and the Ryan family at Cape Dog, just outside the harbour's mouth. North Harbour is somewhat removed from the best cod fishing grounds, further out the Bay, but had fine woodlands and good hunting grounds on the barrens to the west. The community appears in the first census in 1836 with five families; today the population stands at about 160.

A description of tragedy in St. Mary's Bay was carried by the *Daily News* on October 25, 1910.

Oct 25 1910

Another Marine Disaster

Schooner Golden Arrow Lost in Sunday's Storm—Two of the Crew and Three Passengers Drowned—The Captain Washed Ashore

In the storm that raged on Sunday night the schooner Golden Arrow, Thomas Singleton, master, ran ashore at Nancy Key, St Mary's Bay, and became a total wreck. Two of the crew and three passengers were drowned, and Captain Singleton was washed ashore at North Harbor in an exhausted condition. She was bound to St. John's from Placentia with a load of codfish and in the storm and fog lost her bearings and drifted rapidly to destruction. Mr R. J. Devereux, representative for the District of Placentia and St. Mary's, has wired to Magistrate Hogan for the names of the victims in this latest nautical occurrence, as some of the crew and passengers are residents in St. John's and there is considerable anxiety as to the fate of the four other men comprising the crew. It is to be hoped that some of the others may have been rescued, but in the awful weather that prevailed on the night in question such good fortune is improbable. This latest intelligence may not fully reveal all the tragic occurrences of Sunday night's storm and the full toll of the briny may not yet have been paid. As in the Regulus case, the sympathy of the community will be extended to the families of these latest additions to these who have gone down in the deep(and prayers will arise to the Great Throne above that those now missing may have found a haven of shelter from the clutches of the relentless ocean.

LATER

Hon. D. Morison, Minister of Justice, was acquainted of the occurrence by wire to-day from Magistrate Hogan, of St. Mary's. The information received was, to the effect, that the boat Golden Arrow, of Salmonier, Thomas Singleton, master, lost on Sunday night on Nancy Key, St. Mary's Bay. Two of the crew and three passengers were drowned. The master was saved by being washed ashore, and

---

161

Captain Singleton knew this harbour, and his ship-mate, George King, belonged there. The wind was favourable, although blowing at hurricane force. Lying directly in *Golden Arrow*'s route were two hazards: Colinet Island and the more treacherous Nancy Kane (or Key) Rocks.

Without full control of his schooner in the windstorm, Singleton knew he was in danger. Within a moment *Golden Arrow* struck one of the ledges of Nancy Kane Rocks and went to pieces immediately. Thomas Singleton, although a strong swimmer, had no life belt on, and washed ashore near North Harbour. He had escaped the cold water and shipwreck and could not explain why he survived; only to say, "It was miraculous."

The others with him were not so fortunate and per-ished. Lost were George King of North Harbour, married with six children; four unmarried men, brothers Peter and Alphonsus Stamp (sons of Patrick Stamp) of Holyrood; Thomas Ryan, St. Joseph's and Edward Moriarty. In St. John's there was considerable anxiety for it was thought some of the passengers belonged there. The Member of the House of Assembly for the district of Placentia and St. Mary's, Richard Devereaux sent a message to Magistrate W. Hogan at St. Joseph's asking for more details. Nothing further could be added only that the lone survivor was at Cape Dog.

From St. Joseph's and North Harbour, several boat crews searched for remains. One of Goff's (Gough) boats had picked up some wreckage, but no victims. On Friday, October 28th the wrecking tug *Amphitrite*, Captain Lauder, which was at Riverhead went to the scene, but heavy seas prevented a diver from going down. Magistrate Hogan sent this message to St. John's: "Located wrecked schooner about 200 yards from where she struck. Weather too rough for divers to go down. Will likely be able to do so tomorrow." And these, in essence, were the last words on the sunken wreck; she was never again refloated.

Minerva Turns Turtle off Torbay

When a schooner owned by John Fleming of Green Bay pulled into St. John's harbour about nine P.M. on May 16, 1911, she had on board the crew of the schooner *Minerva*. *Minerva* left Pound Cove, Bonavista Bay on May 15th at one P.M.

Her crew were all Bonavista Bay men: Captain Peter Greene, Thomas Greene, James Davis, Frank Howell and Robert Sturge. With their ship in good trim and well-ballasted, they had a good run from Bonavista Bay up to six P.M. when they were off Torbay Head. *Minerva* was a good sailer and had held her own with the other schooners coming up the shore to the eastern Avalon.

About one and half miles off Torbay Head, and running under full sail, a heavy westerly squall struck *Minerva* and threw the ship on her beam ends. It came so quickly that the man at the wheel did not have time to bring the helm "hard down." When the schooner's keel was out of the water, her rudder also lifted out of water and was useless.

Four men on deck were thrown into the water and had to cling to rigging and ropes. The other man in the forecastle barely had time to get to the deck and climb to the rail now high out of water. All five held on for their lives. Gradually the ballast of stone shifted and *Minerva* settled lower. A lifeboat on the lee side was secured but the crew was unable to get it free.

Other schooners that had been in company with *Minerva* were some miles to the windward ahead of her, except Fleming's schooner. She was a half mile behind and the men on watch saw the accident. They bore away to the rescue, launched their boat and took off the five men clinging to *Minerva's* side.

They then rowed around the submerged schooner hoping to see some boxes float from the cabin. Within a few minutes the wind increased, a heavy lop came on and the rescued and rescuers were forced to board the schooner standing by. No belongings were saved.

Before Fleming's boat reached St. John's, the wind blew up a storm and her sails had to be double-reefed until she sailed through The Narrows. All the way around Torbay Head, Captain Greene and some of his crew went to the top rigging to watch the submerged hull. When last seen, *Minerva* appeared to be sinking.

Schooner Turned Turtle Off Torbay Head.

Crew of Five Had Narrow Escape

Besides Clothing, etc., $677.00 Cash Goes to Bottom

Headlines from May 16, 1911 *Daily News* says *Minerva* "turned turtle" and sank.

Captain Greene later spoke of the accident:

I can't account for the schooner turning over. She was well-ballasted and during the nine years I have sailed on her, she was equal to any vessel of her size in Bonavista Bay.

The squall which turned her over was heavy, but *Minerva* had been often hit by even

> stronger winds without any effect. The vessel is
> insured, but the men are heavy losers. They and
> I only have the clothes we stand in.

In addition to clothes, many had money intended for the purchase of home supplies stored in their sea boxes in the cabin: Captain Peter Greene lost $350.00 in cash, Thomas Greene, $257.00 and James Davis, $70.00. Another crewman had considerable money, but carried it on his person. *Minerva* was insured for nine hundred dollars.

The shipwrecked crew called on the Honourable Sydney D. Blandford, Minister of Agriculture and President of St. John's Hotel Facilities, who made arrangements for their accommodations. On May 17th the harbour tug *D.P. Ingraham* left to find the schooner but returned without seeing it.

The last sign of *Minerva* came from another schooner from Heart's Delight, the *St. Bernard*, Captain Henry Reid. He saw two spars somewhere off Torbay Head, but many thought the schooner that "turned turtle" sank sometime after that.

Endurance...and Tragedy

On the night of April 14-15, 1912, the British ocean liner *Titanic* sank with the loss of over fifteen hundred lives after striking an iceberg. Although there was a shortage of lifeboats to accommodate all passengers and crew, the survivors launched several boats and rowed away from the doomed *Titanic*.

Several hundred miles away near the fishing banks off southwestern Newfoundland on that April 15th morning were two men, George Barnes and his dorymate, Arch Bungay, also adrift in their dory. They had no idea of the great marine tragedy unfolding in the mid-Atlantic and, even if they had known, their main task would have been their own survival.

The schooner *T.A. Mahone*, owned by John Rose of Jersey Harbour and captained by Owen Fiander of Coomb's Cove carried seven dories and sixteen men. She left for the banks on April 9, 1912. On April 15, 1912, while fishing on Banquero (Quero) Bank, two dorymen, George Barnes and Arch Bungay of Coomb's Cove went astray from *T.A. Mahone* in dense fog. For Bungay, at age nineteen, it was his first trip to the banks and one never to be forgotten.

For two weeks, both men were adrift and lost without sufficient food or water in near freezing temperatures. Their only food was a ship's biscuit (or hard bread) left aboard the dory from the previous day. Precious drops of water came from the little ice or snow that accumulated on the dory.

On the second night adrift, their dory was caught in a field of Arctic pack ice. A monstrous sea upset the dory and although they managed to upright it, they lost all but two of their trawl tubs. From April 17-26, they were caught in ice which held them for nine cold days. On April 26 they freed the damaged dory from the ice and spent the next three days drifting and using what remaining energy they had bailing the leaky dory.

By this time both men were half-conscious and partly frozen in the bottom of the dory. They may well have succumbed to the cold but for the fact their dory had to be bailed constantly. The extra work may have kept them from freezing to death. They beat the bottom out of one trawl tub and fitted it onto another tub. Taking turns, they used this make-shift shelter in the severe frost, for it was too small for both to get in at the same time.

On the morning of April 29th, they saw the sail of a schooner. Although weak from cold and hunger, they stopped bailing and rowed toward it. The schooner *Francis M*, captained and owned by William Spencer of Fortune, found both men barely alive and on April 28th carried them to the Hamilton Memorial Hospital (administered by the Sisters of Charity, New York) in Sydney, Nova Scotia.

Barnes, whose limbs were more severely frostbitten, was operated on first. On May 9th both arms were amputated as well as his legs at above the knee. When he recovered he had to be fed with a spoon by hospital nurses. Despondent, Barnes felt he would rather die than live a life dependant on others. This, in part, may be why he passed away in the Sydney hospital. Hospital records state the cause of death as gangrene or blood poisoning.

According to his daughter-in-law, Emma (Lee) Barnes of Grand Bank, his last words, or words similar to these, were, "I had a job to make a go of it when I could walk and use the strength of my arms. In this state someone else would have to support me, so what's the use."

When Barnes and Bungay arrived in North Sydney on April 29, 1912, this is how the newspaper *Sydney Post* carried the story. By this time the drama of *Titanic's* loss was still front page news.

On May 10, Bungay, also severely afflicted, had both legs amputated at the knee as well as three fingers from his left hand. While in hospital he received a visit from Sir Edward Morris, Newfoundland's Prime Minister, who said Bungay would receive help. Four months after the operation, a Mr. H. Macdonald of North Sydney presented Bungay with a pair of artificial legs and on December 12, he returned to his Coomb's Cove home.

He contacted Morris to say he wished to learn wireless telegraphy and went to Harbour Breton to take his training. Arch Bungay was subsequently posted to Miller's Passage and later to Ramea, Curling and Port aux Basques. He married Irene Collis of Rencontre East and had four children. His youngest and last child was Richard Winston Clyde who provided much information on his father. Arch Bungay passed away at Stephenville Crossing on May 12, 1972, sixty years after his traumatic ordeal in a dory.

George Barnes, age thirty-three, was married to Hester Vallis of Coomb's Cove and left at least four children — James, George, Abe John and Bessie. Hester later married William Miller of Brunette Island, Fortune Bay, and took two sons to Brunette with her.

Abe John remained in Coomb's Cove and later moved to Grand Bank where he married Emma Lee (who so graciously gave me this information as did Isaac Barnes of Garnish). Like his father, who had died in the Nova Scotian hospital many years before, Abe John followed the sea. He went bank fishing on *Eleanor and Marion*, *Ronald George*, *Blue Foam* and other trawlers. He later lost his life when the trawler *Blue Wave* succumbed to a winter storm in February 1959.

Memorial Service for the Living

On Sunday, September 7, 1914, a memorial service was held in the Grand Bank Methodist Church for two Grand Bank fishermen given up for dead. Dennis Drake, age forty-one, and John Tibbo, forty-two, were missing for such a long that relatives believed they were lost to the sea and the local congregation organized a memorial service for them. Tibbo lived in Grand Bank, but most likely he was born in Harbour Breton or Grand Beach.

Drake and Tibbo were dory fishermen on the Grand Bank schooner *Winnifred Lee* which left Grand Bank in late August for Quero (Banquero) fishing bank. On the third day fishing, both dorymates set out to haul trawls. Fog, the dreaded enemy of bank dorymen, set in and they were unable to locate their mother ship, an all-too-familiar story in the era of bank fishing.

Winnifred Lee (above) In 1916, G. & A. Buffett Ltd,. had this banking schooner built at Shelburne, Nova Scotia. On June 14, 1923, two Grand Bank men — Bernard Lee and John Moore, both married — were drowned on *Winnifred Lee*, Captain George Follett, when their dory upset.

In December 1928 she was sold to A. Lawrence of Bay L'Argent who eventually sold her to Jos and Earl Windsor. On September 7, 1955, she burned in Twillingate harbour.

For three days they drifted in thick fog "a real pea-souper" which only cleared up in the twilight of the third day. About eleven P.M. they sighted a vessel's lights at some distance; it was hard to judge how far the lights were from them. With no means to signal at night, they rowed as hard as their exhausted condition would permit, and after an hour-long pull, drew near the vessel. It turned out to be the Portuguese banker *Senhora Du Gui*, which was practically becalmed. Had there been any wind, Drake and Tibbo would not have been able to overtake her.

Survival Tactics — After Drake and Tibbo arrived home they told the story of how they survived for three days — adrift, lost, with little food and water. At first they rigged a small triangular sail. Drake and Tibbo then took turns rowing and searching for their schooner. As time passed, they could only hope to be rescued by any vessel and realized they had to conserve strength and nourishment as much as possible.

The dory carried a small amount of drinking water and a tin of food. During the first day adrift the castaways agreed they had to drink the water sparingly and not touch the food in the tin for as long as possible. They had no idea how long they would be adrift.

The tin of food was still unopened when Drake and Tibbo were picked up, but the supply of water was practically exhausted. Aboard the Portuguese schooner, which had begun its return voyage to Oporto, they were safe, but no one back home knew they had been rescued. *Senhora Du Gui*'s skipper told them, in broken English, that unless it was possible to transfer the two castaways to a passing vessel, they would have to remain with the schooner until it reached Oporto. He could not go back to Newfoundland.

For twelve days they sailed eastward until the steamer *Davisian* was sighted; a coincidence in itself. It so happened the schooner was on the extreme southern end of the Grand Banks and near the shipping lanes. Normally, the Portuguese schooners travelled further northward, but adverse winds pushed *Senhora Du Gui* south and into the track of *Davisian*.

Davisian passed in the night, but the Portuguese vessel saw the lights and with flares in the rigging hailed the steamer. In response to the signals, the steamer ran alongside and Drake and Tibbo were transferred. Soon afterwards *Davisian* contacted Cape Race which transmitted the news to Grand Bank. It was eighteen days since they left *Winnifred Lee*.

Officers and crew of the steamer raised money for the two Grand Bank fisherman and this fund was increased when the steamer docked in East Boston on August 11. The British consul arranged transportation to Newfoundland via Halifax and Sydney; finally they reached home.

In the intervening eighteen days, relatives and friends assumed they were dead and had made appropriate arrangements. No doubt the memorial church service was forgotten as family members were reunited: Drake had a wife and four children, one of whom was Arthur, a resident of Grand Bank for many years. Tibbo had a wife and three children.

For Grand Bank, which at one time had as many as thirty bankers fishing out of its harbour, tales of men adrift were commonplace. On another occasion, in the summer of 1920, Thomas Forsey and Grandy Matthews strayed away in the dense fog from their fishing schooner *Admiral Dewey*. They drifted for seven days and six nights until a jackboat fishing off Cape St. Mary's spotted the dory and towed the two men to safety. By then, they were near the end of their endurance, not so much from cold or exhaustion, but from hunger. It is believed they were thinking about their eating skin boots: perhaps the tops would have some nourishment.

To reach home, they connected with the westbound coastal steamer *Glencoe*. When the *Admiral Dewey* came into Fortune Bay with flag at half mast, the two men were on the *Glencoe*, also steaming into Grand Bank from Placentia Bay to South Coast ports. *Glencoe*'s captain asked both men if they would know their schooner from a distance and they did, recognizing the schooner and realizing the black flag at half mast was for them. Both the schooner and the two missing men reached Grand Bank about the same time.

Shipwreck at Oderin

Two unusual shipwrecks happened near the Placentia Bay town of Oderin: one in 1893 and the other in 1915 and both involved sailors clinging to rocks for hours to survive.

On June 26, 1893, the schooner *Hattie Collins* of Burin, Captain Moulton — whose first name was not recorded — left for St. John's. The schooner was chartered to merchant and lobster dealer John Warren of Ragged Island (which included the towns of Tack's Beach and John de Gaunt). Warren obtained his supplies from James Baird of St. John's; *Hattie Collins* had aboard a load of lobsters for Baird.

While rounding Merasheen Head, Captain Moulton, seeing his schooner was rather light and that a strong breeze was coming up, hugged the shoreline. He feared, in the open bay, his schooner would "heave out"; thus he wanted to be near a harbour in case the wind intensified.

When near Jude (or Judy, as pronounced) Island, he hauled his logline and thought he could continue for some distance. About ten minutes later, he and his crew realized he was dangerously near Harbour Rock off Oderin. Moulton figured a strong tide brought him near the rock sooner than expected. In the dark the captain didn't see the ledge in time to swing around and *Hattie Collins* grounded.

The men threw over the ship's small boat, but that was immediately smashed to pieces. They then managed to get onto Harbour Rock, which was only barely awash in the heaving seas. That night the seas made a clean breach over the rock and the crew somehow managed to tie themselves to the rocks. As each wave passed over, the men held their breath. When it passed, they braced and breathed deeply for the next one.

In this resourceful way, they somehow managed to survive the night, all the while fighting desperately for their lives. In the morning a small vessel belonging to William Cheeseman and his sons of Rushoon passed by and saw the castaways huddled on the rock. Using the dory, Cheeseman tried to approach the rock from the windward side, but that attempt proved too dangerous. They then rowed around to the leeward side, but could not get near the crag with a raging white sea breaking on it.

But Cheeseman was determined to get them off. He threw a rope onto Harbour Rock and each stranded man was pulled about 120 feet through the water to safety aboard his schooner.

Cheeseman took the men to Rushoon; eventually they reached Ragged Island and home. The wrecked *Hattie Collins* was insured, but not the cargo.

Oderin on Oderin Island in western Placentia Bay lies about thirty kilometers northeast of Marystown. The island, horseshoe-shaped (with its mouth facing west), has a superior natural harbour and was surrounded by fishing grounds which were once some of the best in Placentia Bay. Consequently, from the late 1600s — and possibly earlier — it was a productive fishing station of the French. Its modern name is an English corruption of Audierne, after a coastal town in Brittany. Today it is an abandoned town, but in 1911 its population reached its greatest peak at 240 people.

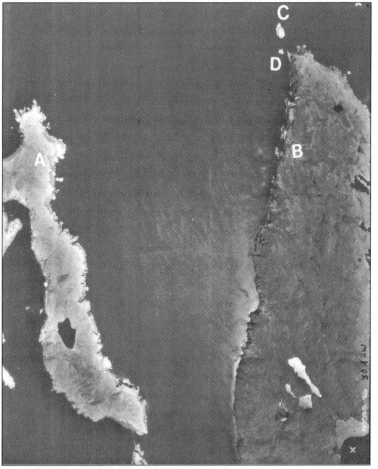

Map courtesy Government of Newfoundland and Labrador, Surveys and Mapping Divi.

From a lookout on Oderin Island (A), to Jude Island (B) is a little over a quarter mile. Gull Rock is (C) and Little Gull Rock (D). For many years, the people of Oderin kept a white cross on Gull Rock (Little Gull Rock is often sea-swept) symbolizing the heroic struggle of the three men.

Oderin planter Richard McGrath was elected a member for Newfoundland's House of Assembly (MHA) for Placentia and St. Mary's in 1861, and later was appointed magistrate there. In 1885 his son James Fanning McGrath established a business at Oderin and later became a MHA. Indeed the latter McGrath plays a part in the next drama of the sea.

On Monday November 1, 1915, *Madonna*, a schooner owned in Placentia and built in Fox Harbour in 1886, left St. John's with general cargo. A small vessel at thirty-eight ton, *Madonna* carried only three crew: Captain Robert Sparrow of Ship Harbour, James Dormidy and his sixteen-year-old son, Michael. James Dormidy, with a splendid physique and in the prime of life, was over six feet tall and weighted about two hundred forty pounds. Although he didn't know it, his strength would be severely tested in the hours ahead.

Madonna reached Fermeuse that evening, but a storm forced Sparrow to wait it out until Friday. The next day she stopped at St. Bride's and went on past Cape St. Mary's at eight A.M. Saturday. Under a stiff easterly wind, she sailed across Placentia Bay passing Long Island at five P.M. Half an hour later, while running the passage between Gull Rock and Oderin island *Madonna* mis-stayed and struck Little Gull Rock, a crag no more than ten feet square.

Immediately all on board knew the vessel was doomed. James Dormidy cut the main sheet allowing the main boom to swing in over the rock and the two men and the boy climbed out on the boom and dropped on this precarious refuge. At high tide the sea swept over Little Gull Rock, but didn't completely cover it. They saw their vessel pound to pieces and sink.

Now they began a fight for life: three helpless men on a small rock with no food or water, night was coming on and a terrible storm raging. To get any kind of a hand-hold on the kelp-covered islet, they edged to the small pinnacle at the top. To this, lying prone, they clung with benumbed hands while sea and cold spray went over them. Throughout the miserable hours of Saturday night, they were almost torn away by the force of waves.

The weather continued with even more fury all Sunday; yet they encouraged each other to tighten their grip on the rocks while hoping for an abatement in the storm. About seven o'clock Sunday evening young Michael Dormidy realized his father was weakening and his strength ebbing.

With a prayer on his lips, the father surrendered his soul to the God who gave it. At eight P.M. he died. Michael, unmindful of his own suffering which by now was increased through pangs of hunger, thirst and exposure, thrust his left arm under his father's waist and held the body until Monday morning. Then a high tide and a heavy sea swept it from him. Michael's left arm was all but useless with the weight and it was a constant battle to hold onto the rock with his right.

Robert Sparrow, a man of sixty-one years, continued to fight for his life until Monday evening. By then exposure, cold and thirst had taken its toll. Young Dormidy saw with feelings of horror his last companion was near death. He was not quite dead when a heavy wave caught Sparrow; he relaxed his grip on the piece of rock and was swallowed up by the waves.

The boy's traumatic situation now played on his mind, for he expected nothing but at any moment a similar fate as what had happened to his father and to his friend. He later said, "I will never forget the horror of the hours of Monday night and Tuesday morning. I was only dimly aware of time passing, but I held on with all my strength with both hands to the rock."

At noon on Tuesday, Alphonsus Melloy, a young boy of Oderin, reported to Magistrate McGrath that he believed he saw someone on Little Gull Rock. Immediately the magistrate engaged four men to investigate. He then looked through his spyglass and saw wreckage along the Jude Island shore and what appeared to be a body on a rock. He knew there had been a shipwreck. Just as the men of Oderin were getting a dory off, another boat came in from the eastward and steered for Little Gull Island.

This was John Pomeroy and his crew from Merasheen Island who found the boy more dead than alive after nearly seventy-two hours on the rock. He brought the unconscious body to Oderin; all who looked at Dormidy agreed he could not possibly recover. But the men in Pomeroy's boat took off their own clothes, stripped the boy of his wet apparel, put on dry clothes and carried him to McGrath's home. The magistrate and his wife placed him in their bed and after giving him stimulants, fed him at intervals for hours with warm milk from a spoon.

After several hours he recovered enough to tell the terrible tale of suffering and the fate of his father and Sparrow. On Wednesday morning Magistrate McGrath sent a crew to try to find the bodies. At six A.M. they found James Dormidy's body. Although about twenty men swept the waters around Little Gull Rock for ten days, Sparrow's remains were never found. It was supposed it did not sink, but drifted west through the reach.

They hooked up a bag of clothes belonging to James Dormidy and, in a stocking, there was fourteen dollars in silver. Michael, who survived despite his slender build, said, "I can never forget the kindness of the Pomeroys, the Magistrate and Mrs. McGrath. I owe them my life."

"Anxiety" As Posted in the Paper

In the era of sailing ships and limited communication, it was common for Newfoundland vessels to be missing for months before their whereabouts was known. Long distance communication in the early 1900s was in its infancy. Usually, when a ship was unreported, local papers voiced concern with an article or brief news item which detailed her destination, the date of leaving port, her captain and sometimes the crew list, and some explanation of what may have happened to the ship.

In certain Newfoundland communities, especially in Conception Bay, these notices of missing ships became known as "anxiety" reports — when words of worry and concern for the safety of sailors and loved ones were published. It became a time of survival, waiting, hoping for family and friends.

The schooner *George A. Wood*, Captain George Winsor of Carbonear, was overdue on a trip to Barbados. She carried fish south and was due to return with a cargo of salt. According to a conversation with Lloyd Rossiter of Carbonear on October 26, 1997, certain families of Carbonear were very concerned for the missing schooner. Lloyd's father, Fred Rossiter, was one of *George A. Wood's* crew.

The tern schooner left Newfoundland in November 1927 with a full load of prime codfish for southern markets. Winsor carried an all-Carbonear crew, the ship arrived at her destination without incident, loaded salt at Turks Island and sailed for St. John's. The ship was relentlessly pounded by extremely adverse winds and rough seas.

Unknown to the families of Carbonear, she sailed to within sight of the St. John's Narrows when a vicious storm blew her back to sea. In the ensuing days of battling gale force winds, her masts were broken and sails were ripped or blown away. She was pushed back across the Atlantic and southward.

For almost three months, nothing was heard from *George A. Wood*. An "anxiety" report was soon to be published. Blinds were drawn, sympathies were offered to the bereaved families and a general sense of despair pervaded the community of Carbonear. *George A. Wood* had been gone so long that people began to think the unspeakable phrase, "She's lost with crew."

But Mrs. Fred Rossiter and Mrs. George Winsor refused to give up hope. Mrs. Rossiter made the usual Christmas pudding that her husband liked so well in the festive season. Then on the eighty-ninth day, one day before the dreaded "anxiety" report was to appear in the paper, schooner *George A. Wood* reported with all crew well. It was February 28, 1928, when the owners received a telegram saying she had arrived in Bridgetown, Barbados, battered but all crew had survived the beating.

Early in December 1929, she made a quick fish-laden voyage to Barbados, loaded 123 puncheons of molasses and set sail for St. John's. On her voyage north, *George A. Wood* was lost on December 30, when she grounded on Sable Island. Captain Winsor, mate William Penney, Robert Penney, all of Carbonear; Clayton Moore, Jersey Harbour; Norman Monster and Bert Thornhill of Fortune reached the island safely.

Built in Nova Scotia, this tern schooner net weight was 120 ton. At one time she was skippered by Harry Brushett of Burin.

Anxiety Felt For Missing Schooner

Considerable anxiety is being felt for the safety of the schooner Letty B., of Cape Broyle, which left here for her home port on Monday afternoon. The vessel is owned by Mr. Carew of Cape Broyle, and was in charge of his son and two others. The last seen of the vessel was about five o'clock on that evening when she was in Petty Harbour "Motion". Captain Winsor, of the Marine and Fisheries, on being informed of the

The schooner *Letty B* was long overdue; subsequently an "anxiety" report appeared in *The Daily News* on January 20, 1928. Owned by Captain Ernest Carew of Cape Broyle, she sprang a leak off Cape Race and was abandoned by her crew: Austen Carew age twenty-three; James Carew, twenty and Stephen Yard, twenty-two. They rowed into Trepassey and finally reported their safe arrival.

Anxiety for *Lornina* — In the fall of 1915, considerable concern arose over the whereabouts of the Witless Bay schooner *Lornina*. She failed to report on a voyage from Quebec to Halifax. In early October she left Quebec laden with a cargo of codfish. At first the owner and relatives of her crew thought the schooner had been abandoned or wrecked. Perhaps her crew had been picked up and carried to another port.

TRAGEDIES OF THE STORM!

A TALE OF DEATH AND DISASTER!

THE "EFFIE M." LOST WITH ALL HANDS!

MAN DASHED TO DEATH AT ARNOLD'S COVE

On September 18, 1907, a sudden gale overwhelmed the fishing fleet returning from Labrador. One of the victims was the schooner *Effie M* of Trinity, Trinity Bay. There was much anxiety in the news reports of the day as shown by this clipping.

Witless Bay, located about thirty kilometres south from

St. John's, was settled in the 1600s. The town had thirty-four people recorded there in 1675 and family names of Dinn, Power, Tobin, Mallowney, Norris, Burk, Maddigan, Carew and Carey were noted. Early settlers relied on the inshore cod fishery and vegetable farming.

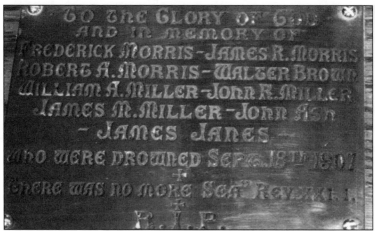

Photo courtesy of Clarence Dewling

Wreckage of *Effie M* was located at Broad Cove, near Old Perlican, on the eastern side of Trinity Bay. There were no survivors. The memorial plaque mounted on a desk/fall-stool and located in St. Matthews Anglican Church in Trouty was dedicated by Rev. C.W. Holland on August 17, 1912.

Listed on the plaque are: Captain Fred Morris, James R. Morris, Robert A. Morris, Walter Brown, William A. Miller, John R. Miller, James M. Miller, John Ash and James Janes. Others lost were George Hiscock, single, son of Robert; James Woolridge, married; James Fleet, Cuckold's Cove; John Pinhorn; Arthur Sexton and his son.

Lornina, owned by the Cashin business of Cape Broyle, was registered to the Honourable Michael Peter Cashin, the Government member for Ferryland district. (M.P. Cashin later became Prime Minister of Newfoundland.) The schooner had a crew of five: Captain John Will Carey, who lived on the south side or Gallow's Cove area of Witless Bay, was married with children; mate Tom Connors; James Tierney, Morgan Lundrigan of Witless Bay who had at least one son, Woodley, living in Witless Bay; Peter Costello of Ferryland and Charles Mason, Carbonear.

Although the exact time and circumstances of her sinking is not known, family tradition puts the date as October

16th or 17th. A story passed down through the Lundrigan family says that at one A.M. on the 17th Mrs. Lundrigan heard a tap on the window. She knew it was her husband, Morgan, at the window saying goodbye.

By December 10, 1915, after six weeks with no report, *Lornina* was posted as missing with crew.

Elliston to the Rescue

After his captain was washed overboard in a storm, John Hickman found himself alone on his vessel from Sunday night to Tuesday morning. It was the "floating shop," the ketch *Yale*, from Burin. Well-stocked with general cargo for trade along the Labrador coast, the little ship with a crew of two — Captain Abram J. Carbage and John Hickman — left St. John's on October 6, 1934, for North West River. Although small at sixteen ton, *Yale* was considered to be an auxiliary yacht; that is she had an engine but could run under sail in fair winds.

Greta Hussey, in her book *Our Life on Lear's Room, Labrador*, describes fishing on the Labrador coast and writes of the trading schooner saying:

> These (traders) were travelling all summer... stocked with dry goods such as knitting wool, dress material and flannel, things needed by the Labradorians. The boats moved from harbour to harbour until all her cargo was sold.
>
> The one we were accustomed to was green in colour and operated by a man by the name of Carbage. On several occasions Mother was taken out to his ship in our motor boat. She would buy things for the family.

It was the usual custom for small traders to arrive in the spring and leave in the fall, but in the fall of 1937

Carbage decided to spend the winter on the Labrador coast. Both men on *Yale* lived in Burin; Carbage, a Jewish merchant, had lived there for twenty years. Hickman was young and inexperienced on the sea.

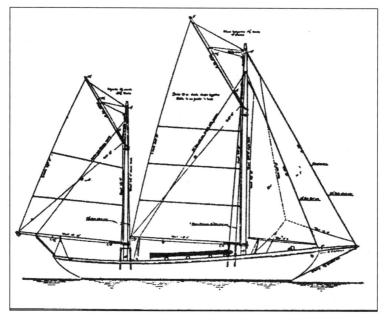

The Yale

Built around 1910 for the Grenfell Mission, *Yale* was forty-three feet long and had an iron keel. With a short mainmast and relatively high foremast, *Yale* was a ketch. She is described as "having no great turn of speed, but good carrying capacity and able in rough water." She had a twenty horse power engine. Merchant Carbage eventually purchased the sixteen ton ketch, but it is not clear what eventually happened to *Yale*.

It was a pleasant day when they pulled out of St. John's harbour at seven A.M. *Yale* was well-loaded with shop goods to be traded for furs or cash, but she made good time. Sometime Sunday evening the two men encountered storm-whipped whitecaps and strong winds. They were forced to shut off the engine and use the sail to keep her head into the high seas. They figured they were somewhere southeast of Cape Bonavista.

By 9:30 A.M. the little craft was so disabled and battered by the storm, Carbage and Hickman had to bail water from the engine room with buckets. The engine and pump had been put out of commission by the force of water going down the hold. While Hickman was bailing, Carbage held the wheel.

A great sea broke over *Yale*, carried away everything on deck and swept the captain over the side. Hickman jumped up from below, but he could do nothing in the dark and boiling ocean to rescue his captain and friend. Somehow, he recovered from the initial trauma of the sudden death of his shipmate and pulled himself together. Despite his youth he had a seaman's knowledge and determination and quickly hauled the little ship's head into the wind.

Hickman was now alone in a storm with little experience in handling a craft. From Sunday night to Tuesday morning he drifted at the mercy of the sea and gale now at its height. *Yale* drifted helplessly Sunday night and when at daylight came on Monday he could see no land. He decided to steer by the sun and at night lay to when the gale subsided.

Early Tuesday morning he sailed within sight of land which he found out later were the hills behind Elliston, Bonavista Bay. Hickman got out the shotgun and fired several signal shots. Fishermen of Elliston heard the shots and saw the little craft. James, William and Benjamin Crewe and Edward Murphy set out in a motor boat to figure out what was wrong.

To their surprise they found one lone young man aboard who had been forty-five hours fighting a fierce gale, struggling to get his small craft to land. Sadly he had to report his captain, Abram Carbage of Burin, lost to the sea. After the storm-damaged *Yale* was towed in, the people of Elliston cared for Hickman with the usual Newfoundland hospitality until he could leave for home and family in Burin. District fishery officer Roland Kean wired Burin's parish priest Reverend Father Miller who notified relatives in Burin.

Perhaps the severity of the storm Hickman conquered can be measured by looking at the fate of schooner *Carrie S* owned and captained by Michael Furlong of St. Brendan's. She discharged a load of birch junks at Elliston on Sunday, left that night and ran into the same gale *Yale* fought. Captain Furlong and his two sons were forced to retreat. But *Carrie S* leaked badly, filled with water and sank at Flynn's Beach, Catalina.

The gear and equipment of the schooner was stored on shore for *Carrie S*, a total wreck, was abandoned and never refloated. Furlong and his sons left for St. Brendan's on the coastal steamer *Home*.

Immigration and the *Mary O'Hara*

One of the earliest stories of Newfoundlanders working out of the large American fishing ports occurred in 1897. When the Gloucester schooner *Lizzie J. Greenleaf*, Captain P. Erickson, disappeared that year, she had seven Newfoundland fishermen in her crew of fifteen. She sailed from

Newfoundland Seamen Lost on *Lizzie J. Greenleaf*, January 1897
William Burgess, age 20, Heart's Content
John Dee, 19, Placentia
Patrick Fitzpatrick, 27, St. John's
William Flynn, 28, Placentia
William Mulcahey, 25, St. John's
Thomas O'Neill, 25, St. John's
George Walsh, 20, Placentia

Gloucester, Massachusetts, on December 26th on a trip to catch halibut and was last seen on January 17, 1897, when another Gloucester schooner hailed and spoke to *Lizzie J. Greenleaf*'s Captain, P. Erickson. She probably foundered in the gale of January 18th.

In the 1920s and 1930s, Newfoundlanders migrated by the hundreds to the eastern United States. Many, like those on *Lizzie J. Greenleaf*, found employment as fishermen in Gloucester and Boston.

Thomas I. Moulton of Lewin's Cove, Placentia Bay, had left Newfoundland for Gloucester many years earlier. He worked on the sea and eventually joined an auxiliary (driven by sail and/or engine) schooner named *Mary O'Hara* as cook. On January 21, 1941, while approaching Boston harbour, *Mary O'Hara* struck barge. What followed can only be best described as "hours of terrifying torture" as eighteen of her twenty-three man crew perished.

While sailing into harbour at night, three men — Captain Fred Wilson, helmsman Gilbert Smith, and Fred Conrad on lookout — occupied the wheelhouse. Twenty were asleep below. Without warning, a rendering, grinding crash shook *Mary O'Hara* as she ploughed at full speed into a black coal barge.

The first man out of the forepeak bunks was Clayton Hines who shouted out to those still below, "She's sinking!" Hines' face was streamed with blood from a severe laceration he received when thrown around in the impact. All the crew, who for the most part were lightly clad, ran on deck. Captain Wilson steered away from the barge and drove *Mary O'Hara* nearly a mile in a futile attempt to reach shoal water before the schooner sank beneath his feet.

It was a cold night; temperatures were well below freezing. *Mary O'Hara*, full of haddock and cod, was also weighed down by ice. Her rigging, bulwarks and decks were thick with ice built up by flying spray and frost. Her two nests of dories, ten in all, were frozen into solid blocks of ice. Wilson and several men worked in vain to chop a boat free while the schooner sped on in a date with death. When the dories floated off deck, they still were two compact lumps of ice.

As *Mary O'Hara* sank, the men swarmed up the ice-coated rigging. She came to a stop on the bottom in forty-nine feet of water. Only four feet of the masthead rigging and a small portion of the foremast remained above the choppy ocean. Twenty-three men, fourteen from Nova Scotia, seven from New England ports and two from Newfoundland, clung for life.

For a time they tried to buoy and cheer each other with conversation. Some prayed, some sang, but their strength gradually waned. In the ensuing hours before daylight, three vessels passed in the night and not hearing the cries and shouts of stranded men, steamed on.

One by one, eighteen plunged to their death in the icy sea off Boston harbour. Frozen fingers and limbs could no longer hold on the cold rigging. After each vessel passed, there were fewer and fewer desperate souls clinging to the rigging. Captain Wilson, born in Lower Pubnico, Nova Scotia, was one of the last to go.

Five remained. Their stamina must have been a little greater, their resolve a little stronger or maybe they were better clad than the others. They lived to see trawler *North Star* bear down and then nose her prow into the rigging to rescue the last survivors of the schooner *Mary O'Hara*. Four were taken off, but the fifth fell from his perch into the icy seas. Fortunately some men from *North Star* threw over the dory and rescued him.

They lived to tell of the anguish experienced as vessels passed by and their lights faded; they lived to tell of the trauma of saying good-bye to friends and workmates dropping to certain death from the rigging. Rescued were two from Boston and three from Nova Scotia: Stanley Conrad of Lunenburg County, Cecil Crowell, Shelburne County and Cecil Larkin of East Pubnico. The two Newfoundlanders lost their lives. Moulton, age forty-eight and married with four or five children, was one of them. John Sheehan, forty-two and married with one child, also perished in the accident. He lived in Gloucester, but was born in Bay Bulls.

Up to the 1920s, the United States welcomed immigrants. Millions came from Europe seeing the country as a golden land of promised liberty. The river of people into the US peaked in 1907 when 1,285,349 immigrants entered. In 1924, the US established a quota system and cut off the free flow. The golden door never closed so tightly, however, that the land ceased to be the "Mother of Exiles." The Statue of Liberty, sent as a gift to the US from France and represented the friendship of the French people, commemorates freedom.

Not only did immigrants come from Europe, but also Canada and Newfoundland. In the years of unrestricted movement, untold hundreds poured into New York, Gloucester, Boston and other American cities from Newfoundland. My own father Charles (and his sister, Rose who married Cyril Fiander of English Harbour West or Harbour Breton) for example, immigrated to the US in 1923 where Charles helped build homes in New York and in the Boston/Quincy area. Charles came back home two or three years later; perhaps he realized the city life in the US was not for him, maybe he yearned for a more rural way and his roots. But come home he did, married my mother and raised his five children in Newfoundland. His sister Rose remained in Boston with her husband and two children, Carol Ann and Alton.

Surviving Hurricane Betsy with Trepassey's Help

Three fishermen from Trepassey, Allan and Lyle Sutton and John Penney, were out tending their fishing gear on August 26, 1956. About two P.M. they had clewed up their day's work; the sea was choppy and they had about three miles to go to reach Trepassey. Hurricane Betsy, one of the worst storms of the season, had roared through from August 19-23. No one ventured on the water during that time but by August 26th, the seas had calmed and winds abated. The Trepassey men decided to leave a bit early as fog was setting in. The Suttons and Penney turned their little boat around and headed home; then one of them heard a sound — a small horn, like a hand held fog horn, blowing.

In the distance, they saw what appeared to be one small boat and it appeared as if two or three gaunt figures were waving from it. Within minutes, the Trepassey men drew alongside. It was three dories, one tied behind the other, and aboard were not three men, but seven. Some lay in the bottom of their craft too tired to get up; all were hungry, thirsty and weak from exposure and exhaustion.

Within minutes they were aboard Sutton's craft. There was enough hot tea for all and the little food aboard was shared around. The Trepassey men tied on the dories that had served as their haven for over seven days and towed them behind. On the way they listened to the story of the shipwreck.

The eighty-five foot *Angela B. Mills*, a sword fishing craft out of Sambro, Nova Scotia, sprang a leak and sank seven and a half days earlier, on August 19th, just hours before Hurricane Betsy struck. Captain Harold Henneberry and his six men — Keith and Melvin Gray, no relation; brothers Charles and Herbert Marryatt, cousin Roy Marryatt and Charlie Burke — abandoned ship. They were about 300 miles from the nearest land mass, the southern tip of the Avalon Peninsula. They had one pair of oars, twenty-three cans of spaghetti or mixed vegetables, three packs of sweet biscuits, a gallon of water, tinned milk and some rum. On the third day they shot a seabird which they tore apart and ate raw.

Some time later, one story said, "They Beat Hurricane Betsy." In that tale Captain Henneberry stated:

> ...that at one point in the high winds it was too stormy even to row. The dories half-filled with water and the oars were whipped from our hands. The winds were thirty miles an hour maybe more. Two of the boys sat huddled with a blanket pulled over the stern to ward off some of the water as they bailed out the rest. They had to do this all night.

With no loss of life and only a few sores, boils and chafed legs, each man had lost about eighteen pounds but had survived a hurricane on the treacherous Atlantic in an open boat.

They were taken to St. John's, lodged in the Red Cross hostel and the next night took a TWA flight home.

Chapter Seven

Abandonment

These yarns of the sea illustrate the hardships and deprivation that crews endured when forced to abandon ship in the North Atlantic. Despite diligent pumping and every effort to keep vessels afloat, hundreds of vessels were claimed by the unforgiving ocean. Most were strained by heavy cargoes of fish, salt or coal; then seams opened in the constant pounding of waves. In a race against time the tired crew pumped constantly while others scanned the horizon for passing ships.

Often no ocean liners passed near the location and there was no rescue ship to save the weary men. The only recourse was to prepare a dory, or ship's lifeboat, and wait until the last possible moment before stepping off the sinking ship.

If the crew sighted a vessel in the distance they signaled, usually by small fires or flares, and hoped the passing ship saw the signal. And sometime the ships didn't see the distressed schooner wallowing in the trough of great combers.

Many local schooners were abandoned at sea and unless they sank immediately or were set afire to prevent them from becoming a menace, the derelict hulls became one of the most common sources of danger in the ocean. Many a missing ship met its fate by running into an abandoned wreck lying on the ocean highways.

Carbonear Crew, Shipwrecked Twice

When they arrived back in Newfoundland, the five men from Carbonear and surrounding area related how they had been shipwrecked twice on one voyage. The second wreck was somewhat of a blessing in disguise.

Captain Arthur Dean, mate Hoyles Chipman, John Pike, Herbert Laing, Edward Winsor and Field Taylor left Merchantman's Harbour, Labrador, on September 14, 1908 in their fishing schooner *Mystery*. Their destination was Gibraltar and from there would proceed onto Greece to discharge their load of salt fish. Robert Duff's business of Carbonear owned the ninety-eight ton, American-built vessel and it was well loaded with over 2700 quintals of salt cod.

But ocean storms can make short work of plans. Captain Dean had sailed three days when a violent ocean storm accosted *Mystery*: seas swept her deck, she began to leak and water steadily gained in the holds despite continuous pumping. To lighten the load, 300 quintals of cargo were thrown over the side.

Mystery drifted at the mercy of wind and seas. On September 20th a wave swept everything moveable from her decks. By the next day, the five men knew the schooner was slowly sinking and they were worn out from constant pumping.

On September 22, the ensign, Newfoundland's flag, was hoisted upside down from the masthead to indicate that there was trouble. Hopefully some passing ship would come near and see the distress signal. Not long after, the crew saw a steamer passing about a mile away going west, but it steamed on, probably not seeing the sinking schooner.

Captain Dean measured the rising water in the hold —

it had gained another three feet. He called his crew together, explained how much time they had left before *Mystery* would be wallowing and awash in the heavy seas. They had to once again handle the pumps to snatch a few more hours before their schooner sank. Dean hoisted some canvas and ran southwest, toward the shipping lanes.

A few hours later, a second steamer came in sight — this one heading east. It saw the distress signal (upside down flag), bore down toward *Mystery* and prepared for a mid-ocean rescue. It was the S.S. *Main* of the North German Line commanded by Captain Jensen.

Jensen sent over a lifeboat manned by *Main*'s second officer and four volunteers. Before stepping off his schooner, Captain Dean set her on fire in the hope she would burn to the water's edge and sink quickly.

The officers and crew S.S. *Main*, bound from New York to Bremen, Germany, treated the shipwrecked sailors with the compassion shown to all distressed mariners. When *Mystery*'s crew arrived in Bremen, they were sent to Hamburg and from there to Grimsby, England. They then travelled to Liverpool to join the S.S. *Ulunda* bound for St. John's, Newfoundland.

But their troubles were not yet over as they were shipwrecked a second time. The S.S. *Ulunda* collided with the Italian barque *Santa Anna* and had to return to Liverpool. The Carbonear seamen mentioned after that, they were not treated favourably aboard *Ulunda* and they were happy to have changed ships. The Board of Trade Officer in Liverpool again arranged for their passage to Newfoundland; this time aboard the Allan Liner S.S. *Mongolian*.

Mystery's crew finally arrived in St. John's on October 26, 1908, where Captain Dean told his story to the local papers.

To Fire a Ship

When the schooner *Mildred*, Captain Wiltshire, arrived in St. John's from Oporto, it had on board another crew. They were Captain George N. Dean of Carbonear and his crew who had lost their brigantine *Lady Napier* in mid-ocean.

Owned by the Job Brothers of St. John's but chartered by Crosbie and Company, *Lady Napier* left St. John's to take 4000 quintals of fish to Bahia, Brazil, on September 5, 1911. Six days later in a storm, the brigantine's rudder head was broken off and she drifted about helplessly. The working and pounding of the rudder in high seas made *Lady Napier* leaky.

Captain Dean took wire and fastened the rudder as best as he could in hope that the vessel could make headway. The jury rig broke away in seas and again his ship became unmanageable; this caused her to leak more. The foremast was smashed and the bulwarks broken. The crew manned the pumps, but it was labour in vain; water continued to rise at a steady rate in the holds.

Up to September 21, *Lady Napier* was at the mercy of the sea. Then the weather abated. At a latitude of 45.49 North, 42.32 West, another schooner, the *Mildred*, sighted the wallowing brigantine and moved close. Captain Wiltshire came aboard and said to Dean that *Lady Napier* should be abandoned. Her condition was such, it would be unlikely the vessel could make any port.

Lady Napier's crew were carried over to *Mildred* in a dory manned by two bank fishermen who were used to handling a dory in high seas. Captain Dean was the last to leave the wreck. To ensure the sinking, oil was thrown over the decks; clothes, blankets or straw-filled mattresses were soaked with oil. A match touched to the rags ensured a conflagration even in the stormiest weather.

Dean also set a fire in the cabin and in the forecastle. He then saturated mats with kerosene, placed them around the butts of the masts and set them ablaze. As *Mildred* pulled away from her, *Lady Napier* was completely enveloped in flames. Both ship and cargo were covered by insurance.

Mildred arrived safely into St. John's on September 25, 1911.

Lusitania, the Rescue Ship

One of the passengers on the Cunard passenger liner *Lusitania* in January 1914 was a reporter for the New York newspaper *World*, Norman Thwaites. Life aboard the British luxury liner may have been without newsworthy incident and Thwaites didn't have much to report on the sea voyage to England. That changed at 2:30 A.M. on January 15 when *Lusitania's* engines stopped in mid-ocean.

The stopping of the engines and a change in the ship's course woke nearly all passengers, including Thwaites. The reporter then came on deck to witness a thrilling drama of lifesaving with the moody Atlantic Ocean as a backdrop.

Through the gloom and whitecaps spanning the choppy seas, Captain D. Dow of the *Lusitania* saw the flare of a torch in the distance. Figuring it was a ship in distress, he changed direction. Most of the crew and nearly all passengers dressed and went on deck to watch an exciting match of man against the sea.

At 3:30 A.M., about an hour later, *Lusitania* pulled alongside a sinking ship. It proved to be the Newfoundland brigantine *Mayflower*. Captain Dow asked for volunteers to man the lifeboat and every able seaman, the stewards and firemen wanted to be part of the rescue. Darkness and a heavy sea would make the work dangerous. First Officer Alexander, another officer and three crew took the lifeboat oars to row the hundred or so yards to the *Mayflower*. For two hours they struggled to manoeuvre near the wallowing vessel. By now the deck of *Mayflower* was awash and her crew had climbed into the rigging.

Dawn was now coming on. Alexander positioned the lifeboat on the leeward side, so as *Mayflower*'s crew could jump into the water and be picked up. There was no way in the heaving waves that the little boat could tie onto the bobbing brigantine. Should the schooner lurch over onto the small craft, it could have upset.

With the lifeboat finally in position, one by one the men clinging to the rigging, but wearing life belts, jumped overboard. Each was grabbed and hauled into *Lusitania*'s lifeboat. Captain Halfyard was the last man to leave his ship. Before the rescuing lifeboat left *Mayflower*'s side, Alexander shouted to Halfyard to set his vessel on fire so that she would not become a dangerous derelict.

Halfyard tried, but high seas came over the side and extinguished the fire. The last that the crew saw of *Mayflower* she was a charred hulk sinking somewhere off the Grand Banks.

The short voyage back to the side of *Lusitania* was fully as dangerous as the outward row. As the lifeboat pulled alongside *Lusitania*, the passengers lining the rails cheered the heroics of Alexander and his boat crew.

When the exhausted seamen were pulled aboard the *Cunarder*, Captain Halfyard collapsed. He was suffering from exposure and delirium. Doctor Pointon, the ship's surgeon, sent him to sick bay where he soon recovered.

The *World* newspaper reporter Thwaites soon interviewed the shipwrecked crew of *Mayflower* and the story he sent by wireless to New York praised them as tough, true "bluenose" sailors; in fact they were all Newfoundlanders. Four lived in St. John's: the captain on Carnell Street, cook William O'Neill on Pleasant Street, Patrick Bowdren on Central Street and John Walsh on Codner's Lane; mate Arthur Snelgrove and Edward Snow belonged to Harbour Grace; Noah Smith, Manuels; and Daniel Carew from Witless Bay. While fighting the Atlantic gale, seaman Snow had been knocked down by a wave and had two ribs broken. He too went into *Lusitania's* sick bay.

Mayflower had left St. John's on September 17, 1913, for Bahia, Brazil, and arrived there November 15th. But the voyage back was one long struggle with gales and head seas which intensified about one hundred miles off Cape Race. Food had run short in the long voyage.

Photo courtesy of Hubert Hall, SHIPSEARCH Marine

Lusitania (above) is well remembered in marine history for another reason. On May 7, 1915, sixteen months after the rescue of *Mayflower's* crew, a German submarine sank the great liner off the Irish coast. *Lusitania* went down in twenty minutes and of the 1,195 lives lost, 128 were American citizens. The ship was unarmed, but the enemy insisted she was carrying materials for the Allied war effort. The incident contributed to the rise of American sentiment in favour of entering the war on the side of Britain and her allies.

On January 12, 1914, three days before *Lusitania*

showed up, *Mayflower* lost its rudder, the sails had been ripped away and the beleaguered brigantine sprang a leak. The crew had lost all belongings and extra clothes.

In a humane gesture *Lusitania*'s passengers collected a large sum of money for the rescuers and the rescued. The two officers of the lifeboat crew received gold watches, the remaining boat crew £15 each and *Mayflower*'s men £15 each. The latter arrived back in St. John's on February 6, 1914.

Mayflower, owned by Goodridge and Sons of St. John's, was the eighth ship out of eleven owned by Goodridge lost at sea — only *Rosina*, *Minnie* and *Clementine* remained. Lost or wrecked were *Devonia*, *Energy*, *Bella Rosa*, *Grace*, *Amanda*, *Algeria*, *Viola*, and now the *Mayflower*.

No Time to Celebrate

Burn! To survive they had to burn everything combustible — doors, booms, bulwarks, even rope. New Year's Eve and New Year's Day slipped past, but there was no celebration in this fight to the finish in a sea tale which took place on *Euphrates*, a small cargo-carrying steamer plying a regular run from St. John's to Bell Island.

Her crew were local seamen: Captain George Dawe and stoker Anthony Taylor belonged to Port-de-Grave, but lived in St. John's; mate John Somerton, seaman Fred Somerton and the cook Azariah Churchill were residents of Portugal Cove, Conception Bay and engineer William French, Bay Roberts. On this particular trip, George Dawe replaced his brother, Jabez, who had been stricken with a heart attack. George Dawe later ran a grocery story at 176 Duckworth Street, St. John's.

On December 28, 1920, the S.S. *Euphrates* slipped

away from the coast of Newfoundland and was never seen again — the crew of the St. John's, harbour tug *D.P. Ingraham* caught a final fleeting glimpse while the tug was off Cape St. Francis. For several days relatives and friends in Portugal Cove and Port-de-Grave wondered if *Euphrates'* men were alive or if they too had been claimed by the sea. Then on January 3, 1921, a telegram came to the Minister of Shipping at St. John's. It had been relayed from the wireless station at Cape Race to her agents, the Neal brothers of the Bell Island Steamship Company:

> Taken all crew off *EUPHRATES* in sinking condition. Lat. 44.24 North, Long. 45.27 West. Dangerous to navigation. Inform St. John's, Nfld.
>
> (Signed) Jones, Master *GALILEO*

When S.S. *Euphrates* left Bell Island on the morning of December 28 to return to St. John's, the wind was strong but nothing the little ship couldn't handle. She was light in ballast as all cargo had been discharged and she carried no passengers. As *Euphrates* rounded Cape St. Francis, conditions changed — for the worse. The wind increased from the southeast and soon intensified to gale force accompanied by thick snow.

While *Euphrates* was off Flatrock, the St. John's harbour tug *D.P. Ingraham* saw the steamer partially obscured by snow and this final sighting, when reported, increased fears that *Euphrates* was in trouble. In the silence of the next three or four days many thought she had foundered with all crew.

Days passed and anxiety grew. Were Captain Dawe and his men safe? Had they put into another port? Were they driven off to sea? Perhaps wrecked somewhere? For a week there was no word on the whereabouts or fate of *Euphrates*.

Then the telegram (above) arrived at St. John's via

Cape Race from the ocean liner *Galileo*. Behind it was a story of hardship and endurance which only came to light when *Galileo* docked in New York harbour.

On that December day when the blizzard struck, *Euphrates* steamed on until the crew could hear the foghorn on Cape Spear. Nothing could be seen except thick snow. Dawe wisely decided to heave to and wait until the storm blew over or abated. In the night the weather cleared and the crew could see the lights of St. John's. They tried to reach The Narrows, but within two miles of safety, the wind veered suddenly to the northwest and came on with hurricane force.

Captain Dawe decided to let *Euphrates* drift with the wind rather than attempt to steam against it — to "run before the wind" would take them far out to sea. By daylight the next morning, December 29, there was no sign of land. They looked in vain toward the western horizon for the friendly outline of Cape St. Francis or Cape Spear.

Still No Word of Ss. Euphrate:

The owners of the steamer Euphrates are still anxiously awaiting some word of her but up to press hour to day nothing was known and the worst is now feared. The Euphrate plied between this port and Bell Isle as a freight carrier and left Bell Isle on Tuesday morning at 11 o'clock She was seen off Pouch Cove by the tug D. P. Ingraham which was tow ing a Danish schooner to Carbonear About that time snow squalls wer beginning and before 1 o'clock th weather was extremely thick wit the glass falling rapidly, so much s that the Sachem which left here o the same forenoon for Liverpool, pu back to await an improvement i conditions. Nothing was seen of th Euphrates since she was passed) b: the Ingraham altho the tug searche the shore as well as possible yester day, it being thought that perhap the little steamer went ashore in on of the dense snow squalls. There i a hope that she put off to sea bu had she done so it is likely that she would have got back by now. Th Euphrates has been in the local trad for many years, and for the past 6 o: 8 has been on the St. John's-Bell Island route. There was not a cent of insurance on her. Her crew num bered six men whose names are: George Dawe. St. John's, Captain: William French, Bay Roberts, Engi neer; Anthony Taylor. St. John's. Fireman; Azariah Churchill, Fred Somerton, and John Somerton. Portugal Cove, deck hands.

Anxiety surfaced in print with this December 1920 report of the missing steamer: "The owners ...are still anxiously awaiting some word of her and the worst is now feared." Owners David Neal and Mr. Colbourne had gone out in the S.S. *Mary*, another of Neal's steamers, and searched unsuccessfully.

To run before the wind was the safest course, but with inherent hardships. Regular coastal voyages from Bell Island to St. John's took four or five hours; thus the steamer had enough food for that length of time. As well it carried only a ton or two of coal for the steam engine. Now food and fuel on *Euphrates*, pushed many miles from land and already a day overdue, dwindled to nothing.

First the coal supply ran out and every piece of wood on board had to be burned to keep the steam boilers going. By December 31, every scrap of bread, hard tack, potatoes and other vegetables had been eaten. Six exhausted men held no celebration to usher in the New Year, 1921; in fact, a fight for life was shaping up. Their battle intensified as *Euphrates* took a battering from the mountainous seas pounding her planking and gradually opened seams.

In a memoir found in the files of *Daily News* (March 27, 1958) one of the crew reported:

> ...The ship was beginning to leak. On December 29, the engineer reported coal was running short and food was nearly gone. The bunkers were empty and a reserve store of 1 1/2 ton of coal in Number One hold had to be used. All hands were now without food and no one had slept since leaving Bell Island.
>
> By the evening of the 31st all the coal was consumed. We broke down the bulkheads and used the wood for fuel. By New Year's Day all woodwork had been burned in order to keep up enough steam to work the pumps.

For five days and nights the men had little sleep and less food. Finally all hope seemed lost, with no fuel, it became almost impossible to keep *Euphrates'* pumps going and her head to the wind. In a last ditch effort, the exhausted men chopped up the cargo boom, the derricks and even the mooring ropes to feed the fire. Just as the supply of combustible material was used, someone spotted a steamer in the distance. In response to a distress signal raised on *Euphrates*, the ship turned toward them.

It was two P.M. January 3rd. Five days had passed since the crew left Bell Island and they were now situated in the transatlantic shipping lanes southeast of Cape Race.

This vessel proved to be the S.S. *Galileo* bound from Antwerp to New York. Such a storm had swept the Atlantic, *Galileo's* lifeboats were smashed. When the ship drew close and Captain Dawe signalled they wished to be taken off, *Galileo's* Captain Jones replied they had no lifeboats; they had been damaged by heavy seas. The crew of *Euphrates* had to lower their boat and row to the rescue ship. *Galileo* made a lee for them to cross in the choppy seas — seas so rough it was impossible to hoist the lifeboat aboard and it had to be set adrift.

Photo courtesy of Mona Petten

The crew of *Euphrates*, Captain Dawe is second from the left; Anthony Taylor may on the far left. The others — John and Fred Somerton, William French and Azariah Churchill — are not identified.

Euphrates, now waterlogged and wallowing, soon

went down. Captain Dawe and his men lost all their belongings and the vessel was uninsured, but they didn't complain for each felt lucky to have escaped with his life.

Within a day or so, the shipwrecked men arrived in New York where agent J.M. Devine arranged for their journey home via Boston and Nova Scotia. At North Sydney, Mr. Shano looked after them and on January 16, they arrived in St. John's by train from Port aux Basques. Nineteen days had passed since they left Bell Island for a trip that normally would take a few hours to complete.

Bay Roberts Seamen on *Clintonia*

Some years ago I described (in my book *Survive the Savage Sea*) the hardships the crew of the two-masted schooner *Clintonia* endured when they abandoned their ship at sea. It happened on November 3, 1921 but only two of her crew's names were given at that time: Captain W.H. Bradbury and the cook Arthur Kelly.

Clintonia's crew had been several days searching the horizon for a passing ship. While bound from Placentia to Portugal, their schooner was battered by an Atlantic storm. When the tern vessel *Jean Wakely* came by, Captain Bradbury gave orders to abandon ship but, before doing so, attempted to set *Clintonia* afire to prevent her from becoming a menace to navigation.

In the process of dousing the cabin with gasoline, the captain and Kelly were severely burned when the oil lamp exploded. Thus only two names of a compliment of seven — the two treated for injuries — were reported by the media of the day. However, since the time of my story of the *Clintonia*, new information has come to light.

Not long ago I received a letter from Lewis E. Mercer of St. John's whose father, Thomas, was also on the storm-battered schooner that night over seventy years ago. Lewis, by virtue of his father relating the tales of the sea to a son, knew the names of the other crew — all of Bay Roberts: Thomas Mercer, Captain Bradbury's brother Archibald Bradbury, Richard Crane, Robert Dale and Arthur Menchions.

Lewis Mercer concluded his appreciated piece of correspondence saying that in later years his father, Thomas, turned away from a life at sea and worked for the Western Union Cable Company at Bay Roberts until he retired.

Chapter Eight

War

During the last two years of the Great War, sailors knew their vessels had little chance of making a voyage across the North Atlantic without being intercepted by a German submarine. German U-boats preyed on enemy ships sinking unarmed merchantmen on sight. Those merchantmen were wooden, sail-driven schooners, unarmed and carried only salt fish for Greece, Portugal or Spain, or fishery salt from Cadiz or Setubal on the east to west voyage.

Quite often submarine commanders showed a special humanity toward the crews of these lonely sailing vessels they were forced to sink. If the crew was not taken prisoner aboard an enemy warship, time was often allowed to let the crews get away in their lifeboat. Then the schooners were destroyed usually by planted bombs — the more expensive torpedoes were reserved for larger, more prestigious targets.

Two of the five stories are of World War Two vintage and both are of Newfoundland crews forced to abandon ship in the mid-Atlantic.

McClure: Victim of an Enemy Sub

Several months after the outbreak of World War One, the German war machine resorted to their submarine fleet to bring Britain to her knees. By January 1917 the Germans, convinced they could starve Britain in five months, entered into unrestricted submarine warfare.

To the enemy this policy, at least in its initial stages, was spectacularly effective. Allied shipping losses increased throughout the war reaching a peak of 869,000 in April 1917. The Germans invented or improved the self-propelling underwater torpedo and perfected the use of the submarine or U-boat. Schooners became easy targets.

By the time the war ended, enemy submarines had sunk at least twenty Newfoundland schooners — one which fell prey was the 191 ton *McClure*. She

Crew of *McClure*, March 1917
Captain Augustus Taylor, age 34, Carbonear
William Bailey, Twillingate
Charlie Steven ?, Twillingate
Allen Barrett, St. John's
Bert Noseworthy, St. John's
mate Bert Wells, Twillingate, son of Philip Wells, Twillingate

was built in Tatamagouche, Nova Scotia, in 1900 and was subsequently owned by J.T. Moulton of Burgeo and chartered by George N. Barr's business of St. John's. *McClure* was a tern schooner, i.e. three masts, and measured 104 long and twenty-seven feet wide.

On March 13, 1917 she left Newfoundland laden with salt cod for Naples. On May 22, as the crew neared the European coast, they kept a sharp lookout for submarines. Just as it seemed as if *McClure* would safely make the British protectorate of Gibraltar and then the Mediterranean Sea, helmsman Allen Barrett saw a submarine. He sent word to the captain and both Taylor and mate Wells agreed it was best to 'heave to' and stop as the sub moved closer.

All sails were dropped and the lifeboat was readied for launching. The Newfoundland crew knew their schooner, carrying food to Europe, would be sent to the bottom. Soon a German landing party of four men rowed up in a small boat and boarded *McClure*. The head of this group, a lieutenant, had one time bomb placed in the forecastle and another aft. About ten minutes after the schooner was abandoned, explosions ripped apart the Newfoundland tern schooner and she quickly sank.

The crew were ordered into *McClure*'s lifeboat taking with them food, provisions, oilskins, and Captain Taylor's charts and sextant. They rowed for a day and a half until late that night when an Italian destroyer spotted the boat and took them aboard.

Photo courtesy of Maritime History Archives,, MUN

Captain Augustus Taylor, lost at sea in December 1917. Earlier that year he escaped with his life when a German sub intercepted and sank his schooner *McClure*. He next sailed on a Twillingate vessel *Sidney Smith* (above), but she failed to report and is posted "Lost at Sea."

The first thing the commander of the Italian ship wanted to know was the nationality of the castaways. Taylor replied, "British subjects from Newfoundland." Knowing that Newfoundland schooners frequented Cadiz, the destroyer landed the men there. *McClure's* crew were well-cared for by the Spanish people; eventually they joined a Newfoundland vessel and landed in St. John's.

Unfortunately, a few months after this misadventure at sea, Captain Taylor and mate Bert Wells were lost on the tern schooner *Sidney Smith*. Their crewmates were Eli Hawkins and Henry Porter, both of Change Islands and cook Stewart Hull of Twillingate. *Sidney Smith*, laden with fish for Europe, left Twillingate in early December and never reported. The cause remains unknown: faulty repairs which caused the vessel to leak and founder at sea, a mid-Atlantic storm or an encounter with an unfriendly German submarine.

Sole Survivor

As far as he could tell, at the reiterating of his story, Oliver Batt was the only survivor. During the Atlantic battles at sea in World War One, Oliver Batt of Herring Neck, Newfoundland, was twenty-one years old and serving in the Royal Navy. His British naval ship was cruising somewhere off Europe when on September 21, on the very day Oliver celebrated his birthday, his ship was torpedoed.

While recuperating from his ordeal at Royal Hamadryad Seamen's Hospital at Cardiff, Wales, Batt wrote his mother to let her know he was okay. The hardship and trauma of his experiences recently came to light when the letter was re-discovered in the Batt family Bible in Herring Neck. Oliver had passed away in 1961 and the letter was sent to his daughter, Doris, residing in Corner Brook.

The story of Oliver Batt's struggle to survive is

recounted through his letter. He writes that his ship (which is not identified in the letter) was battling a typical Atlantic storm when about twelve o'clock in the night, an enemy torpedo exploded amidships. "It was a wonderful rough night, with wind and rain," he explained to his mother. "We were only left port two days before getting torpedoed. It was on my birthday, 21st September."

According to Batt, the crew was not expecting to encounter a sub at that time:

> I was on watch at the gun, just going to relieve my mate when all of a sudden the enemy fired. I still stuck to the gun but he (the enemy) didn't show himself.
>
> We didn't have time for anything and we were not able to get over the boats. She only stopped on the water or stayed afloat for two or three minutes so you can fancy what an explosion it was.
>
> Then every man for himself and one God for us all. We put on our life belts and rushed to the main deck. By that time she was keeled right over on the starboard side. One boat was lowered, but no one could get in.

Batt remembered that two shipmates were behind him when he jumped. He wisely took off his oilskins, but kept on his life belt. When he hit the water which was "quite a distance down" he went under, but quickly floated up. He wrote:

> I made haste and swam clear of the sinking ship. I pulled off my sea boots in the water. It was, you know, terrible with so many in the water together.
>
> Well, I didn't get a bit excited as I knew that if I did all would be over. It was about ten past twelve then. I was swimming around about half an hour and speaking to some of my shipmates.

They didn't know what to do — no boat to get in and the sea so rough.

It was a fine thing for me that I could swim. I got hold of a plank and I could fancy in the dark there was a boat. It was a long distance and there was so much crying in the water, it was terrible.

After this Batt saw no more of his shipmates and assumed none were saved. He was alone on a dark night, miles from land holding on to a plank. But as he says he kept his wits about him:

Well, I reached the boat all right, but she was bottom up and I climbed up on the bottom. When I got up there was one more fellow. He could not understand me and I could not understand him. (Batt doesn't explain why there was a language barrier or if this man was injured or in shock).

We were drifting to sea fast on the bottom of this boat. You may fancy what it's like in heavy sea on the bottom of a boat. It was a long time before daylight so I made the other fellow keep his hand on the keel, but you know we had all we wanted to do to keep hold of her.

The sea was running right over her. He got washed off twice, but I managed to get him on her again. He was with me till daylight when the poor fellow died; he got so cold. So I let him go and still hung on myself.

Batt confided to his mother that his biggest fear at this moment was getting downhearted himself; perhaps relinquishing somewhat in his desperate fight for life and losing his grip on the slippery bottom. But, he kept his faith in God, lived in hope of rescue and said to himself, "Where there is life, there is hope."

I was on the bottom of the boat until twelve o'clock in the day before being taken off. Just twelve hours. I had all hope given up. I was, as I found out later, twelve miles from land when I looked astern and saw a ship coming. She was coming right for me so I held up my hand, and up alongside she came.

They tried a long time before they could get in (near the overturned boat). It was too rough to lower the ship's lifeboat, but they managed to throw a line to me and I tied it around me. They pulled me in. I never thought of seeing land again.

Batt reiterates his strong religious upbringing as taught and instilled by his family: "Trust in the Lord and He will save you." Aboard the rescue ship he was treated well, given warm dry clothes and hot food. He then went to a bunk for much-needed sleep.

When the rescue vessel arrived in port, Oliver Batt was taken to hospital. He needed only rest for he had no other injuries or illness. Naturally he was a hero in the Welsh town and everyone asked him, "How did you endure it? How did you hold on to the bottom of a boat for twelve hours?" Batt simply replied, "It was a matter of life or death."

He waited to hear of other survivors, but had no knowledge if any had made it. He wrote that "by my next letter I can explain which ships were involved and if others had been rescued." But no other letter by Oliver has been located.

He concludes his missive to his mother saying, "Don't worry. I am all right, but my chums are gone. I felt the sadness more after I was picked up. Good-bye with loving wishes."

Author's note: I searched for the name of Batt's ship. After much research since receiving his letter, I saw Batt's photo in William Coaker's book *Twenty Years of the F.P.U.* the young seaman wears the HMS *Valiant* navy hat. During

the war at sea Britain lost many ships, some with few survivors, although *Valiant* was not a casualty. It is possible he
served on *Valiant* after his ordeal.

Batt, along with Chesley Kearley, Darius Hurley, Philip
Blandford, Chesley Miles and Eric Woodford of
Twillingate, Herring Neck, Too Good Arm and vicinity,
enlisted in April 1916; thus his sea action came after 1916.
When Batt returned from Europe in 1919, he was brought
first to Nova Scotia and Sydney's *Daily Post* of March 27,
1919, described his ordeal. Batt, a gun crew officer on the
merchant ship *Poseley* which carried general cargo from
Cardiff to France, said, "About midnight, September 21,
1918, a single torpedo crushed *Poseley* like an eggshell
and it sank before a single lifeboat could be lowered. The
entire sixty aboard jumped into the water and I'm the only
one left alive to tell the story."

Oliver Batt was the sole survivor of a World
War One sinking. In this photo he wears the
navy cap of the HMS *Briton*. This ship was first
called *Calypso*, a British cruiser and a training
and drill ship brought to Newfoundland for the
Royal Newfoundland Reserve. Two years into
World War One she was re-named *Briton*, but
was generally referred to as the "Old Calypso."

Peril by Sea; Peril on Land

Nowadays we tend to think, and justly and rightly so,
of the dangers faced by Newfoundland mariners
during World War Two — those who fought in the
Royal Navy or with the merchant marine branch. But the

focus of this story is those intrepid seamen of the Great War of 1914-1918.

In those years many more sailing craft plied the ocean; at least twelve Newfoundland schooners were intercepted, shelled or bombed and sunk by the enemy. The crews of three — *Jean* owned in St. John's, *Duchess of Cornwall* of Burgeo, and *Dictator*, English Harbour West — were taken prisoner aboard an enemy raider and carried to concentration camps in Germany.

Early in her career the two-masted schooner *Dictator* was owned in Grand Bank by fish exporters Forward and Tibbo. In a list of schooners fishing out of Grand Bank in 1912, *Dictator* is shown as obtaining 1600 quintals under Captain J. Hiscock. Netting about 100 ton and 115 feet long, she was built in the United States around 1900. At the time of her final voyage overseas, she was owned by Henry E. Petite of Mose Ambrose and operated out of English Harbour West.

She carried a hardy group of south coast seamen: Captain Thomas Fiander of English Harbour West, Thomas Bowdridge, Burgeo and Henry Banfield, Charles Blagdon, Leo Bungay and James Parsons. The place of residence of the last four is not clear although they are names common on Newfoundland's south coast.

On June 12, 1918, *Dictator* left Cadiz, Spain, loaded with salt and was about 580 miles off Newfoundland when on June 18th the crew sighted a German submarine. Three shells were fired at the schooner and the crew immediately threw over a lifeboat to escape. They were ordered to row to the sub where Captain Fiander was taken aboard. For half an hour he was questioned; then the rest of *Dictator*'s crew was ordered to board the submarine.

A German crew made a trip to the helpless Newfoundland vessel, gathered all the food available and then set off bombs that blew *Dictator* apart. Within a few moments the schooner that an hour or so before had been their workplace and home on the sea, sank to the bottom.

Photo courtesy of Hubert Hall, SHIPSEARCH Marine

U139, launched in Germany in December 1917, was the type that intercepted the English Harbour West schooner *Dictator*. *U139* was three hundred eleven feet long, carried six torpedo tubes and four guns on deck (one is not visible).

For twenty-two days the six men were kept prisoners on board the U-boat. Food was not bad and they were allowed on deck for short periods to stretch their legs. On July 28, 1918, they arrived in Germany, and were taken to Kiel where they spent seventeen days in prison. Eventually they were transferred to Dulmen, a soldiers' prison camp where they were imprisoned for a month.

The final stop was Brandenburg. This prisoner of war camp became their place of residence until the armistice was signed on November 11, 1918. At Brandenburg, *Dictator*'s mate Leo Bungay died from pneumonia for he had been put to hard labour despite his illness. James Parsons was killed by a train being diverted to a side track.

The remaining four were, like all the other hundreds of prisoners at the camp, forced to work hard. They received barely enough food to keep alive. One of the strange coincidences of the story of imprisonment was a story told by Thomas Bowdridge. On the German ship or at the camp, he met other Burgeo men from the tern schooner *Duchess of Cornwall* who were also prisoners. Their schooner had been shelled and all seven Burgeo men were taken prisoner. It was a happy occasion and many stories of home and sea life were swapped.

In later years, Alf Anderson of the *Duchess of Cornwall*

who lived to a good age and resided in Burgeo, told his stories of life in the concentration camp. According to his tale, prisoners would be left two or three days without food. The guards would bring in trays and plates of hot food to smell and to see; then would take it away to eat the food themselves. Bread and water was the usual fare for those like Anderson.

At any rate, four of six of *Dictator*'s crew lived to return to their south coast homes (all of *Duchess of Cornwall*'s crew survived). When the armistice was signed they were taken to Copenhagen, Denmark, from there to England and arrived at Nova Scotia on the liner *Empress of Britain* on January 30, 1919. Captain Thomas Fiander left Copenhagen four days previous to the others and reached Newfoundland first to tell his story of capture on the high seas and imprisonment in Germany.

Seven Days in a Leaky Boat

The enemy ship had the appearance of an old tramp ship flying the Swedish flag, not a gun on her to be seen. They were all sheltered from our view with dummy lifeboats made of canvas.

We were contented enough about her until 'boom boom' went the shells. The first shot took us in the bow, second shot took down the funnel and Marconi wires, a direct hit. The third shot took the engine room.

I was just past the funnel on the promenade deck when the wires came down across my head. I got hit in the side by a piece of shrapnel which gave me a slight wound.

We scarcely had time to get our life jackets. He must have fired 20 shots without ceasing and we lost every garment of our clothes. After awhile he ceased firing and we managed to lower our lifeboats. He then gave us the signal to come aboard. Five of our men were wounded, which they took to their hospital on board and finally they took us to a prison below deck.

— Raymond Stoodley's "Memoirs" on the sinking of S.S. *Davisian*, July 10th, 1940

That was just the beginning of trouble. Ray Stoodley and fellow Newfoundlander William Peckford, age thirty-two and born in Change Islands, survived the shelling and sinking. In later years Stoodley recorded his story of war and hardship.

It was July 10, 1940, and the battle of the Atlantic was in full swing. The steamer *Davisian* was steaming along 420 miles east of Bermuda when it crossed paths with the German auxiliary cruiser *Narvik*.

Stoodley, a young man at sea many miles from his hometown of Grand Bank, was in the merchant marines; in essence he and his shipmates helped carry valuable supplies overseas on an unarmed freighter. He, Peckford and the rest of *Davisian*'s compliment were "taken down below and locked up. The next morning about forty more [prisoners] from another room were put in with us. We learned that they were taken prisoner from the tanker *British Petrol* which they had sunk one month ago to the day we were shelled."

Narvick cruised the seas looking for other victims. On July 13, she sighted another ship. Every crewman was called to his station. Stoodley, locked up below, felt the engines vibrating furiously, heard the klaxon horns and knew the whole German ship was in action. Six inch guns pounded overhead. The guard, a man with a machine gun at the ready, told the prisoners to have lifejackets handy. The greatest worry was that the attack could be on a British destroyer. No doubt they experienced a sea battle with mixed feelings for if the German ship were success-ful, British sailors would die. Should *Narvick* lose, Stoodley and fellow prisoners would have little chance locked below.

Soon action stopped; most likely it was a successful strike, but the POW's were not informed of this. The enemy decided there wasn't enough food aboard for sixty-five prisoners and plans were made to set them adrift. In his war memoir, Stoodley wrote:

> We were put into three lifeboats. Two of "King John's" lifeboats were used and we were put in *Narvick's* large one at the mercy of the winds and tide with no position (bearings) whatever. The captain of "King John" told us we were about 269 miles from Guadelope, a French island in the east Caribbean Sea.
>
> So we steered west southwest for seven days. After a couple of nights, we lost sight of the other life boats; so we drifted on. We had three Spiller Ship's biscuits every 24 hours and about half a pint of water.
>
> Twenty-five men, all crammed into a small boat, leaking very badly. We had to keep watches steady, throwing water where the boat was full of shrapnel holes.

German armed raider *Widder* (above) built in 1929 for the Hamburg Amerika Line and christened *Neumark*. She was renamed *Widder* and converted to a raider in 1940. It was a raider like this which found and sank the freighter *Davisian*.

On the second night, Ray Stoodley's lifeboat became separated from the other two and he never learned the fate of the others. He clearly remembered rowing and bailing water for seven days and nights and that "We saw land on Friday night, with only enough water left for one more day. Saturday morning we decided to land on the beach to look for water."

Officers from *Davisian* and *British Petrol* had charge of the lifeboat which was now offshore from some deserted island which as far as they could determine, must have been in the Caribbean or West Indies. First Officer A. Smart, a Scotsman, and Third Officer Victor Harrison decided to breech the reef extending the whole beach.

Stoodley recalled:

> So we straightened her up and let go before the breakers. As she touched, we jumped into the water to our throats. Men were placed around the sides of the boat and we ran her in on the beach where a few went in search of drinking water. While they were filling the small kegs, the rest of us stood in the water to keep the boat in position.
>
> Finally we were ready to leave and the task of getting the boat off was no easy one. Smart selected four oarsmen, of which we two Newfoundlanders (Stoodley and Peckford) were to man the oars with two others. One sea broke over her stern and filled the boat about half full, a very difficult task. But with energy and skill, we got off over the reef.
>
> To our surprise we discovered we had one man left ashore who was scared of water and missed his jump into the lifeboat. It was almost impossible to go in over the reef for one man, so Third Officer Harrison took a rope and tied it around his waist. He leaped into the water amid foaming seas and swam ashore, tied the rope

around the man and we pulled him on board the
boat. The Third Officer swam back.

Photo courtesy of Hubert Hall, SHIPSEARCH Marine

(Above) Side view of steamer *Davisian* at the dock. She was sunk July 10, 1940 by an
enemy warship.

Seaman Ray Stoodley (right) suffered from the effects
of his long row. He and his shipmates rowed for seven
days, and consequentely Stoodley's fingers and
hands were severely deformed for the remainder of
his life.
    Ray Stoodley passed away in Grand Bank in
1952.

Photo courtesy of Tom Stoodley

The twenty-five men figured they were close to Samoa
Bay in the Republic of Dominica. Determined to rescue
themselves, they rowed the coastline near the main island,
Dominican Republic, looking for a safe harbour. After several hours, a ship came up behind them, altered course
and came near. S.S. *Leif* had found the survivors while they
were still forty-five miles from any harbour. As they
climbed up the ship's ladder, Stoodley remembered that

"we were all feeling very much exhausted, so men began to fall onto the deck, and within a few minutes were asleep."

Ray Stoodley, William Peckford and the others were taken on board, given dry clothes, food, a warm bath and bed. In time, they reached Puerto Plata, Dominican Republic, where the British Consulate arranged to get the men to their respective homeland, England, Canada or Newfoundland. Ray Stoodley came to Grand Bank from Halifax on the MV *Icehunter*, captained by Ben Snook.

William Peckford suffered no long term disability from his ordeal and later moved to Gander where he worked as an electrician. He passed away in 1969.

Photo courtesy of Marie Cook

Wreck of steamer *Empire Energy* at Big Brook, near Cook's Harbour on the tip of the Great Northern Peninsula. The bow section has broken up from wave action and lies on the beach (right). She was the only vessel to wreck on Newfoundland side of the Strait of Belle Isle during the war.

Empire Energy ran aground on Nov 4, 1941, while en route from New York to Belfast via Sydney, Nova Scotia. This vessel was built in Rostock, Germany, in 1923 as the *Grete*, sold to Italy in 1934 and renamed *Gabbiano*, then taken by the British as a "war prize" on June 10, 1940.

In February 2000, I received several beautiful photos of a shipwreck which the sender could not identify. Subsequently, to determine which ship this was, I went to archival newspapers and consulted with those who live near Big Brook or who have done extensive research on World War Two casualties.

The wreck lies on the shores of Big Brook, a small fishing settlement of five to ten families located between Eddies Cove East and Cape Norman on the Great Northern Peninsula. According to local knowledge, the iron wreck is a British steamer and was filled with loose corn or in sacks. The people of Raleigh, located across the bay from Big Brook, fed their dog teams all winter on the corn. It could also be brewed for beer or much stronger drink, probably a version of corn liquor or "white lightning."

Sometime during the Second World War, a German submarine chased the vessel and it grounded. Big Brook is situated at a narrow point in the Strait of Belle Isle; the Strait route could have been used to avoid the presence of subs in regular sea lanes.

Today the ship is on the beach about two or three minutes walk from the road near Big Brook.

Photo courtesy of Marie Cook

Close-up of stern of the Big Brook wreck. Little is left of the port side and the bow which have been exposed to wind and wave for over fifty years. *Empire Energy* netted 6989 ton and was 440 feet long. Two days after she grounded a tug came to pull her off, but failed. Her crew left on the tug.

Humber Arm (above) was torpedoed by a German U-boat south of Ireland on July 8, 1940, while en route to England with newsprint. At the time of her loss she carried twenty crew; sixteen from Bay of Islands, three from Port aux Basques and Captain J.R. Morbey. There was no loss of life.

Humber Arm, net tonnage 3,500 and 445 foot long, was built for the first paper company, the Newfoundland Pulp & Paper Company at Corner Brook. *Humber Arm* loaded newsprint after the mill went into production on August 24, 1925 The first to command the ship was Captain Charles Cross who died on board at sea; he was succeeded by Captains Dunn, Lidstone, Bennett and Morbey.

"Get Us a Life Boat"

With these words two men from Belleoram jumped into action. For long enough they stood and watched seamen freezing and suffering on an offshore wreck. Now it was time for a rescue, a time to do something.

The wreck was an American sub chaser, commanded by Captain French, bound from Halifax to Argentia. Known only by her number, *S.C. 709* she lay on her side on the bar in the mouth of Louisbourg Harbour on January 22, 1943. For twenty-four hours others had tried to get out to the wreck, but until Clarence Mullins and John Hillier stepped forward, little was accomplished.

S.C. 709, a 120 foot long United States ship, was headed for Argentia from Halifax in January 1943. She carried three guns, twenty depth charges and a crew of twenty-four. On January 20, the weather changed and over the course of the next two days, thick ice formed on her superstructure and she developed a list. The ice-encrusted sub chaser, while attempting to find shelter, stranded on a ledge in the mouth of Louisbourg harbour.

All her crew were ordered topside with life jackets. For twenty-four hours various attempts were made to get to the stranded ship, but terrible winter weather prevented rescue. The Canadian Navy harbour craft of Louisbourg tried but gave up. The crew of vessel *Lady Laurier* shot a line to *S.C. 709*, but in the low visibility and high seas each attempt failed. It was feared the U.S. ship would capsize or its men, many lightly clad, would freeze to death if another night passed.

One ship moored in Louisbourg was the Norwegian barquentine *Angelus* commanded by Edward Jensen of Lunenburg. Among his nine crew, were several Newfoundlanders including Clarence Mullins and John Hillier, both of Belleoram. They saw the plight of the stranded American sailors and sized up the situation.

Mullins and Hillier asked for permission to take two dories from *Angelus* and, with two other men, carried the dories to Burying Ground Point (now a part of the National Park near Louisbourg) and launched them. Contending with the wind and sea, they managed to row to the stricken ship.

S.C. 709's Captain French had the eight worst sailors ready to transfer. While other larger rescue craft were getting near, the two Newfoundlanders made about three trips to land taking two men per trip. Eventually as vessels from Louisbourg reached the wreck, the rest of the crew were taken off. Observers at the scene wrote about the condition of *S.C. 709*'s men:

> The crew were all standing on the deck, and were they ever cold. They couldn't straighten out their hands to hold a rescue line. They were on the deck of that thing from eleven o'clock one day to eleven o'clock the next day with below zero weather. Nothing to cover themselves with, some with bare feet, some with shoes.

So impressed was the town of Louisbourg with the rescue that the mayor, M.S. Huntington, went aboard *Angelus* on January 25th to find out the names of the four men involved in the rescue. These he entered into his personal diary which Huntington kept for sixty years.

But that spring the Battle of the Atlantic was in full swing and *Angelus* found itself in the middle of the conflict. She had gone to Barbados with a cargo of fish; her crew: Captain Jensen, Hillier, Mullins, first mate Arthur Holman, his twenty-year old son Alexander Holman, both of Belleoram; Cecil Hardiman of Grand Bank and four other men from various Atlantic ports.

Photo courtesy of Ron Caplan

An indistinct view of barquentine *Angelus* Courtesy Ron Caplan of Nova Scotia who interviewed Walter Boudreau, one of the ship's survivors.

Angelus sailed from Barbados on April 28. On May 19th she met her fate. A submarine surfaced about four miles away, fired a shot that fell into the sea on the barquentine's port side, and then closed in. The sub commander gave Captain Jensen and his crew twenty-five minutes to prepare a lifeboat and launch it. Soon a barrage of shells put *Angelus* to the bottom and the U-boat disappeared leaving the men in the middle of the ocean.

They put up the sail and shaped a course for Cape Sable, Nova Scotia. For a day or so the weather was fair, but on May 22-23 a gale arose with a heavy sea. The lifeboat capsized several times, all provisions were lost, and the men, although they uprighted the boat, were quickly drained of energy. Captain Jensen drowned when the boat capsized and within the next twenty-four hours seven more men perished.

On May 24, only two remained, mate Arthur Holman (who had watched his son die of exposure in his arms) and Walter Boudreau. The next day a plane spotted them; then an American destroyer which had been alerted by the plane picked them up. The two survivors of *Angelus* were landed at Portland, Maine, and eventually sent by train to Halifax.

Thus did three men from Belleoram and one from Grand Bank pay a price for war. Ironically John Hillier and Clarence Mullins, who had bravely rescued American sailors from *S.C. 709* only four months before, perished at sea in loss of the *Angelus*.

This was not the first tragedy to affect the Mullins family of Newfoundland's south coast. In December 1931, the thirty-ton *Martha E.* disappeared in the fall of the year. Aboard were Captain Peter Mullins, his two sons Roland and Randell of Harbour Breton and seventy-three year old Fred Moore of Jersey Harbour. They had landed their fish in Nova Scotia and landed coal for south coast ports, but disappeared en route.

Chapter Nine

People

The maritime history of Newfoundland and Labrador is filled with names of people who have journeyed all over the world by sea and land. Many have won fame and riches; others were ordinary folks who performed heroic deeds or contributed to the betterment of our world. In my accumulation of material of the sea and ships, the following eight stories were appropriately placed in this chapter: unique, intriguing and fascinating people.

In the St. Pierre Slammer

In a 1940 school booklet there's a story of a daring escape from wrongful imprisonment in St. Pierre. The story was passed on through family tradition and is true as written by Jane Forsey, the great, great granddaughter of the central character, Captain John Symes.

On February 11, 1823, John Symes (which later became Simms in Grand Bank) married Jane Hickman. Sometime in 1837, Captain John Symes left Grand Bank in his small vessel, but went into the port of St. Pierre for shelter. Authorities imprisoned the crew, all of whom were from Grand Bank, saying they had broken the laws of the French colony.

The Englishmen didn't deny the violation of French law, but explained to the police they had broken the law unknowingly. Nevertheless their pleas of ignorance fell on deaf ears and they were thrown in a St. Pierre jail for several months. They knew their families back home were deeply concerned for not only were the breadwinners of the household gone for an extended period, but wives and loved ones knew the men were not criminals nor had broken the law. Also there hadn't been a trial.

Friends and relations in Grand Bank were distraught and worried when they learned what had happened. No one was allowed to see them, but the prisoners could receive tobacco and food. The captain's wife, Jane (Hickman) Symes who at the time was pregnant, baked a loaf of bread and cleverly concealed a knife inside it.

Little by little, the men cut a hole in the prison wall. To hide their work, they smeared tobacco juice on the fresh cuttings. Finally the hole was large enough to squeeze through and one night when clouds covered the light of the moon, they escaped. They took a dory from the beach and, after many hours of hard rowing, reached Fortune.

It was early morning when they arrived. Not wanting to be seen in prison clothes, the men hid all day under the dory which they had pulled up on the beach and turned over. When darkness came they walked the five or six miles to Grand Bank where they were greeted by joyful family and friends.

In the intervening time while the men were in jail, a baby boy had been born to the Captain's wife. She called the child Jabez, a Biblical name meaning "born in sorrow."

Ah, our valiant and resourceful pioneers, unlucky and unjustly treated, but they were "Born on the Edge of the Ocean" and their wit and determination pulled them through. I'm grateful for this story which comes mainly from a booklet the U.C. *Record* of Grand Bank, 1940, and the descendants of the captain: Hazel Milley, Helen (Forsey) and Jane. In 1860 Jabez Symes married Martha Forsey, a distant relative of mine.

Bound Down for South Australia

In 1852, when the brig *Sybil* sailed out of St. John's harbour with Newfoundland settlers bound for Australia, no one really knew what happened to the people on board. Some wrote letters back home saying they had arrived safely or had settled in, but apart from that, not much was known of them.

In 1851, gold was discovered in southeastern Australia. Immigrants flooded in; many from English speaking countries — Canada, England and Ireland. 150 years ago the spirit of a new venture and leaving home must have been a daunting prospect and an inherently more dangerous voyage. Yet anticipated rewards — gold, land, a new life "down under" — probably compensated for any hardships.

As far as is known only one ship, in that era of colonization and gold rush, left Newfoundland bound for Australia. In the summer of 1852 several opportunistic young men bought the 100 ton brigantine *Sybil*, encouraged others to join including several families, and on November 18th headed through The Narrows on a journey destined to take them halfway around the world.

It was such an unusual and perhaps historic occurrence, bits and pieces of the story appeared occasionally in local print. One of the first times the event re-surfaced in the newspaper was in the October 21, 1899 edition of the *Evening Telegram*.

THE MUSTY PAST.

MANY old persons will well remember the departure, in the ship *Sybil*, of a large number of immigrants, about 50 years ago, from St. John's to Port Philip, South Australia. The following names are taken from the list:—Messrs. Ritchie, wife and four children, Beaton, wife and child; Moore, wife and four children; Kingwell and wife; Shaiu and wife; Watt, wife and child; McB. Brodie and wife; Vey and wife; H. Fleming and wife; Fourrie, Wylie, R. Fleming, Muir, Belcher, Wheatley, Allan, Frazer, Clough, McLennan, J. McPherson, Ed. Meileish, Williams, Sinclair, Murphy; Misses Murphy, Fourrie, Wylie and Mrs. Hoggart. The above names are taken from an old newspaper and handed to us for publication. No doubt there are persons living here at the present time that will be interested in the above reminiscences.

Over 100 years ago the *Evening Telegram* reminisced about the ship load of emigrants that headed for Australia in 1852. This clipping is from October 21, 1899.

The article says "...many older persons will remember the departure in the ship *Sybil*, a large number of emigrants from St. John's to Port Philip, South Australia." It concludes with the names of the passengers and crew: Messrs. Ritchie, his wife and four children; Vey and wife; single men Fleming, MacPherson, Williams and so on. Several couples with their children and many young men made the voyage — the names of all are at the end of this story.

A second version of this adventure appears in a small but historically valuable book entitled *When Was That?* compiled and published by Dr. H.M. Mosdell in 1923 in St. John's. *When Was That?*, a book of dates and facts, is arranged alphabetically. He documents this singular event saying:

> "*Sybil*: brigt. 100 tons, purchased by number of people of St. John's, chiefly young men — clerks and mechanics — sailed from St. John's for Australia with seventy emigrants November 16, 1852."

Who were these "number of people"? Did they actually arrive? Where did they settle? Do we have kinfolk down under, descendants of those brave pioneers? An examination of Australian shipping records shows that the ship *Sybil* did indeed reach Australia and stopped at Port Philip (since renamed Melbourne) on St. Patrick's Day, 1853. Many of them settled in Geelong, near Melbourne. The list of those aboard (actually fifty-three men, women and children) closely matches, with some slight spelling differences, the *Telegram* list of 1899.

On their arrival in Port Philip, the passengers and crew sold *Sybil* and got half their voyage expense money back. On the voyage south — via the Cape of Good Hope, across the Indian Ocean and then the South Pacific — the crew was paid one shilling a month. *Sybil* had an active career trading around Australia's coast until some years later she was wrecked near Port Curtis, Queensland.

Sybil passenger Robert Murphy, whose occupation is listed as a joiner, or finished carpenter, married Ellen Murphy (no relation) in the Presbyterian Church in Geelong on April 18, 1853 — witnesses were fellow passengers Peter and Sarah Jane Ritchie.

It is known from the Vey family tradition that James Vey, a watch maker and repairman when he lived in St. John's in

Crew and passengers bound to Australia, 1854
Mr. Charles and Mary Beaton, 5 boys and one girl
Peter and Charlotte (Mc)Brodie
Andrew and his sister Mary Fairrie
Hamilton and Mary Fleming
Capt. John and Catherine Hoggart
John and Mary Kingwell & infant child
Alexander and Emma Moore, 2 boys and a girl
Robert and Ellen Murphy
Peter and Sarah Jane Ritchie, 3 boys and a girl
William and Mary Thane
James and Dinah Vey
John and Ellen Watt, an infant and one boy
Patrick and Kate Wiley

The single men were:

E.H.W. Belcher	George E. Clow
Robert Fleming	Allan Frazer
John MacPherson	George McLennan
Edward Melleish	David Muir
Charles Sinclair	James Wheatley
Stephen Williams	

1852, settled in Geelong. A check of the Australian telephone directory shows no Vey's in Geelong, but three families in nearby Melbourne. The name Moore in the directory has 170 entries, no doubt many descended from the children of Newfoundlanders Alexander and Emma Moore.

As an epilogue to this story of adventure and immigration, at least one person wrote a letter back to a St. John's newspaper. Allan Frazer's letter of January 24, 1853, is postmarked Cape of Good Hope. In his long and descriptive letter (of which part is given here) he says:

> We stood off in the Bay off St. John's until 8 o'clock waiting for another passenger who came aboard, then we bore away on our course to Australia. The scene on board *Sybil* baffles description: a small and crowded vessel, men, women and children huddled together each

more sick than the other. The ship with a tremendous deck load laboured heavily.

We had fair wind for seven days except on Sunday night after leaving when we encountered a heavy gale in the Gulf of St. Lawrence. We shipped a sea which threw us on beam ends, carried away the weather bulwark and rail, the seats on the quarter deck, a lot of buckets, fowls and other items. Fortunately all hands were in bed except the watch otherwise some may have been washed overboard. But otherwise our sweet little craft rode over tremendous seas like a duck and behaved gallantly.

We divided ourselves into two messes for eating. Our officers are all efficient and trustworthy men, our crew thorough seamen, our vessel safe and seaworthy, and passengers respectable and sociable. Mr. Wheatley was appointed ship's husband...taking charge of water and provisions. We owe a great deal of our comfort to his foresight and determination.

...On our arrival in Cape Town we were rather surprised to hear that we had made the quickest passage for the season...

Photo courtesy of Eileen Thistle

Captain Jacob Davis of Port aux Basques owned several schooners: *Mary Emma* and then *Beta*. Davis bought *Winged Arrow* around 1900 for the halibut fishery. During one of his trips, a dory went astray off Codroy Island in a storm. Davis would not leave until he searched for the dory in the storm; eventually it got back safely. An hour of so after the two men and all crew were aboard, *Winged Arrow* struck a rock and sank.

Davis then purchased the 120 ton American yacht *Brunhilda* (above) in Boston. Brunhilda, at 120 feet long and twenty-five feet wide, was built in 1885. As a yacht owned by the wealthy of New England she had had a fine career and had elaborate fittings including a music room complete with a white piano.

But days of leisure changed to labour in Newfoundland waters. Captain Davis used *Brunhilda* in the coasting trade for food, supplies and coal. On one voyage Davis bought dishes at Halifax and brought them to his home in Port aux Basques. The fancy, beautiful dishes originally came from San Francisco and because of the 1906 San Francisco earthquake ended up on the eastern seaboard market.

Around 1923, Captain sold *Brunhilda* to McRea's business of Harbour Grace. She went down while carrying coal from Sydney to Newfoundland. Davis' business in Port aux Basques was located in what is now the Coleman's store. In the lower level he dealt in general supplies and food especially flour; upstairs he kept nets and dories as well as a large sewing machine for making and repairing sails. Capt. Davis passed away around 1942 at age ninety-one.

Captain John Burke,
Balladeer Johnny Burke

Captain John Burke of St. John's had a notable life at sea. In 1850 he was in command of the vessel *Kingalock*, owned by the Honourable Laurence O'Brien. While on a voyage from Hamburg, Germany, to St. John's Burke came upon a ship in distress in mid-ocean. The American ship *Tarquin* commanded by Captain Moody with his crew of seventeen, sailed from Quebec to London with a cargo of lumber. While battling an Atlantic storm. the ship became leaky and eventually waterlogged. The crew had no way to get off the sinking vessel until Burke rescued them. As a reward for his deed, Captain John Burke was presented with a "binocular glass" or telescope by Captain Moody.

Some years after that rescue, Captain Burke took command of the brig *Nautilus*. In the book *The History of Burin* this ship is noted as: "On January 1, 1865, the brig *Nautilus* was lost at Petty Harbour Motion with Captain Burke, his son and three crew. This vessel was owned by John Marshall, Burin, and at John's death in 1853 was willed to his son, Matthew Marshall."

In late December 1864, *Nautilus* arrived off the eastern Avalon Peninsula laden with coal for Laurence O'Brien's business in St. John's. Although the exact cause of the disaster is not clear, it is known *Nautilus* sank off Petty Harbour. Captain John Burke, his fourteen year old son, William, mate William Bell, cook John Dealy and seaman Timothy Lane perished. The three survivors were William Dwyer, James Foran and Edward Cashin.

Captain John Burke was fifty-five when he was drowned on *Nautilus*. His wife (Sarah Rutledge) was left to raise seven surviving children. His third child was Johnny Burke who later became known as "The Bard of Prescott Street" — the composer/singer of well-known Newfoundland folk songs such as "The Kelligrews Soiree" and "The Trinity Cake."

On February 3, 1865, news reached St. John's through the paper *Newfoundlander* that the bodies of Captain Burke and two of his crew had been recovered in the waters off Petty Harbour. Burke was an uncle of Archbishop Michael Francis Howley.

Photo courtesy of NF and Lab. Tourist Dev. Office

Petty Harbour, where Captain John Burke lost his life, is shown here in the 1950s when cod was salted and dried on the stages and flakes. Structures such as these were used in Newfoundland for four and a half centuries until 1950s when fresh frozen cod replaced the salt-dried product.

Newfoundland Dories in Bella Coola, British Columbia

In around 1910, Newfoundland dories made their debut on opposite ends of Canada: Bella Coola River and its channel in British Columbia. The man who built them was Captain John Tuck of Fortune.

Tuck was born and raised in Fortune. He followed the sea as a young man and eventually captained his own vessels. In 1886, for example, he commanded the schooner *George A. Tuck*, a seventy-five ton schooner launched in Fortune earlier that year. Captain Tuck first left Fortune in 1903 with his wife Clarissa (Hillier) and two young children, Alice and Donalda, to seek medical help in Nova Scotia for his wife.

After the death of Clarissa, Tuck eventually remarried a Chapman girl from Harbour Breton, Newfoundland. He returned to Fortune and his life on the sea, but in 1910 he and his wife decided to leave Newfoundland for British Columbia and sold his home to his brother William.

Captain John settled in Bella Coola, a remote fishing village at the head of a fiord 600 miles north of Vancouver and accessible by boat. Why he chose to go there is not clear, but Bella Coola was a prime fishing community and that may have attracted the Newfoundlander in Tuck's blood.

In British Columbia Captain Tuck found employment as a fisherman, a contractor, and a boat builder, but for his own pleasure he built Newfoundland dories and skiffs. Many West Coast fishermen and seamen expressed great interest in the unique construction and gathered around his small shipyard to watch. Tuck, of course, was not long explaining the advantages and benefits of Newfoundland small boats. Captain Tuck was quick to demonstrate his craft.

He died in February 1943 at the age of eighty-three. His daughter Ann (by the second marriage) went into the interior of British Columbia as a schoolteacher and is said to have visited her pupils on horseback. She married a man from Montana and started a ranch at Williams Lake, B.C. They had a large family with six boys and one girl.

Photo courtesy of Steven Stacey

Captain John Tuck and his craft of Newfoundland design on Bella Coola River, British Columbia. His descendants (and perhaps his influence in small boat design) remain in British Columbia today.

Captain on Christmas Day: William Ayres of Fortune

Certainly William "Billy" Ayres of Fortune had an unforgettable experience when he was summoned "on deck" by his captain. Ayres was twenty-three years old and a seaman on the schooner *Ambition*. This in itself is not unusual nor significant; many young Newfoundland sailors stood before the mast as young as fourteen and were veteran seamen by age twenty-three. However, Ayres was suddenly thrust into a position of command almost at a moment's notice.

In December 1912 *Ambition*, while under command of Captain Albert Dyett of St. Jacques, delivered coal from Sydney to Twillingate. Billy Ayres was one of his crew. On the return voyage from Twillingate to Fortune Bay, somewhere off the eastern Avalon Peninsula, *Ambition* was running before a vicious gale when, on Christmas Day, the schooner shipped a sea which washed the captain overboard. Dyett, age thirty-seven, was never seen again.

Ayres was taken by the same wave from the deck, landed on top of the cabin house where he grabbed a line and clung for his life. When the wave passed over the deck, he climbed down into the cabin to report to the rest of the crew that the captain had been washed overboard and drowned.

Ayres knew the rudiments of navigation for he had become good friends with Dyett over the course of the voyage and the captain had shown him how to calculate position by sextant and chart. Ayres was elected or made captain by the rest of the crew and, two days after, made his first landfall at Cape Chapeau Rouge near St. Lawrence. When *Ambition* safely docked in St. Lawrence, he had completed his first voyage as captain, but he also had the melancholy and difficult task of contacting St. Jacques to report the untimely death of Albert Dyett.

The Dyett family name is rare in Newfoundland today, but between 1900 to the 1950s the Dyetts (Edgar G. Dyett) owned a prosperous business in St. Jacques which served many communities at the head of Fortune Bay. In the salt fish export trade, the company sent schooners to the banks and foreign-going vessels to Europe.

The family opened a retail general store, James Dyett and Sons, in 1917 and following James' death in

1938, son Edgar G. Dyett took over the business until 1955. The business was sold in 1978.

One of their largest vessels, the *Grand Falls*, was lost at sea. Launched in April 1910 at Shelburne, Nova Scotia, and classed as a semi-knockabout, the tern (or three-masted) *Grand Falls* was one of the fastest schooners plying the European trade routes. She measured 121 feet long with a twenty-six feet beam, and registered 145 ton.

Clipping of Grand Falls news. Anxiety surfaces in local papers about the whereabouts of Dyett's tern schooner *Grand Falls*. "Grave fears are now entertained..." it said. The vessel never reported.

Vessel Long Overdue.

Grave fears are now entertained for the schooner Grand Falls, which is over seventy days out from Marystown to Oporto, with a cargo of fish. Owing to the recent storms that swept the Atlantic the opinion is expressed that the vessel has foundered but it is earnestly hoped that the crew have been picked up. The Grand Falls was of semi-knockabout construction and perhaps the fastest sailing vessel engaged in the foreign fish trade.

Grand Falls was owned jointly by the Dyetts of St. Jacques, and Rendells business of St. John's. In early January 1914, she became overdue, seventy days out from Harbour Breton to Oporto laden with salt fish. A series of storms had swept the Atlantic which might have overpowered the schooner; she disappeared taking a crew of Fortune Bay seamen with her. Unfortunately her crew list has not been recorded, although it is known that from 1911 to 1913 she was commanded by Captain Augustus Taylor of Carbonear.

Dyett's schooner *Ambition* was later sold, but Ayres went on to skipper other vessels including *Olive Evans*. Built in Mahone Bay, Nova Scotia, in 1905 *Olive Evans* was acquired for the coasting/trading business by Captain William P. Evans of Grand Bank. According to family knowledge, *Olive Evans* had been a rum-runner before Evans owned her and had false bottoms built into the bunks. She was sold in 1921 to George T. Dixon's business of Fortune who put Captain William Ayres in command.

Olive Evans sprang a leak and sank on December 2, 1921, north of Port aux Basques, but close to shore. Ayres and his crew threw over the dory and stood by the schooner until she went down, then rowed ashore to the land only about a gunshot away. At that point the Newfoundland railway line ran near the shoreline for several miles; the shipwrecked crew walked up to the track and flagged down the next train headed to Port aux Basques.

So ends some interesting and unique facets of Captain "Billy" Ayres of Fortune, Newfoundland — one of those intrepid seamen who answered the call of the sea. He passed away in 1975.

Mystery of the Poem: Loss of the *Loyalty*

Poet, songwriter and educator Art Scammell, son of Archibald and Sarah (Torraville) Scammell, was born at Change Islands, Notre Dame Bay, in 1913.

Scammell is probably best known as the composer of the song "The Squid Jiggin' Ground" which he wrote at the age of fifteen while fishing with his father. In his lifetime, Scammell composed many songs, some of which were for special occasions: "A Sealer's Song", a satirical look at the controversy surrounding the seal hunt; "The Shooting of the Bawks", a defence of the right of rural people to kill seabirds for food; and in 1966 "The Newfoundland Come Home Song."

Scammell wrote many humorous short stories, poems and reminiscences and, like most writers, the young poet/songwriter sought out newspapers and magazines which would publish his humour and satire. What follows then may be one of Scammell's songs, uncredited.

The schooner *Loyalty* was wrecked at Lumsden on December 20, 1927. She carried food and supplies for Change Islands, but before it reached home she battled a winter storm on Newfoundland's Northeast coast or "Straight Shore." Not much has been recorded of this event except what appears in the *Fishermen's Advocate* on January 10, 1928.

The piece was written at Change Islands — the schooner and crew belonged there. Could the writer (identified only as "Santa Claus") be the fifteen-year-old Art Scammell poking fun at the old schooner and the circumstances of the shipwreck? In his book *Collected Works* (1990)

Loss of the Schooner *Loyalty*

Captain Bown has reached safely home,
The *Loyalty*'s days are o'er
She held out bravely to the end,
But she'll plough the waves no more.

Mr. James Bown was her captain,
She carried a jolly crew,
The bravest sailor on that ship
Was our dear friend, Jos. LeDrew.

The captain and crew of the *Loyalty*
Toiled hard to get her along,
But they had to run her in Loo Cove,
Her rudder was nearly gone.

The *Loyalty*'s strength was failed her,
Before she left the town;
She managed to reach Cat Harbour,
Then the old ship soon went down.

The crew were kindly treated,
When the schooner they had to leave,
Till the good old steamer *Prospero*
Brought them home on Christmas Eve.

For the loss of such a schooner
No captain can be blamed,
Before starting for that journey
She should have been condemned.

The crew belonged to Change Islands,
John Roberts owned the schooner,
He sent them to town with a load of fish
But he thought they would reach home sooner.

If Mr. Roberts can get the insurance,
There'll be no need to frown.
He can soon get another schooner
For our dear friend Captain Bown.

The people all along the Lumsden shore
Their names are too many to utter,
But this is the winter they'll all get fat,
They will live on beef and butter.

(Signed) Santa Claus
Change Islands, January 1928

Scammell makes no mention of this poem nor of the ship-wreck. By his own admission not all of his published work appears in this compilation.

Critchell of *Patara*

The discovery of casks of cod liver oil on September 21, 1932, off Drum Head, Nova Scotia, gave rise to a sea mystery. The casks indicated some vessel had been in trouble or was lost. Drum Head is located on Nova Scotia's eastern shore, south of Cape Canso and there some fishermen found three casks — two filled with cod liver oil, the other with water. Not long after and near the same location, an empty dory drifted in. The dory was marked *L.A. Dunton*, a fishing schooner out of Gloucester.

When Nova Scotian authorities contacted Gloucester it was learned that *Patara*, one of Gloucester's last all-sail schooners, was overdue and had indeed carried dories from the banking schooner *L.A. Dunton* on deck.

Patara, built by Ernst Ship Builders of Mahone Bay in 1921, was used first in the fisheries and then for rum running. As a rum runner she was apprehended by the American Coast Guard and taken to New York, where she was purchased by Captain Ben Pine and the Atlantic Supply Company. Under Pine she was engaged in strictly legal business — fishing and collecting fish. Pine was a prominent and frequent rival to Angus Walters and the *Bluenose* for the Fishermen's Trophy.

On August 13, in command of Captain Matthew L. Critchell of Bucksport, Maine (and formerly of Belleoram, Newfoundland), *Patara* sailed from Gloucester for Domino Run, Labrador. There she loaded salt fish and 105 barrels of cod liver oil, left for Gloucester on September 3, but due to strong winds was forced in Long Point, Quebec. On

September 7th she left, but then seemed to disappear for no one could account for her whereabouts. A gale had swept Cape Breton around September 9-11; and only this could explain *Patara's* loss.

Upon receiving the news of debris off Nova Scotia, Captain Pine stated, "She is one of the last New England schooners depending on canvas alone. She had been re-rigged, caulked and outfitted with a new suit of sail before she left Gloucester. She should withstand that recent gale so I am not giving her up yet."

But more evidence of *Patara's* loss came when the British steamer *Hazelwood* passed the wooden super-structure of a schooner off southern Labrador. That helped confirm her fate; American papers on October 7th declared, "Give up Overdue Sch. *Patara* as Lost."

Patara carried a crew of six and, according to owner Ben Pine, a "guest." Just before *Patara* left on her last voyage, a young man named Arthur Schmidt, age eighteen, asked permission to sail on the schooner. He told Pine he was on vacation and his home was in San Francisco. This was confirmed by Pine who, in mid-September, received a telegram from the boy's mother asking if he had sailed on the schooner. He wired back saying the boy had sailed on *Patara* as a guest.

Pine was faced with reporting his death at sea as well as the other six: Critchell, William Delaney, James F. Hallett, Francis Lloyd, John Rose and Philip Mason, all listed as living in or near Gloucester. Today the Critchell name is rare in Newfoundland; indeed Seary's book of Newfoundland names lists it as "rare" and originating at Belleoram. Matthew Critchell was forty-eight when he disappeared on *Patara*.

It was as if *Patara*, built on the shores of Nova Scotia, had returned home for her final hours. As well, her loss mirrored the disappearance of the renown Gloucester schooner *Columbia*, which vanished with all hands near

Sable Island. With the loss of both schooners, only two of Gloucester's great sailing fleet remained: *Thomas Gorton* and *Elsie*, the latter a competitor in the sailing race for the Fishermen's Trophy.

Gloucester Seamen's Memorial showing Critchell's name.

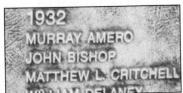

Photos courtesy of Jean (Critchell) Clothier

The Untimely End of the Seneff

In the beginning everything went well and it might have been another routine voyage for a veteran captain in charge of a stalwart ship. But three days out of port, conditions changed as they are known to do in treacherous November. Soon the trip became a battle of man against the elements. When it was over the ocean had claimed another victory; ironically not because of the weather but from another unforeseen circumstance. Fortunately Captain William Swain and his six crew survived and returned to St. John's safe and sound.

A half century ago sea traffic in and around Conception Bay was much greater than it is today. In those years North East Fisheries of Harbour Grace had their draggers ply the Grand Banks for cod and haddock. Collector vessels gathered fish and berries from around the coast and freighters carried products to the United States. Of course with the high volume of sea traffic came the inevitable wreck and tale of woe.

Under grey skies, and a hint of dirty weather, the motor vessel *Seneff* slipped out of Harbour Grace on November 23, 1955. She was bound for Gloucester, Massachusetts, with a cargo of frozen cod fillets and blueberries. Weather grew progressively worse. Seventy-two hours out of port and off Nova Scotia, heavy seas and wind, sometimes reaching gale force, lashed the 212 ton freighter.

About eleven P.M. on November 26, the wind moderated to about twenty-five miles per hour west northwest. But the seas and low visibility had the helmsman worried. "Skipper," he said to Swain who stood beside him, "what a spate of weather. B'Jasus, I don't know if I've ever been out in a night like this!"

By this time most of the crew had gathered in the wheelhouse and they could see the occasional flash of a light. Captain Swain calculated this to be the Canso lighthouse located abeam about five and a half miles away. The crew collectively breathed a sigh of relief. It looked as if *Seneff* had weathered another storm and the crew — Swain, engineer Charles Swain (his son), second engineer Eli Dowden, cook Graham Martin, seamen Leonard Cooney, Charles Dowden and George Swain — might reach the safe haven at Canso. Swain said:

> The ship was making about eight miles per hour and the seas were calming down. We passed White Point bell buoy and steered a course west one-half south; soon after we struck something like an old wreck under water. It hit about four feet on the starboard side and in the center of the engine room.
>
> It went through the plate striking the pro-

peller. Our exact location was latitude 45.11 North, longitude 61.03 West. I immediately stopped the ship and went to the engine room to make an investigation only to find the water running in. It certainly looked as if the object we struck had ripped off a plate.

I radioed Canso for assistance and the *Golden Nugget*, owned by Captain Clayton Munroe of Canso came to our assistance, as did other ships. By the time the *Golden Nugget* reached us, the after part of the *Seneff* was awash.

Photo courtesy of Maritime History Archive, MUN

In 1922 the *M.V. Seneff* (above) was commanded by Captain George Barbour and later by George Norman of Catalina. Her last captain, William Swain was born in Perry's Cove and lived in Carbonear all his married life. Swain also ran the ferry from Portugal Cove to Bell Island. He passed away in 1976 at age seventy-six.

No captain wants to surrender his ship to the sea and Swain especially liked the faithful *Seneff*. He treasured his vessel's every movement and could recount its long history. She was one of four sister ships built in the Great Lakes as coal burning minesweepers for World War One: *Malakoff, Lutzen, Sevastopol* and the *Seneff*. Job Brothers of St. John's acquired the latter three with the *Malakoff* (see photo in Chapter One, Story Twelve) becoming the Government bait supply ship. Eventually Jobs converted *Seneff* to a diesel engine and added refrigeration units in her holds.

Now the time came for Captain Swain to say farewell. He remembered:

> Somehow the *Golden Nugget* fastened a towline on our sinking ship. Plans were to tow *Seneff* to Canso, but after ten minutes the cable broke. Another attempt to get a towline secured failed and *Seneff* sank about a half mile west of White Point bell buoy.
>
> I did everything in my power to save my ship and crew. I saved the crew, but not the ship. I was the last person to leave *Seneff* and I stood by to watch her go down. It seemed as if part of me had disappeared beneath the surface.

In a way it was hard to comprehend. The rugged *Seneff*, which had been through two world wars and countless storms, rode out one of the season's most vicious gales, only to run into a derelict, an old wreck lying off Nova Scotia. In the end this put *Seneff* to the bottom.

Captain William Swain, a veteran seaman and captain had clashed with the sea several times before. In one trying experience in 1933 he found himself alone for fourteen hours on a small vessel called the *Ruby M*. The vessel ran into trouble off Flambro Head, located about eight kilometers south of Bay de Verde.

Two of the three men aboard left to row to Bay de Verde for assistance. They reached there all right, found the assistance, but were unable to get back to *Ruby M*. Seas and winds prevented any ship from leaving Bay de Verde that day. Swain was alone in a storm on a small vessel, unable to rescue himself or to alert others to his predicament.

Fortunately Captain Arthur Dean of Carbonear in the MV *Lincoln* saw the lonely *Ruby M* and steamed over. Dean quickly had Swain taken off and a tow line put aboard. Captain Swain remarked at that time, "I was never so glad to see another ship's lights."

Photo courtesy of Hubert Hall, SHIPSEARCH Marine, Yarmouth, NS

M.V. *Seneff* (above left) and a foreign ship *Stina Dan* await cargo at Carbonear. To the far right is the M.V. *Icehunter.*

Swain was part of *Lincoln*'s crew in 1943. She approached The Narrows to enter St. John's, but was cut down by the *Shulamite* — *Lincoln* sank in seven minutes. *Shulamite*, a Government cutter, carried the crew into St. John's. At the time William Swain's son Charles, then sixteen years of age, was second engineer and his adopted son, Joseph, chief engineer.

The closest time he came to death on the sea was when *Seneff* stranded on the dreaded "Sisters" shoal off Halifax in a 1953 hurricane. In later years Captain Swain, who was the only one injured in the mishap, referred to that misadventure as a "miracle" that *Seneff* came off the rocks and no one was lost.

Photo courtesy of Alex Hardy

In the days after his heroic deeds, Ernest Thornhill was awarded the George Medal for Bravery by Queen Elizabeth and a Silver Medal for the Royal Canadian Humane Association. When the dragger *Cape Agulhas* (above) grounded off Portuguese Cove, Nova Scotia on January 6, 1956, Thornhill jumped overboard with a rope.

He swam 200 feet through the rocks and surf, picking up many severe gashes and a broken leg on the way. He secured a lifeline around a rock, enabling his eighteen mates to make shore. *Cape Agulhas* slipped under a short time after.

Hospitalized for ten days and in bed at home for three months, he was later awarded the Commonwealth's highest award for bravery for a civilian.

He died at sea on January 26, 1962, at age thirty-seven. When struck by a lashing cable aboard his dragger *Red Diamond III*, Thornhill suffered broken legs and internal injuries. He was transfered to the liner *Queen Frederika* but passed away.

Ernest Thornhill was born in Fortune, Newfoundland, and moved in 1956 to West Dover near Halifax, Nova Scotia. He was married with six children.

Chapter Ten

Murder

Murder: the elements of mystery, secrecy, unraveling clues, solving the crime, the means, motive and opportunity make murder stories and unsolved crimes staple reading material. The following are five crimes connected with the ocean. The first four are in chronological order, but the final titbit I saved until my last entry. You see, the main character once lived in my home town, and while there is no written proof "wrongful death" ever happened, family and local tradition says it certainly did.

Dastardly Deed at Mouse Island

In terms of the great number of victims, perhaps one of the most atrocious acts of crime on the high seas happened on Mouse Island, Port aux Basques, many years ago.

The passenger ship *Lady Sherbrooke* was intentionally wrecked on July 19, 1831; and that day became the last day of existence for 268 people who lost their lives for insurance money.

Not much has been written or documented of this tale: the Newfoundland newspapers published in 1831 rarely contained news from the west and south coasts and early Newfoundland settlers, while proficient in oral story-telling, wrote little to describe this event.

Genealogy helps explain the crime. Two obituaries (and there may be others) located by descendants mention the wreck: one comes from John Laird, a survivor of the sinking of *Lady Sherbrooke*. Laird, who was born near Letterkenny, Ireland, lost three children, his wife and five siblings. Another brother survived. They were two of the few people who survived, as noted in Laird's obituary.

What happened off Port aux Basques on that July day?

Nearly a month before she arrived off Mouse Island *Lady Sherbrooke*, filled with immigrant Irish farmers and pioneers, left Londonderry in northwest Ireland headed for Quebec. However Quebec was not the final stop for the passengers; many had their sights set on the fertile and available farmlands of southern Ontario.

Under the command of the diabolical Captain Gambles, the 377 ton *Lady Sherbrooke* set sail with a full load: twenty crew as well as 278 immigrants and their luggage. Although many were farmers, others were adventurers eager to seek new lands and to make their fortune in the New World.

Up to mid-July the voyage was smooth and without incident. The first sight of land, somewhere off the south coast of Newfoundland, brought all to the decks and the sunshine, thankful and happy the long journey was over. Some celebrated with an Irish jig, a pint or two, joyous laughter and merriment.

Captain Gambles probably didn't take part in the festivities for he had other thoughts that crowded out the cheer and excitement. It has been documented that the immigrants and certain ship's officers were not on the best of terms. Captain Gambles was believed to be a heavy drinker and, on seeing his passengers' celebrations, remarked, "They are merry this evening but by daylight they may be in Hell!"

Ariel view of Port aux Basques: the town (A); Ferry Terminal (B); Channel Head Island (C); the section of town called "Mouse Island" (D); and the islet Mouse Island (E) where the Irish immigrant ship *Lady Sherbrooke* wrecked taking 268 lives.

According to a report written in Halifax on August 22, 1831 that describes the wreck, at twelve o'clock one of the seamen called out from the forecastle, "There's rocks on the lee bow!"

Instantly there was confusion on board. Those below rushed on deck. An attempt was made to tack the ship, but the wind was so light, it failed. Stern first, the vessel drove ashore at Mouse Island and in less than ten minutes completely broke up.

Apparently *Lady Sherbrooke* was intentionally wrecked for the monies Gambles would collect on the ship later, but he had no idea there would be such an appalling loss of life.

The crew managed to launch the boats and fill them with men, women and children, but in the heavy surf pounding the little island, they capsized. Most of the passengers and nearly all crew perished. One survivor saw his wife and seven children drown before his eyes. Another man, a member of a family group which included sixteen people, parents, children and grandparents, was almost carried to the sea bottom by the undertow. He was a powerful swimmer and managed to save himself and one son. His wife, who had 120 gold sovereigns sewn into her clothing, was dragged down by the weight and was never seen again.

Those who lived clung to sections of the wreck or were thrown by waves on the cliffs. At twelve noon the next day, some Port aux Basques fishermen discovered the survivors and the wreckage. Thirty people — the captain, mate Richard Codner, a sailor and twenty-seven passengers — had reached shore safely. Many bodies of the 268 lost washed ashore near Cape Ray.

Several survivors were taken to Channel/Port aux Basques by local boats and, some days later, Captain Monro in the schooner *Pomona* took them to Halifax.

Hugh Coyle, a single man from Tipperary, spent a night in the cold water, but was found by a fishing boat and taken to the United States. His descendants (some of whom live in Minnesota and Iowa today) have his obituary which specifically mentions the shipwreck:

> ...He sailed to America in the ship *Lady Sherbrooke*, which was wrecked near the coast of Nova Scotia [sic] in the night. He being a good swimmer, swam to a rock and was picked up the next morning by some fishermen...

The Royal Gazette
And Newfoundland Advertiser.

Fear God: Honor the King.   *Oldfield*

| Vol. XXIV. | TUESDAY, September 3, 1831. | No. 1255. |

SAINT JOHN'S: Printed and Published by JOHN RYAN, Printer to the KING'S MOST EXCELLENT MAJESTY, at his Office, *King's Place*.

DREADFUL SHIPWRECK.—A schooner recently arrived from St. George's Bay, brings intelligence of a disastrous shipwreck, attended with the most melancholy loss of lives, on the western coast of this island. The barque *Lady Sherbrook*, from Londonderry, bound to Quebec, with between 300 and 400 passengers, men, women, and children, ran on shore in a thick fog on Tuesday, the 19th July last, outside of Port aux Basques, near Cape Ray, and became a total wreck when, dreadful to relate! out of the whole of the passengers and crew, only *forty*, amongst whom were the master and mate, were preserved from a watery grave.—The master of the schooner touched at Port aux Basques on his way round, and obtained the above particulars from some of the unfortunate survivors, who were about being conveyed in a coasting schooner to Sydney.— He also reports having sailed through a great number of dead bodies in the vicinity of the awful catastrophe. *Newfoundlander.*

Very little evidence of a dire deed at Mouse Island exists today. The one or two newspapers of 1831 were based in St. John's and news coming from Newfoundland's west coast was limited. A newspaper in Halifax sent the story to *The Royal Gazette* which printed the scant details on September 13, 1831. One quote of the mass murder said it was "...a disastrous shipwreck with the most melancholy loss of lives on the western coast of this island of the barque *Lady Sherbrooke*."

John Laird, who lost nearly all his immediate family and his personal possessions even to his cap, was taken to New York by a ship going there. Eventually he ended up in Ontario — his original destination. Laird married, settled in Haysville, Wilmot township in Ontario. When he passed away in 1879 his obituary specifically states he survived "...the *Lady Sherbrooke* wrecked off the coast of Newfoundland...The captain was afterward tried and condemned to be hanged for wrecking the vessel for the insurance money."

Muɾdeɾ on *Lake Simcoe*

In the early part of the 1900s Baine Johnson and Company's barquentine *Lake Simcoe* made the news often. None was good news.

The first of three unfortunate incidents happened in early September 1912 when *Lake Simcoe* left St. John's for Brazil with her crew: Captain Andrew Wilson, Jack Fitzgerald, bosun Harvey Williams, Fred Nolan, Harry Penney, John Duke, John Sears, James Finn, John Coady and a seaman named Power.

She hadn't sailed far when Captain Wilson stopped a fight between Duke and Coady. Seven days out, on September 12, twenty-one year old seaman John Sears fell to the deck from the yardarm where he and Duke had been taking in the top gallant sail.

What had happened was not an accident. Duke, who was thought to be friends with Sears, had drawn his knife, plunged it into Sears' throat and the young man climbed down or fell to the deck, mortally wounded. When *Lake Simcoe* arrived in Pernambuco, Brazil, Duke was arrested, held on a charge of murder and kept below deck until the ship arrived back in St. John's.

Sears belonged to St. John's, but was an orphan raised at Mount Cashel. Duke, forty-two years old, had a wife and several children. News of the murder reached St. John's before the ship arrived; the newspaper *Daily News* ran an account of it in the October 21, 1912 edition.

Crowds of people gathered at King's Wharf to get a look at Duke as he was escorted from the ship to prison to await trial. As he walked along Water Street in chains, people come out from the shops to stare. At the murder trial, evidence determined Duke suffered from paranoia and thought someone was about to kill him. His DT's, or delirium tremens (called 'drunken horrors' in local language), followed his bouts with alcohol and fits of insanity. The twelve man jury found Duke guilty of murder while insane and thus he escaped hanging. He passed away years later at the Waterford Hospital.

WAS SEAMAN SEARS MURDERED?

Report has it that seaman Sears, of the barqt. Lake Simcoe, whose death occurred Sept. 12th, seven days after leaving port, was the victim of foul play. According to messages received, it is alleged the unfortunate seaman, with another seaman named Duke, went aloft to take in the topgallant sail, and while the two sailors were on the yard arm, Duke drew his knife from its sheath, plunged it into Sears and he fell to the deck dead. What led to the stabbing has not been made known. On arrival at Pernambuco, Duke was arrested, and held on the charge of murder, and it is likely he will be brought on here for trial. The victim of the stabbing was 22 years old, and a native of St. John's. He was reared at Mount Cashel, his parents having died many years ago. Duke is also a native of St. John's, is about 42 years old, is married with a wife and several children.

Up to the date of Duke's trial, local papers speculated on what actually happened. (*Daily News* October 21, 1912)

A few months after Sears' death, Captain Andrew Wilson had the sad duty of sending word to Baine Johnson and Company that on December 26, 1912, a St. John's seaman washed overboard and drowned. *Lake Simcoe* left St. John's on December 18th again bound for Brazil. During a severe storm on December 25-26, heavy seas stove in the cabin doors and skylights, flooded the cabin and swept the decks of everything moveable. The barquentine's mainsail had to be cut away and part of the cargo thrown overboard in order to save the ship.

Mate James Finn, who was a crewman when Sears had been murdered, was washed overboard during the storm. His body was never recovered. When the telegram from Captain Wilson reached St. John's, J.C. Hepburn of Baine Johnson met with Reverend Dr. Greene who broke the news to Finn's widow and relatives. James Finn, a quiet man and very attentive to his duties, was thirty-three years old and had earned his ship master's qualifications four years previously.

In a little over one year the sea had claimed three members of the Finn family: John, lost on S.S. *Erna*; Thomas Finn when the schooner *Grace* disappeared and James on *Lake Simcoe*.

Lake Simcoe continued her overseas voyages during the war. In the fall of 1915 she disappeared, probably a victim of a German submarine. Although Captain Wilson was not in command, eleven men disappeared with her: Daniel Carew, son of Stephen Carew of Witless Bay; John Coady, son of Margaret Coady of 78 Lime Street, St. John's; William Eason, son of Isaac Eason of Manuels; Richard Fleming, husband of Mary Ann Fleming, Spaniard's Bay; Silas M. Halfyard, husband of Jessie, 23 Carnell Street, St. John's; Patrick Kirby, brother of James and John Kirby, St. John's; E. Newhook, son of Richard Newhook, Trinity; Noah Smith, husband of Martha Smith of Manuels; Thomas White, husband of Annie White, 24 Casey Street, St. John's and two whose residence is not clear, H.N. Peppas and Duncan Briely.

Marion: A Murder Mystery?

The story of the loss of the fishing schooner *Marion* in 1915 is one of the best-known tales in Newfoundland's maritime history. Bud Davidge and Sim Savoury (the recording group "Simani") researched her loss in the 1980s, put the story to verse and song and the subsequent ballad became very popular in Newfoundland. When their interview with Kezia (Miles), Blagdon, Cecil Blagdon and Stephen John Blagdon, who were relatives of some of *Marion's* lost crewmen, played on the CBC television program "Land and Sea" it further popularized the story.

The schooner *Marion* was owned by Burkes of St. Jacques. Denis Burke and his brothers had had this schooner for at least four years. A mention is made of her in the May 25, 1911, edition of the *Evening Telegram* when her Captain Denham reported two dorymen, Emberley and Smith, were drowned on May 11. Smith left a wife and three children.

According to local knowledge on June 15, 1915, *Marion* left St. Pierre headed for the banks. Apparently — and this was never proven in court and there was no physical evidence to support it — a French trawler followed the schooner, rammed it at sea, and all seventeen men were lost. It is said that the captain of the French trawler had had a fight, either physical or verbal, with *Marion's* Captain, Ike "Jones" Skinner in a St. Pierre bar the night before *Marion* sailed. The final confrontation came at sea and since "dead men tell no tales", no one from the ill-fated schooner would tell what happened. No allegations of wrong doing or protests were ever filed nor was there an official investigation carried out.

Marion, outfitted and baited for bank fishing, would have been gone two to three weeks. When she didn't report into St. Jacques or Boxey, where several crewmen lived, another week or two went by before the alarm was raised that *Marion* was missing. Thus one would have to look weeks — perhaps months — after mid-June 1915 for newspaper reports on the loss of the *Marion*. However, Newfoundland papers are strangely silent carrying very little about her disappearance.

Only one article (that this researcher could find) appeared in newspapers. In a *Daily News* feature "Year of Events" published December 31, 1915, the *Marion* crew is listed.

Her captain was Isaac Skinner of Boxey, age thirty-two and often referred to as Ike "Jones." Others from Boxey were Charles William Skinner, twenty-three, Wilson Skinner, Morgan Miles, Frank Clems, Isaac Miles, and Arthur Miles. Two men were from Coomb's Cove — Samuel Vallis, age twenty-three and Angus Vallis, the youngest aboard at seventeen years.

Five were from English Harbour West: Samuel Strowbridge, Thomas Penney, Cecil V. Fiander and brothers John George Childs and Thomas R. Childs. As a matter of interest, they were sons of David "Pappy"

Crew of the *Marion*, Lost 1917	
John George Childs	William Pittman
Thomas R. Childs	Joseph Quann
Frank Clems	Charles W. Skinner
Cecil Fiander	Isaac Skinner
Thomas Hardy	Wilson Skinner
Arthur Miles	Samuel Strowbridge
Isaac Miles	Angus Vallis
Morgan Miles	Samuel Vallis
Thomas Penney	

Childs. David Childs came from England in 1848 as a stowaway, landed at Harbour Breton and moved permanently to English Harbour West, but the sea took three of his sons, two on the *Marion* and another on the *Effie May Petite*. He passed away at the age of 94 in 1942.

Marion's William Pittman lived in Doctor's Harbour, Fortune Bay; Joseph Quann, Miller's Passage; Thomas Hardy's place of residence is not clear, but he probably belonged to Rencontre East. Nearly all lived on the Connaigre Peninsula in towns relatively close together; many were related and left wives and children to grieve.

What could have happened to these seventeen men? Could *Marion* have foundered, sprung a leak and went down, perhaps quickly? This is unlikely, as no storms were reported for that period. As well, the men should have had time to get a lifeboat or dory off. If she reached the banks and sank, there probably were other schooners nearby. By all reports, *Marion's* owners kept their vessel sound and well-maintained. Indeed when she left St. Pierre in June

1915, *Marion* had been on the St. Pierre slip for minor repairs or caulking.

Marion fished off St. Pierre (probably the St. Pierre Bank or the grounds off Rose Blanche) in the early stages of World War One. Is it possible she have been intercepted by an enemy submarine and sent to the bottom? There were sinkings of Nova Scotian schooners as early as January 1915. For example, on January 14, 1915, off the coast of South America the German converted cruiser *Kron Prinz Wilhelm* approached schooner *Wilfred M* and demanded the crew leave the ship. Once they boarded the battleship, she gave a broad side of shells into the helpless schooner and in a short time it sank. The crew survived.

Near England in the month of August 1915, there were two merchant ships and seventeen fishing vessels sent to the bottom by German submarines. In those skirmishes, there was little loss of life for generally the enemy, during World War One at least, gave the crews of merchant ships it intended to sink time to abandon ship in a lifeboat.

The greatest thrust of the German U-boat came in 1917. *Marion* disappeared in 1915, two years before that. There doesn't appear to be any reports of a small fishing schooner shelled or torpedoed off St. Pierre in June 1915. Assuming *Marion* was destroyed with crew by the enemy, it seems odd that no other Newfoundland schooners were sunk or had contact with a U-boat in that time frame.

Could *Marion* have been rammed accidentally by a larger ship or ocean liner? Several Newfoundland schooners were lost when speeding ocean steamers cut them down at night or in dense fog. Two prime examples come from Burin: in August 1894 the liner *Majestic* ran into the fishing vessel *Antelope*, cutting her in two and killing two Burin men. In October 1900, the fishing schooner *Henry M. Martin* of Burin was rammed by a steamer at Cape Pine. Six of her eight crew were saved and taken to Sydney, Nova Scotia. Usually these accidents were reported, but there were cases of collisions at sea (on which fishermen survived), where the ocean liners did not stop to render assistance.

The *Evening Telegram* for June 28, 1915, says that a French trawler *La Provance* put into St. John's for repairs to its rudder. Of course this may have had nothing to do with the disappearance of the St. Jacques schooner. Yet the possibility exists *Marion* may have been accidentally cut down.

And of course there is the theory that *Marion* was intentionally rammed by another larger ship. Why this theory? It is said that a French trawler commanded by a man who disliked Captain Ike Jones followed *Marion* to sea. There, out of sight of prying eyes, the trawler ploughed into the defenseless schooner. In strange, unique folk stories passed on through the generations on our island, no matter how implausible, there is always an element of truth. Thus it may be entirely correct that the St. Jacques schooner and her men met with foul play.

Most mysterious is a letter reportedly sent to a newspaper by the French trawler captain many years after the incident when he resided in Montreal. He was dying and wished to confess. Confess he did to those around him, but it is said he also sent a letter of remorse to a paper. Which paper and when? Was there ever a protest or an investigation carried out in Newfoundland or St. Pierre/France? These are questions which, like the disappearance of the *Marion*, are yet unanswered.

Mutiny in Placentia Bay

Harbour Buffett, once a thriving fishing and shipping port in Placentia Bay, often saw vessels from European ports docking to load salt fish. The flags of Portugal, Spain and Denmark flew from the top masts of foreign vessels and life was good in the busy island town. In December 1922, the Danish schooner *Centaurus* pulled into port, but life aboard this ship had been decidedly unpleasant.

Indeed the captain and mate were taken to St. John's and held for eight days on suspicion of murder — a deed most foul, brought about by mutiny which arose and was played out in a grim scene in the few miles between Harbour Buffett and Spencer's Cove, Placentia Bay. Both towns, situated on Long Island, were a few miles apart by land, but several miles by sea. Captain Kristian Rasmussen, mate Erik Knudsen and two members of *Centaurus'* crew were detained at His Majesty's Penitentiary, St. John's, on a charge of murder.

The sailing vessel *Centaurus* left Alberto Wareham's premises at Spencer's Cove at ten A.M. on December 19, 1922, bound for Harbour Buffett. At W.W. Wareham's business, she would complete her loading. The wind was fair and she rounded the northern end of Long Island. While rounding this point of land the captain and mate, who were unfamiliar with water depth and hidden shoals in that location, had an argument regarding *Centaurus* position. In order to consult the charts and to discuss their position, both went into the cabin where their voices grew louder and louder.

The noise attracted one seaman on *Centaurus*, a man named Kristian Jacob Lorentzen. Lorentzen, a big strapping man and over six feet tall, also went into the cabin, and told both captain and mate that neither one of them knew their job. Lorentzen's voice became more agitated and he began to shout and rave. He was soon obnoxious and began to bully the two ship's officers.

Rasmussen and Knudsen ordered Lorentzen to the deck, but the insolent sailor refused. Instead he attacked his captain! Mate Knudsen who attempted to separate them was also assaulted. The fight in the cabin lasted over half an hour and ended when Lorentzen ran on deck, barred the cabin door and kept the two men imprisoned below.

This situation lasted several hours despite several attempts by the captain and mate to gain control of the deck. Lorentzen would meet them at the doorway and kick them in the face if their heads appeared in the companionway.

Finally Rasmussen and Knudsen reached the deck — the captain was armed with a gun in order to frighten or to calm the distraught sailor. This had little effect and only served to enrage Lorentzen more — he grappled with the captain and, in the scuffle, the gun went off. No damage was done for the shot went into the sea. Seeing the captain armed and ready to shoot, Lorentzen turned his attention to the unarmed mate and tried to push him overboard.

The ship's chief officers then stopped, for the battle with the enraged bull of a man had worn them down. Both men went below; again Lorentzen barred the companionway door. By now it was nearing four o'clock in the evening. The weather had turned into a typical December snowstorm and *Centaurus* drifted dangerously close to land.

Lorentzen realized this too and practically took charge of the schooner. Grabbing the wheel, he ran *Centaurus* out into Placentia Bay some three or four miles. As the captain made another attempt to break out of his confinement, the man saw him and ran down to slam shut the companionway door. This time Captain Rasmussen had his gun and just as the sliding hatch of the entrance was closing, he shot to frighten or to warn Lorentzen. The mutinous sailor received the shot in the left arm near the elbow. He immediately went forward where another crewman dressed the wound to stop the gush of blood.

A few minutes later, Lorentzen came on deck and, of his own accord, stripped the bandages off and again ranted around deck. This time he was more subdued. Rasmussen and other crew members looked after him, replaced the bandages, and he was taken to the cabin. He lay on the captain's berth, white and weak.

Within two hours he had bled to death; a post mortem examination later confirmed this.

By the time the scuffle was over, the wind had changed. *Centaurus* beat back into Harbour Buffett and she made anchorage five hours after the sailor died. Rasmussen reported the matter immediately to authorities in Harbour Buffett and the arrest of the captain and mate followed. They, and *Centaurus'* two sailors as witnesses, were transported to St. John's.

Following the investigation by the Department of Justice, the two accused were released for no evidence could be found for murder, but an act of self-defense in the face of a mutiny by Lorentzen. On January 3, 1923, all four took the train to Placentia to join *Centaurus* awaiting in Harbour Buffett. Harbour Buffett at this time had a population of about 400, and no doubt the whole town was abuzz with news of *Centaurus* and the story of murder and self-defense.

The Danish Consul in St. John's, The Honourable Tasker Cook, sent a full report to the Danish authorities. *Centaurus*, now freed to sail again, was short-handed with the death of one crewman. The captain hired a young man named Pomeroy from either Red Island or Merasheen Island, Placentia Bay.

On February 7, *Centaurus* slipped out of Harbour Buffett and headed to Oporto, Portugal, with her load of fish. But the Danish ship never arrived there nor, as far as could be determined, any port. By July 16th that year after enquiries came from Denmark on her whereabouts, *Centaurus* was posted as "Lost with Crew" — presumed to have gone down taking Captain Kristian Rasmussen, mate Erik Knudsen, two Danish sailors and one Placentia Bay man with her.

Mysterious Ritual Brings Death

I n 1906, Edwin James Welsh of Grand Bank died a mysterious death under unusual circumstances in Oporto, Portugal. Born in Spoon Cove, (today Epworth near Burin), in 1860, Welsh moved to Grand Bank where his name appears in the town's 1898 Census as a fisherman. He had sailed to Oporto on one of Grand Bank's foreign-going schooners.

Enterprising businessmen of Grand Bank began shipping salt-dry fish overseas to Europe about 1890. Previous to this, local exporters sent fish to Harbour Breton or St. John's, but eventually became independent exporters themselves and bypassed the St. John's merchants.

In earlier years, the 4800 mile round trip was made in banking schooners which averaged between 60 to 120 ton. Between 1910 and the 1930s the tern, was more economical. In 1910 the two-masted schooner *Mary A. Whalen* had a third mast added to increase speed for long ocean voyages. Grand Bank's first true three-master was Samuel Harris' *Dorothy Louise*, built in 1910. The last foreign-going tern was *General Wood* which was sold in 1942 to a business in the West Indies.

Fishing is a spring/summer occupation and, in winter, bank fishermen often joined the "foreign-going" two-masted bankers or the terns for work. These ships carried fish to Spain, Portugal and Greece and brought back salt for the curing of fish. Welsh sailed to Portugal on a Newfoundland schooner, probably out of Grand Bank, to discharge dried fish.

While there, the crew was subjected to brainwashing or was forced into a ritual intended to make them change their religion or belief. Exactly who the culprits were is not clear. The Newfoundland seamen had to dance around a fire, chant, sing ritualistic songs and in general renounce their faith. Edwin Welsh refused to do so and was made to walk the plank to which he went to his death.

To save their own lives, the other men from the Newfoundland schooner went along with the ritual, but made their escape and returned home to report Welsh's death. He was married to Emma Jane Hickman and had eight children: Harriet, James, Amelia, Selena, Charles, Dinah, George Samuel and Anne Belle.

Early photo (c. 1930s) of Grand Bank in the years when Portugese steamers visited and two and three masted schooners carried the salt fish products to Spain and Portugal. Two steamers in the background are flanked by a forest of masts and spars of banking schooners.

After Word

Occasionally I read and refer to Newfoundland "fact" books that were in vogue and were published many years ago. Mosdell's *When Was That?* published in 1923 is a personal favourite of mine. Often I wish I could find the original sources the writer used; then it would be a matter of checking or verifying a story for oneself. That is why I chose to compile (what I termed at least) an after word or epilogue to this volume which contains the main sources for the stories.

Thus, in case a future reader may think a particular story is a product of someone's over fertile gray matter, I feel a need to document where each story originated.

Much of the information about towns came from my own files, the *Encyclopedia of Newfoundland and Labrador, Volumes I-V*, or information gathered in various Newfoundland archives.

A prime and essential source are those people who wrote, called or whom I met personally. It would be remiss here if I did not give my gratitude to those people who contacted me about wrecks, ships and people. Some corresponded through e-mail, others by letters and phone calls. I like to think we worked together, my correspondents and I, solving a mystery of the sea. And there were many mysteries solved: information of ship losses, crew lists and death at sea. The reader will see them, as acknowledgments, in the sources listed below. Others loaned photos to illustrate the stories and I thank these people for sharing their pictures and knowledge.

Several stories are brief and have gaps, especially of those ships which disappeared at sea. Often an archival search revealed little or nothing (that I could find, at least). I would like to think that publications like this will stimulate other future researchers to thoroughly investigate odd and intriguing circumstances. Perhaps more of the missing pieces can be put together.

A debt of gratitude to several people: William Chapman who read the early manuscript with a keen eye, gave advice and further encouragement; Jack Keeping, Fortune, for many statistics and vital information and to Hubert Hall of SHIPSEARCH Marine, Yarmouth, Nova Scotia for many photos and statistical data. Then too I have to thank my family and friends for putting up with me in the "computer room"; they knew something would come out of it.

Sources by Chapter

CHAPTER 1 – UNUSUAL

TIGRESS
— Written correspondence from Philip Badcock, Virginia, who had audio taped several older residents of Carbonear and area in the 1970s
— *Newfoundlander* May 13, 1873
— Telegraph April 22, 1874
— *Evening Telegram* June 26, 1963
— *Caladonia Courier* July 3, 1875

MORNA
— *Evening Telegram* August 11, 17, 22 and 28, 1888
— the poem appeared on November 27, 1888

HENRY M. MARTIN
— *Evening Telegram* October 3 and 6, 1900

H.M.S. *DRAKE*
— St. John's *Daily News* July 14, 1864
— personal visit to St. Shotts, Summer 1999

HELEN F. STEWART
— *Herald* June?, 1911

MAPLE LEAF
— Unidentified newspaper clipping dated March 1912
— the various examples of rewards were taken from James Murphy's booklet *Newfoundland Heroes of the Sea*, published in 1923

WILFRED MARCUS
— Personal correspondence with Jerome Walsh, Marystown
— *Evening Telegram* January 31, 1919

ELIZABETH RODWAY and *LOWELL PARKS*
— *Daily News* February 27, 1922

"MIRACULOUS ESCAPE"
— A ship (unidentified) story taken from *Family Fireside* 1928

"ARMED INSURRECTION IN PLACENTIA BAY"
— Personal conversation with Dr. Leslie Harris and Otto Kelland
— *Encyclopaedia of Newfoundland and Labrador* "Placentia Bay"

NOTRE DAME
— Daily News August 12, 1935
— William Pierce's story from an undated *Evening Telegram* column

NATIONAL IV
— Personal correspondence from William Chapman, North Sydney
— *Atlantic Guardian* November 1946
— clipping found in shipwreck files, Public Archives of Newfoundland and Labrador

NYODA
— Evening Telegram September 10, 1938

CHAPTER 2 – WRECK

CALITRO
— *Evening Telegram* May 21 and June 7, 1894

BELLE OF BURGEO
— *Daily News* September 12, 1919

SOURIS BELLE
— *Evening Telegram* June 2, 1909

BELLE HADDON
— *Daily Columnist* November 18, 1890
— personal conversation with Roland Abbott, Musgrave Harbour

HENRY FORD
— Personal correspondence from Patrick Scalli, Gloucester, MA and Luke Payne, Cow Head, NF
— *Western Star* June 20 and 27, 1928.

NAUPHILA
— *Cape Breton Post* December 15,1948

M. & G. FOWLOW
— *Daily News* October 8 and November 16, 1949

NORSYA ex *SHULAMITE*
— Personal conversation with Clem Miles, Marystown
— Written correspondence from Joseph Day, North Sydney
— *Cape Breton Post* September 22?, 1953

MARVITA
— Personal conversation with Clyde Collins, St. John's formerly of Lamaline
— *Daily News* July 17, 1954

CAMPERDOWN
— Personal conversation with William Lockyer, Marystown
— written correspondence with Ray Bursey, Fogo
— *Evening Telegram* March 31, 1960

TERRA NOVA
— *Evening Telegram* April 8, 1964

FENMORE
— *Evening Telegram* October 17 and November 22, 1960

CHAPTER 3 – FATALITIES

ORIENT
— *Daily News* May 7, 1959
— *Harbour Grace Standard* June 26, 1875

ORTOLAN
— *The Times* October 27, 1877

EXEL, N.P. CHRISTIAN and *HEBE*
— *Daily News* March 25, 1957
— further information on Hebe in personal correspondence with Betty and Eric Jerrett, Bay Roberts Heritage Society

JESSIE
— Personal and written correspondence from Phyllis (Rendell) Steiner, Lexington, MA, Gertrude Mercer, Boyds Cove, NF, William Cooper and Ralph Douglas (Sr.), Grand Bank, NF

- *Daily News* April 16, 1907
- personal visit to Brunette Island, Summer 1994, and gravestone information from Brunette Island

LUCY HOUSE
- Personal conversation with Ena and Ken Edwards, St. Lawrence; John Ben Warren, Grand Bank
- unidentified newspaper clipping, no date
- *Orangism* in Grand Bank, unpublished booklet, Grand Bank, 1987

ARTIZAN
- *Evening Telegram* March 22, 1917

HILLCREST
- *Daily News* March 6, 1926
- *Fisherman's Advocate* March 12, 1926

ANNIE L. JOHNSON
- Personal conversation with Maxine (Johnson) Turner, sister of the victim
- *Daily News* July 26, 1950

CHAPTER 4 – DISAPPEARANCE

CHARLES PICKLES
- Church Records, Grand Bank
- personal conversation with Roy Noseworthy, Pouch Cove

SUCCESS
- Written correspondence with Beverley Warford, Fortune Harbour/Point Lemington and Maggie Croke, Fortune Harbour/Buchans
- *Evening Telegram* December 15, 1880

OCEAN FRIEND
- *Twillingate Sun* October 1, 1887

REASON
- Personal conversation with Joe Smith, Fortune
- *Halifax Herald* October 10, 1892

PHYLLIS
— Personal and written correspondence with Marion Baker, St. John's

DOROTHY LOUISE/BEATRICE/GRACE AND OTHERS:
— Various newspapers of November 1911 to April 1912
— gravestone inscriptions and church records

RELIANCE
— Personal conversation with Gordon Bradley, Bonavista

ERNA
— Written correspondence with MaDonna Conners, Suffolk, Virginia
— *Daily News* April 13 and 23, 1912

SAGUA LA GRANDE
— Personal conversation with Captain George Jones, St.John's
— newspaper clipping of *Family Fireside*, date unknown

LUCY ANN COX
— *Family Fireside* November 1928
— personal correspondence with William Chapman, North Sydney

GEORGE B. COCHRANE
— Personal conversation with Walter Collins, St. John's, son of William Collins of *George B. Cochrane*
— *Evening Telegram* Jan 31, 1929
— *Fishermen's Advocate* Feb 1 and 15, March 8, 1929
— *Daily News* January 28, 29, and 31, February 2 and 4, 1929

BARBARA AND RONNIE
— Written correspondence from Bert Griffon, Nova Scotia, formerly of Jersey Harbour
— personal conversation with ? Courtney, brother of Charles Courtney and Clarence Vautier, LaPoile/St. John's
— *Western Star* January 4, 1952

MAYFALL
— *Evening Telegram* January 5, 1952

SWILE
— Written correspondence from Doris (Mason) Stead, Niagara Falls, Ontario formerly of Port Union.
— Note: no newspaper account of her final days in Newfoundland or of her disappearance could be located. The story of her loss is from verbal sources, many of whom, like Lance Blackmore, were from Port Union/Catalina
— *Fisherman's Advocate* May 24, 1929 and March 7, 1930

PORT KERWIN
— Personal conversation with Stan and Christine (Hillier) Osmond, Grand Bank
— *Evening Telegram* January 15, 1976
— *Daily News* January 16 and 19, 1976

CHAPTER 5 – DEBRIS

GEORGE WASHINGTON and GEORGE CROMWELL
— Personal conversation with Gordon Bradley, Bonavista who alerted me to the loss of William Roper and the steamer *George Cromwell*
— *New York Times* February 17, 1877
— *Morning Chronicle* February 24, 1877
— *Daily News* October 6, 1909

SNOWBIRD
— Written information from Maureen Thoms, Newfoundland and Betty Hamilton Of Middleton, MA (great granddaughter of the captain)
— *Evening Telegram* November 3, 1955
— *Daily News* July 10 and 11, 1894
— *Harbour Grace Standard* July 3, 1894

LUCERNE
— Written and personal correspondence with Carolyn Cockerline, Niagara Falls, Ontario and Roy Winsor, St. John's (grandson of crewman Augustus Winsor)
— *Evening Telegram* February 15, 1901
— *Daily News* February 16, 18 and 19, 1901

GEORGE MAY
— Personal conversation with Everett Bishop, Grand Falls

— *Daily News* October 17, 1912
— *Evening Telegram* October 17, 18 and 19, 1912

BONNIE LASS
— Personal correspondence with Lucy (Power) Dobbin, Seal Cove, Conception Bay South
— *Daily News* September 27, 28 and October 2, 1916

H.V. MORRIS
— Personal correspondence from Clarence Dewling, archivist at Trinity
— *Evening Telegram* September 30, 1916

CHAPTER 6 – SURVIVAL

HOPE
— Written correspondence from Sandy MacEwen, Phoenix, AZ
— *Evening Telegram* December 1, 1881

MARY F. HARRIS
— Personal conversation with Clyde Forsey, Max Grandy and Hattie (Noseworthy) Russell, Grand Bank
— *Evening Telegram* October 7, 1887

MARY JOSEPH
— *Evening Telegram* August 21, 1888

GOLDEN ARROW
— unidentified newspaper clipping from PANL

MINERVA
— *Daily News* May 16, 1911

T.A. MAHONE
— Personal conversation with Emma (Lee) and son John Barnes, Grand Bank and Max Barnes, Philip's Head, the latter two grandsons of George Barnes
— unidentified newspaper clipping; "Offbeat History" in *Evening Telegram* April 28, 1962
— written and personal correspondence from Clyde Bungay of Fredericton, NB, son of Arch Bungay

HATTIE COLLINS
— *Evening Telegram* June 26, 1893

MADONNA
— *Evening Telegram* November ? 1915
— *Mail and Advocate* December 4, 1915

WINNIFRED LEE
— Written correspondence from Roberta (Misacura) Sheedy, Gloucester, Massachusetts
ʼ — *Daily News* June 19, 1928
— unidentified newspaper clipping from Gloucester, Massachusetts

GEORGE A. WOOD
— Personal conversation with Lloyd Rossiter, Carbonear whose father was crewman on this vessel

LORNINA
— written correspondence with Tom Barnwell, Stanton, Michigan
— *Daily News* December 10, 1915

LETTY B
— *Daily News* January 20, 1928

EFFIE M
— Personal correspondence with Clarence Dewling, Trinity
— *Daily News* September 23, 1907

YALE
— *Daily News* October 11 and 16, 1934
— Greta Hussey *Our Life on Lear's Room, Labrador* Printed by Robinson Blackmore, 1981, page 31 and 56
— R. Tayor's article "Mower Ketch was Grenfell Mission's Intrepid Workhorse" in Grenfell mission booklet, date undetermined.

MARY O'HARA
— *Western Star* date undetermined

LIZZIE J. GREENLEAF
— *Harbour Grace Standard*, March 12, 1897

L & H MCDONALD
— unidentified newspaper clipping dated April ?, 1931.

ANGELA B. MILLS
— *Chronicle Herald* August 28, 1956
— *Weekend Magazine* Vol. 7, No. 31, 1957

CHAPTER 7 – ABANDONMENT

MYSTERY
— Unidentified article from PANL

LADY NAPIER
— Unidentified newspaper clipping

MAYFLOWER
— *Evening Herald* February 6, 1914

EUPHRATES
— Personal conversation and written correspondence from Mona Petten, Port-de-Grave
— *Daily News* December 31, 1920 and March 27, 1958
— two unidentified newspaper clippings – one entitled "News Item of By-Gone Years: Loss of S.S. *Euphrates*"

CLINTONIA
— Written correspondence from Lewis E. Mercer, St. John's
— *Daily News* November 7, 1921

CHAPTER 8 – WAR

MCCLURE
— Lehr, G. and Anita Best. *Come and I Will Sing You*. St. John's: Breakwater, 1985

SYDNEY SMITH
— an unidentified newspaper clipping in Newfoundland Historical Society files.

"SOLE SURVIVOR"
— Personal correspondence from Lew Grimes, Herring Neck;

Lloyd Batt, Bay Verte and Doris (Batt) Parsons, Corner Brook
— information taken from an unidentified newspaper clipping
— Coaker, William (ed.) *Twenty Years of the Fisherman's Protective Union*, 1930
— *Sydney Daily Post* September 27, 1919

DICTATOR
— Personal conversation with Clifford Bowridge of Burgeo who had a relative on *Dictator*
— *Evening Telegram* January 31, 1919 (from *Morning Chronicle*, Halifax)

DAVISON
— Written/verbal correspondence from Thomas Stoodley, Hibb's Cove, and Ray Stoodley, St. John's, the sons of Raymond Stoodley; verbal correspondence with Shirley (Peckford) Sooley, Ontario, daughter of William Peckford

EMPIRE ENERGY
— Marie Cook, Grand Falls and Ross Manuel, St. Anthony

ANGELUS
— *Evening Telegram* June 4, 1943
— "Louisbourg Fishermen Rescue U.S. Seamen" in *Cape Breton Magazine* January 1986
— C/O's report of loss of *S.U. 709*, Department of Navy, USA, March 12, 1943

CHAPTER 9 – PEOPLE

"IN THE ST. PIERRE SLAMMER"
— Written correspondence from Helen (Forsey) Milley and Hazel Milley
— *U. C. School Record* Robert Carr, ed., Grand Bank, 1941

SYBIL
— Written correspondence from several of descendants of Newfoundland/Australian settlers including Roger Murphy, Burlington, England; Debbie Klimeck, Victoria, Australia; written correspondence from John McRea, St. John's, Elaine Kranjc, Australia, and John Oakes, Victoria, Australia
— letter in *Newfoundland Express* (Letter dated January 24, 1853)

— *Evening Telegram* October 21, 1899
— internet site for Australian immigrants at www.users.on.net/proformat/auspass.html (Public Record Archives, Victoria's Archives)
— Mosdell, H.M. *When Was That?* St. John's, Trade and Print Publishers, 1923;

BRUNHILDA
— personal correspondence from Eileen (Downing) Thistle, Corner Brook/Port aux Basques

NAUTILUS
— Written and verbal correspondence with John O'Mara, St. John's, a descendant of the Burkes
— *History of Burin* Senior Citizens Committee, 1977
— *Evening Telegram* January 26, 1960
— unidentified newspaper clippings of January 1 and February 3, 1865

"FELLOW FROM FORTUNE AT BELLA COOLA, B.C."
— Written correspondence from Stephen Stacey, Ontario, grandson of Captain Tuck, William Chapman, North Sydney, and Margaret Mullins, Fortune

AMBITION
— Personal conversation with the Ayres descendants
— unidentified newspaper clipping

PATARA
— Personal correspondence with Jean (Critchell) Clothier, New Mexico, daughter of Captain Critchell (Author's note: because our search of dates and circumstances, Matthew Critchell's name was added to the Gloucester Memorial to Lost Seamen)
— *Gloucester Daily Times* September 24, 1932
— *Halifax Herald* September 24 and 26, 1932

SENEFF
— *Family Fireside* November 1955

CAPE AGULHAS
— *Halifax Chronicle* January 7, 1956
— *Evening Telegram* January 29, 1962
— personal conversation with Margaret Mullins, Fortune

CHAPTER 10 - MURDER

LADY SHERBROOKE
— Personal correspondence (including the obituaries of survivors Hugh Coyle and John Laird) from Mary Henderson, Wisconsin and Judy (Peake) Lingard, Toronto, ON, respectively
— *Royal Gazette* August 16, September 13, 1831

LAKE SIMCOE
— *Daily News* October 21, 1912
— unidentified newspaper clipping dated January 22, 1913

MARION
— Personal conversation with Stephen Blagdon, Boxey; Bud and John Davidge, English Harbour West and Clarenville
— written correspondence from David Benson, Tors Cove
— *Daily News* "Year of Events" December 31, 1915
— *Wake of the Schooners* Robert Parsons, Creative Publishers, 1993
— "A Fortune Bay Christmas" from *Land and Sea*, CBC Television, December 1986

CENTARUS
— *Evening Telegram* January 4, 1923
— Personal conversation with Stewart Dicks, St. John's/Harbour Buffett

"MYSTERIOUS RITUAL BRINGS DEATH"
— Personal conversation with a descendant of the Welsh family

Index of Ships and Towns

285